WHIPPING BOY

WHIPPING BOY

THE FORTY-YEAR SEARCH FOR
MY TWELVE-YEAR-OLD BULLY

ALLEN KURZWEIL

HARPER

An Imprint of HarperCollins*Publishers*

An extension of this copyright page appears on 290.

FIRST EDITION

Library of Congress Cataloging-in-Publication Data has been applied for.

ISBN: 978-0-06-226948-5

15 16 17 18 19   OV/RRD   10 9 8 7 6 5 4 3 2 1

In memory of my father, for the things he invented

With gratitude to my mother, for the things she preserved

CONTENTS

This is a work of nonfiction.

No names have been changed.

PART I

SWITZERLAND

In the little world in which children have their existence whosoever brings them up, there is nothing so finely perceived and so finely felt, as injustice.

Charles Dickens, *Great Expectations*

My youthful innocence suffered an injury. It was a slight scratch, which in the course of time grew into a gaping wound that cut deep into my flesh and did not close.

Hans Keilson, *The Death of the Adversary*

CONFESSION

You've been a menace and a muse. A beacon and a roadblock. My jailer and my travel agent.

You have this uncanny habit of popping up in the most unexpected places. During a walk through the Louvre. At the back of a bar. In the lyrics of a Broadway show tune.

If *The Da Vinci Code* shows up on TV or if I'm playing foosball with my son, if I spot a certain kind of fountain pen or a particular brand of wristwatch, there's a good chance I'll find myself thinking of you.

The prompts aren't always that subtle. A few years back, a credit card company website summoned the obsession directly with a password hint: "Who was your archrival when you were growing up?"

Without a second thought, I entered the name of the boy who entered my life when I was ten years old—entered my life and reshaped it forever: C-E-S-A-R A-U-G-U-S-T-U-S.

RULES AND RANKS

Even if I hadn't bunked with a kid named Cesar Augustus, memories
of the Swiss boarding school that brought us together surely would
have stuck. The eccentric imperatives of the institution's forward-
thinking founder and the exotic backgrounds of the teachers he
employed, the daily meditations promoting liberty and the thirty-six-
page handbook that curtailed it, the lessons in swordsmanship and elocution, the alpine expeditions, cold showers and soybean steaks . . .
all of it was way, *way* too strange to forget.

Established on an mountain plain high above Geneva in 1949,
Aiglon (pronounced *EGG-lawn*) was the brainchild of John Corlette,
a headstrong, asthmatic Englishman with a singular vision of what a
boarding school should be: regimented yet free-spirited, full of fearless high-altitude adventure and moral enlightenment. JC—yes, that's
how the founder chose to be addressed—believed physical fitness and
spiritual reflection nurtured body and soul and that obedience was a
prerequisite for independence.

"Freedom," he declared, "is an exceedingly difficult commodity
to handle. To do so requires very strict training and discipline. At
Aiglon such training and discipline are not only provided; they are
enjoyed."

Well, not by me, they weren't. As the school's youngest pupil, the
runt of the litter, I found myself at the very bottom of a pseudo-military
pyramid codified in the aforementioned handbook. I received a copy
of *Rules and Ranks* the day I arrived, September 1, 1971, and was
given a written test on its contents a few weeks later.

Every lower-schooler entered Aiglon a so-called no-rank, with
promotion to junior green badge summarily awarded to all but the
most noncompliant plebe. The appearance of hard work, academic
achievement, physical prowess, or moral rectitude (translation:
brownnosing) paved the way for further upgrades, first to junior red

badge, then to silver eagle, and from there to the lofty rank of golden eagle. A new sweater pin accompanied each promotion, as did a correlative bump in the pocket money handed out each Wednesday afternoon.

Upper-schoolers could climb even higher through JC's Rank System by becoming standard-bearer candidates, then standard-bearers, then captains, and finally (for the two most even-keeled and charismatic pupils in the school) head girl and guardian, the latter honorific optimistically filched from Plato's *Republic*.

Nuanced enough? Not for JC. He tweaked the protocol further by introducing stars. I recall this small refinement because the School Council promoted me to junior green badge *star* soon after I took first place at a regional track meet. (Two months later, I was stripped of the spangle when a dining-hall monitor caught me shirking my duties.) As a junior red badge star, the highest rank I achieved, my weekly "pay" was pegged at five Swiss francs, or roughly $1.25. Although the school took care of laundry, haircuts, postage, and paper, it was up to me to cover all miscellaneous expenses, and at Aiglon those expenses included fines.

Say the house captain caught me flicking a towel or the dining-hall monitor noticed I was tilting backward in my chair. Suppose the outside tidiness captain found grease on my camping gear or his residential counterpart observed that I'd left a light on during

John Corlette (1911–1977), founder of Aiglon College, known as JC.

the day. Any one of those slipups could trigger a fine of twenty to fifty centimes. And don't for a second think a parent could cover those charges. External financial assistance was, at least in principle, banned from campus.

"The moment a student is given extra sums of money over and above his earned income, the education value of the system is destroyed," JC noted in a brochure sent to my mother. The regulations tied to this apocalyptic premise were spelled out in the "Money and Trade" section of the *Rules*:

> *All and any currency exceeding five francs in total value must be handed to your housemaster at the beginning of each term. Any other money received by you during the term for birthdays, etc. must be handed in at once.*

I was ten and terrified. I obeyed JC's monetary restrictions. Most older students did not. Aiglon sustained a robust black-market economy dependent on all sorts of unsanctioned revenue streams. (Cesar, for example, did a brisk business reselling movie posters and pock-

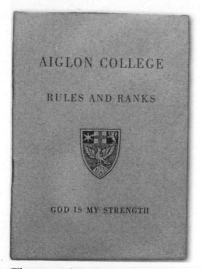

The cover of the thirty-six-page student handbook, circa 1972.

etknives.) But heaven help anyone who got caught with "funds in excess of nine francs" (about two dollars). One of the nicest and most respected seniors, nabbed in flagrante delicto with a Diners Club card, got the boot two weeks before he was to graduate.

Money wasn't the school's only mechanism of control. Public tally boards also instilled discipline. Red marks—earned for feats of physical, spiritual, or academic virtue—signaled success and paved the way for promotions and *bons*, tissue-paper vouchers distributed by housemasters and accepted among local shopkeepers in lieu of cash. Black marks, on the other hand, could result in a pensum, a two-page assignment on a subject of a prefect's choosing ("The Virtues of Thrift," "The Sex Life of the Sand Fly," etc.). Since I was too young to be saddled with written penalties, my waywardness usually resulted in "laps"—punishment runs requiring me to dash to a stone bridge and back, a hillside circuit of about a mile. Late for class? Laps. In the hallway after lights-out? Laps. Spotted crossing the invisible one-meter barrier surrounding the assistant housemaster's VW Bug? Caught "being slimy," "exhibiting loutish behavior," or "micturating on a football pitch"? Laps, laps, and more laps.

The surveillance of conduct wasn't restricted to adults. Each of the school's five alphabetically named houses—Alpina, Belvedere, Clairmont, Delaware, and Exeter—operated under its own student-run bureaucracy. House captains managed prefects, prefects kept tabs on monitors, and monitors oversaw the rest of us. Everyone had at least one house chore. Besides serving as a yogurt carrier—a low-level job not to be confused with the more exalted position of yogurt *checker*—I also was compelled to provide assistance to a shower monitor with an imperial name.

WIENERWALD

Let's rewind for a moment. How does a ten-year-old Jewish kid from New York end up at a Swiss boarding school founded by a mystically inclined Christian Englishman? For years, I had a ready response to that question: "My mother warehoused me in Aiglon while she was test-driving her third husband."

But that glibness is misleading and unfair. I *wanted* to go to Aiglon. I *campaigned* to attend. And I did so for reasons that can be traced back to the alpine passions of another ten-year-old Jewish kid.

My father, born in Vienna in 1911, was raised to love the mountains. In a journal he kept as a young boy, he drew pictures inspired by his weekend hikes through the Vienna Woods—sketches of mountain ranges, flowers (snowdrops in particular), hound dogs, and deer. When he turned twelve, my father joined the local chapter of a socialist scouting organization called the Rote Falken, or Red Hawks. With like-minded leftists, he hiked, rope-climbed, and skied the Wienerwald and the Alps. Those adventures, and pretty much every other pleasure in his life, ceased once Hitler came to power. In 1938, he was arrested, along with most of his comrades. Yet unlike them, he managed to get himself released. Soon after he fled to England— the details of the escape are fuzzy—and from there immigrated to the United States, where he found work as a mechanical engineer.

After the war, my father returned to Europe under the European Recovery Program, known informally as the Marshall Plan. Whenever he wasn't designing machinery—everything from room-size metal lathes to a tabletop "Automatic Orange Juicer"—he'd head for the Alps. By 1958, he had lined up enough consulting work among Italian machine-tool manufacturers to resettle in Milan with his second wife (my mother), two stepchildren, and a pair of handmade hiking boots. I was born two years later.

All of which is a roundabout way of explaining why I spent winter holidays in Switzerland. My father would load Mom, my much older half siblings, Ron and Vivien, and me into his Chevy Impala—an elegant, powerful, and generously proportioned first-generation import purchased by an engineer who was himself an elegant, powerful, and generously proportioned first-generation import. He'd then drive the family to Villars, a sleepy village in the Vaud, a French-speaking canton celebrated for its watchmakers, ski slopes, and international boarding schools.

A preference for the rustic charms of Villars over the glitz of Gstaad or Saint Moritz shouldn't suggest that my father was immune to luxury. Quite the opposite. A classic example of what the Swiss call

a *Cüpli-Sozialist*, or champagne socialist, he spent lavishly on friends
and family and, in particular, on me. While his generosity found
expression throughout the year, my father, lapsed Jew that he was,
waited until Christmastime to go whole hog, transforming the Villars of my early childhood into a life-size snow globe filled with Steiff
animals, LEGO bricks, Märklin trains, milk chocolate, and candy.
(It was my father who introduced me to Sugus taffies, a superior an-
tecedent to Starbursts.)

Dad was particularly immoderate when it came to winter gear. My
closet in Milan quickly filled with goose-down snowsuits and double-
bladed skates, wooden skis and leather lace-up boots small enough to
have hung from the Chevy's rearview mirror. Not that Dad himself did
much skiing or hiking by the time I came along. Arteriosclerosis and
severe angina made prolonged exertion impossible. Yet even in sickness
he found a way to honor the Alps. He kept his meds in a silver pillbox
shaped like the iconic whis-
key cask associated with the
Saint Bernard rescue dogs
once bred for alpine rescue.

When I turned four, my
father had a heart exam.
That exam led to further
tests, and the tests revealed
he had cancer. He rejected
the treatment options recommended by the local doctors,
arguing that Italian hospitals
were far more life threatening
than any disease. When my
mother finally strong-armed
him into consulting an on-
cologist in the United States,
it was too late. Dad spent his

*One of the thousands of photographs my
father took of me in Villars. I'm around three
in this one.*

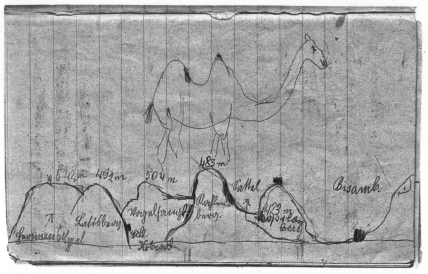

A sketch from a notebook my father started when he was ten years old.

Further evidence that my father, Robert Kurzweil, loved the mountains.

final Christmas in a New York hospital bed and died in a morphine haze on April 19, 1966. He was fifty-four and I was five.

Widowed in a foreign land, Mom saw no future for us in Italy. She moved me, along with Ron and Vivien—both bound for college—into an apartment on the Upper West Side of Manhattan. The new place was sparsely furnished and bleak, made bleaker still by the sorrow of its two principal occupants.

While my father was alive, our home had been filled with his photography. (He always traveled with a boxy Rolleiflex camera strapped around his neck.) One long corridor of the Milan apartment had been given over to a set of images he'd shot of me, age three, tottering down a dirt road above Villars. After our relocation stateside, those photos never got rehung. In fact, no image taken by my father, or *of* my father, was displayed.

Such acts of wholesale erasure were not unusual in the 1960s. Grief experts commonly advised widows with young children to banish all physical reminders of the deceased and to shroud in euphemism any reference to death. So when I was told that my father had gone to his "resting place," I felt confident he'd eventually get bored, wake up, and rejoin his family.

Mom did what the shrink advised her to do; she kept me home the day of the funeral. It was only at the Yahrzeit ceremony a year later (again with the therapist's approval) that she brought me to my father's gravesite. When, as Jewish tradition dictates, my mother placed a rock on the headstone, I had a meltdown.

"Stop!" I screamed.

Mom froze, confused by my outburst.

"Stop! You're hurting Daddy!"

"But sweetie."

"You're standing on him! You're crushing him! Get off! Get off!"

"But—"

"*GET OFF!*" I shoved my mother off my father's body and ran away in a blind fury. She remembers it taking the better part of the afternoon to find me. I was discovered weeping, inconsolably, behind a marble crypt.

Even as my notions of death matured, I continued to dream of a father-son reunion. A survey of the Manhattan phone book, conducted when I was eight, revealed that a "Kurzweil, Robert" resided a few blocks away from our apartment. While Mom was out, I would sometimes start to dial the number listed in the directory. But only once, as far as I remember, did I have the courage to allow the call to go through. I hung up before Kurzweil, Robert, answered. I couldn't handle the possibility that the voice on the other end of the line belonged to my father. Or worse, that it didn't. I never dialed the number again.

I don't remember much about my father. In point of fact, I have only one clear memory. It's in early March 1966. Daytime. I'm standing at one end of a long hallway when, from the other end, I hear the sound of squeaking wheels. I look and see Dad rolling toward me on a hospital gurney. When he reaches the spot where I'm standing, he takes hold of my hand and gives it a squeeze. I can't recall what he says to me or what I say to him, but I retain the physical sensation of my hand in his, and I can still see the watch he has strapped to his wrist. I remember the face of that watch more vividly than the face of its owner.

THE MARXIST

With my father gone, Mom needed to figure out a way to pay the bills. After reviewing her options—managing a family-owned granite and marble warehouse or becoming a professor of sociology—she chose the latter path. That meant getting a PhD, which in turn meant writing a doctoral thesis. She wrote her dissertation on Italian industrialists, a familiar subject given my father's commercial pursuits. Still, the research required a year of fieldwork in Italy. For the single mother of a ten-year-old that presented certain logistical challenges—challenges further complicated by the extracurricular attentions of a Marxist sociologist for whom Mom was working part-time. I realized pretty quickly that while she was pursuing her degree, the Marxist was pursuing her. So intense was his ardor that he took a sabbatical from his post as a professor at Amherst College and joined her in Italy.

And where did that leave me? Mom suggested that I spend sixth grade at an English boarding school in Villars.

In Villars? She might as well have proposed Disney World, which, everyone knew, was just about to open down in Florida. No, this was better than Disney World. Mom was giving me a chance to return to a realm I imbued with far more magic than any trademarked magic kingdom.

Before the start of school, Mom took me on a road trip through Italy. First stop: Bologna, to pick up the Marxist's spanking new river-blue Audi 100 LS automatic. (My father wasn't the only champagne socialist in my mother's life.) The vehicle came fully loaded—sunroof, tinted glass, FM stereo. It also included a couple of hidden charges: the Marxist's two French daughters, ages eleven and thirteen.

The girls were even more put off by the travel arrangements than I was. Although fluent in English, they boxed me out of all backseat diversion by restricting their conversations to French and German. When not conspiring against their de facto stepbrother, or squabbling between themselves, Anna and Antonia would gang up on their father. At one point, the bickering became sufficiently unbearable that the Marxist halted the Audi, dumped his elder daughter, Anna, by the side of the road, and zoomed away. It took

My mother, Edith Kurzweil, circa 1972.

my mother the better part of an hour to convince him to turn around and retrieve her.

The girls weren't the only troublemakers sitting in the back of the Audi. I pulled my weight, too. It wasn't hard. I campaigned against museum visits, sang Beatles tunes to drown out the Bach, and undermined travel schedules by wandering off at rest stops. Every guardrail of every Esso station became a tightrope stretched over a pit full of poisonous snakes, a volcano covered in molten lava, a lake stocked with piranhas.

It was this sort of impromptu escapism that caused me to scramble onto the roof of a seaside *pensione*. While searching for pirates through a spyglass fashioned out of two clenched hands, I tripped on a terra-cotta tile and, to avoid breaking my neck, lunged for, and caught, a tree branch. Then, with equal grace and dexterity, I planted my foot in a hornet's nest the size of a soccer ball. The ER doctor who treated me was so impressed by the broad constellation of welts dotting my body that he rustled up a camera to document the attack.

THREE SAINTS AND AN EMPEROR

After surviving stepsisters and hornets, it was a relief to return to Villars—the alpine wonderland inextricably linked to my father. I made a friend the very first day at school, even before settling in. His name was Woody. I think we hit it off as quickly as we did because we were both newly arrived no-rank Yanks. "That puts us at the bottom of the food chain," Woody said. I admitted not knowing what the phrase *food chain* meant, so drawing on his knowledge of sharks—Woody *loved* sharks—he explained the term and proposed we stick together. I agreed, then dragged my brass-cornered trunk up the spiral staircase of Belvedere, a converted hotel that served as the principal dormitory for the lower-school boys of Aiglon. My room, at the very top of a tower, accommodated five metal bunks in a space originally intended for two. Although the room had a balcony that opened onto a breathtaking section of the Alps that my father had climbed before the *Anschluss*, I'd be lying if I said I took much notice of the views. My focus was directed inward, at the four roommates I'd be bunking with: three Americans and a kid from Manila.

The first of the Americans I met was named Paul. His father was an ex-cavalry officer who organized pheasant shoots on country estates throughout Europe and the Americas. His mother was an heiress to a banking fortune who arranged charity events. Paul lived in a château outside Paris. Next was a Kentucky boy named Joseph. Joseph's family owned horses and McDonald's franchises. The last of my three American roommates was Timothy, the son of a successful New York stockbroker and a lover of Broadway show tunes.

That left Cesar, an overweight twelve-year-old with an easy smile and an unruly mop of coal-black hair. Cesar (pronounced *say-CZAR*) was rumored to be the son of the chief of security (or some similarly high-level official) under Ferdinand Marcos. At the time, I knew nothing about the Filipino strongman, but I had heard of Caesar Augustus.* (In fifth-grade history, I did two units on ancient Rome.)

Shortly after the start of the school year, Cesar approached to offer some practical advice. "You know what that tree is used for?" I recall him saying as he pointed from a fifth-floor balcony at a distant pine. "If there's a fire and we can't use the stairs, I'll have to throw you into that tree. But you don't have to worry," he reassured me. "The small branches at the

*Cesar was born Cesar Augusto Viana III, but had his middle name Anglicized while at Aiglon.

My pal Woody Anderson (left) with Assistant Master Patrick Roberts.

My dorm room, at the top of the Belvedere tower, and the looming pine.

top of the tree will break your fall, and the bigger ones down below will catch you."

Whether Cesar believed what he told me or not, I can't say. All I know is he made *me* believe it. And once I believed it, I began to worry.

The nightmares started a few days later. They were always the same: a never-ending tumble through the burning branches of a hu-mongous tree. I tried to stay awake to stave off the dreams. With my head under the covers, I'd stare at the bright green numbers on my watch—the same watch my father was wearing when the gurney men wheeled him away—and calculate the time remaining until the floor waker would pound on our door and end my terror, if only until the following night.

BANISTER SURFING

I wasn't especially studious during the year I spent in Switzer-land—my bookishness only emerged in high school—but I had a great time hiking, skiing, and goofing off. Sometimes my buddy Woody and I would finagle permission chits and visit the smoke shop at the base of Belvedere, where we'd purchase Mars bars and Sugus candies, and survey the shop's prodigious knife display. Other times we'd go "surfing," which meant sliding down the hand-rail of the Belvedere banister, a spiral of hardwood that ran from the top of the tower to a newel post five floors below. Balance not being my strong suit, I never achieved the grace of Woody's descents. Nor could I control my dismount, something most older boys nailed with the flourish of Olympic gymnasts. Still, like all residents of Belvedere, I helped buff the rail to the high sheen of a polished credenza.

The bond between Woody and me extended beyond banister surfing. One time we had a race to see who could change the fastest into the No. 1 Dress uniform mandated for Saturday and Sunday dinners. Woody won by keeping his school tie knotted and threaded through the button-down collar of his shirt, a trick I soon adopted. We were also fierce rivals in foosball, though neither of us played at the level of the senior boys. How could we? Table time tended to be governed by strength and standing, and we had precious little of either. That made us obvious targets for boys in search of easy prey.

Woody handled their unwanted attentions better than I ever did. He was fearless. His knowledge of shark behavior, I suspect, taught him that sometimes the best way to respond to attack is with a swift punch in the nose. I, on the other hand, took my cue from the chamois, the mountain goat mascot of my intramural sports team, and avoided conflict by bouncing from one perch to another, relying on ceaseless movement to keep me out of danger.

That same ceaseless movement (plus more than my share of punishment laps) eventually caught the attention of Derek Berry, the school's ruddy-faced director of activities. He put me on the track team. I loved running and excelled in the sixty-meter dash until, a month into the season, a teammate, wearing track spikes, stepped on my foot. The resulting puncture wound required the school's medical officer, Docteur Méan, to stitch me up. (I suspect he did so a bit too hastily. To this day, whenever the barometer drops in wintertime, a sharp pain cramps my foot and summons up memories of the unforgettably named doctor.)

"Eat It, Nosey"

I was, as already noted, the youngest student in the school. That was the most obvious strike against me. There were others. I was the fatherless son of a middle-class mother in a holding pen of privilege, an institution larded with the sons and daughters of royals and movie stars, diplomats, foreign correspondents, army officers, and spies. Strike two. And I was a Jew, one of only six or seven. Strike three.

Anti-Semitism might explain why, soon after my arrival, Cesar began calling me Nosey.

"Nosey, do this." "Nosey, do that." To enhance the slur, Cesar took to forming a *C* with thumb and index finger, pressing it around his nose to exaggerate its profile.

Ethnic cliché aside, I'm sure I *was* a little nosy, sneaking peeks at Cesar's knife collection, asking way too many questions, desperately doing whatever I could to fit in. At dinner one night, I made the mistake of flattering Cesar about his tolerance for hot sauce. (He kept a private stash in the room.) Although he appeared to disregard my pandering, I should have known the gears were turning when I noticed that he'd slipped a slice of bread into his pocket. No one in Belvedere swiped bread. Baked once a month, the notorious *pain intégral* had a mass density that rivaled lead.*

Up in the tower later that night, I watched as Cesar planted himself by the window and busied himself rolling bits of the purloined *pain* into pea-sized pellets.

---

*To appreciate the material properties of the bread served at Aiglon, consider this observation, made by a student reflecting on an ill-fated hiking expedition: "The weather turned and we were trapped there for two days and food had to be dropped from a ski plane. I still remember the net baskets of school bread breaking on impact." The payload itself was undamaged.

"What are you making?" I asked.

"Don't be so nosy, Nosey," he replied, adding his two-finger flourish.

Cesar arranged a half dozen bread pellets in single file on the windowsill and saturated each with a dollop of hot sauce. It was obvious by the way he kept grinning at me that I was implicated in his plans. How only became clear after lights-out, when he approached my bunk, cupping a cured pepper pellet in the palm of his hand. "Eat it, Nosey."

Cesar, age twelve.

I refused so he motioned to Paul, a highly suggestible giant with an uneven gait and pronounced underbite. Paul lumbered over and repeated the command.

I had no choice. I popped the pellet in my mouth and swallowed it whole. The homemade fireball numbed my throat, but that was pretty much it. I felt quite pleased, even slightly cocky, that I had passed the test without flinching.

Cesar walked back to the window, plucked another pepper pellet from the sill, and returned. "Eat it, Nosey," he said again. "Only this time make sure you chew."

Cesar was big. Paul was huge. What choice did I have? I placed the second pellet in my mouth and bit down. It had a lot more kick. I was still waving a hand in front of my mouth when Cesar held out another pellet. No command was necessary. It wasn't long after I bit down on the third fireball that I began to whimper, and then cry, my tears triggered both by the physiological effects of the chili sauce and by the glee of its purveyors.

Cesar eventually authorized me to rinse out my mouth, but by then the damage was done. The episode left a bitter taste in my mouth long after the burning subsided.

"THOSE WHO SUFFER ARE OFTEN CLOSER TO GOD"

Okay, an obvious question: Did I complain to someone in charge? The answer is no. It never even occurred to me to rat out my roommates. For all the rhetoric of communitarian governance, Aiglon was very much a *British* boarding school. The divide between child and adult was as distinct and hazardous as a glacial crevasse. Teachers took a dim view of tattletales, and so did their charges.

The Alps, as seen from the Belvedere dining hall.

And even if I had mustered the courage to snitch, where would I have taken my grievances?

The Belvedere housemaster? To quote the man himself: "Not bloody likely." He and his wife made it perfectly clear that they hadn't been hired to mollycoddle their charges. During the first week of school, the forbidding couple had forced a homesick twelve-year-old, struck down by the flu, to clean up his own vomit.

JC? He wasn't an option, either. He would have told me to look inward. A line from *Julius Caesar*, which he often recited during morning meditation, summed up his perspective: "The fault, dear Brutus, is not in our stars, but in ourselves." Besides, JC was rarely in residence. Fragile health had necessitated a "rest cure," which blossomed into an around-the-world pilgrimage, a search for the "cosmic intelligence of the Divine" requiring lengthy stays in the ashram of an Indian mystic and the commune of some Bay Area "Jesus freaks." (The quotes are pulled from an update he sent to the school.)

I found Group Captain Watts, the acting headmaster during JC's spiritual road trip, nearly as unapproachable. A Bible-quoting fighter pilot who strode about campus with a chunk of shrapnel lodged in his shoulder—a souvenir picked up while dogfighting Messerschmitts during the Battle of Britain—"Groupie" scared the shit out of me.

If I'd been older, Madame Duttweiler, the Aiglon fencing master, could have provided practical instruction adaptable to my needs. But her lessons in swordsmanship were restricted to upper-school students.

No, my only potential ally, and an unlikely one at that, was Lady Forbes, the school's eighty-two-year-old elocution teacher. A one-time opera diva fond of cat's-eye glasses, fake pearls, and capacious leather pocketbooks, Lady Forbes ran a pretty tight ship, often chastening in-attentive students with a quotation from some Eastern philosopher or

Lady Luia Forbes.

a line plucked from the Psalms. "Be still," she would command, her exquisite diction undermined by the hissing of loose-fitting dentures, "and know that I am God."

Had she felt so inclined, Lady Forbes could have made quick work of Cesar. Unfortunately, she shared JC's faith in self-reflection. Although she had more heart than the haggis* she prepared at Castle Forbes, she also believed in self-reliance, and the redemptive power of personal struggle. She was fond of telling her charges: "Those who suffer are often nearer to God than those who have never known pain."

Exes

One thing more than any other rescued me from the tyranny of the Belvedere tower. It was called expedition. Modeled on the teachings of Kurt Hahn, the founder of Outward Bound and JC's mentor (before the two educators had a bilious falling-out), expedition, or ex, was a mountaineering program designed to promote "character-training through adventure."

Exes at Aiglon took two forms: long and short. The so-called longs, chaperoned affairs lasting a fortnight, combined vigorous hikes with

---

*Before embracing vegetarianism, Lady Forbes was an accomplished chef with a special fondness for organ meats. Her bilingual cookery book, *Dinner Is Served* (Lima, Peru, 1941), contains recipes for haggis, tongue with almonds, veal kidney a la Liége-oise, and (her signature dish) thin-sliced calf-brain cocktail sandwiches.

age-appropriate cultural activities. My most memorable long included a series of perilous day climbs, a tour of the Nestlé chocolate factory (a visit I can still narrate minute by minute), and a descent into the dungeons of the Château de Chillon, a lakeside castle commemorated by Byron in a sonnet I once knew by heart.

Longs were fun, but it was the shorts that filled me with intemperate delight.

Though it's unthinkable today, back in 1971 the school had no qualms dispatching three or four unchaperoned boys into a harsh and unforgiving terrain with a few francs, some beat-up camping gear, a compass, and a map. In his capacity as expeditions master, Derek Berry would sometimes monitor the movements of the younger teams from a distance, aided by a pair of high-powered German binoculars. But as a general rule, surveillance during overnight outings was rare. Where we hiked and camped, and what grub we bought with our five-franc per diems, was left up to us.

My off-campus delinquency was all pretty innocent. I ate white bread, guzzled sodas (banned by JC because of the "drugs" they con-

tained), and played mumblety-peg with knives that exceeded the blade length sanctioned by the *Rules*. The older boys were more daring. One upperclassman I admired regularly skied off-piste during avalanche season. Another hired a helicopter to fly him over the route of an expedition he was supposed to complete on foot. Probably the most extravagant act of weekend dereliction took place just before I arrived. A student deviated from his

Expeditions master Derek Berry in 1971.

authorized itinerary by hitching a ride to Geneva and jumping on a plane bound for New York. He began his transatlantic ex on a Friday and by five p.m. that Sunday he was back at school, with the expeditions master none the wiser.

I enjoyed the autumn exes, but it's the winter ones that remain most vivid. I had a funky pair of skis fitted with all-terrain bindings that could be adapted both to downhill and cross-country conditions. (The toes were hinged and the heels could be disengaged.) I could even ski *up*hill by strapping on a pair of "skins."* Every aspect of the snowy hikes was exhilarating. They left me feeling filthy and cleansed, exhausted and energized. And they awakened dormant memories of Villars when my father was alive. On Sunday nights it was often a struggle just to climb into bed. Yet I welcomed the fatigue; it allowed me to sleep, nightmare-free, until the floor waker pounded on the door early Monday morning.

VERRUCAS

Typically, the school day began at seven a.m., with roll call and physical training: ten minutes of fresh-air squat thrusts, jumping jacks, and deep knee bends. PT was followed by cold showers. JC believed daily applications of "heat, cold, and wet" promoted "the irrigation of the glandular and lymphatic systems" by flushing out the "toxins" and "relative stagnation" brought on by sleep. The icy morning hosedowns were only mildly unpleasant, especially by comparison to the warm showers required in the afternoons.

When naked boys congregate, private parts inevitably receive public scrutiny. Although this fundamental law of human nature was

---

*A technical clarification: Before advances in synthetics, the "skins" fitted to the bottoms of skis to enhance traction were generally fashioned from the pelts of baby seals. (A pup's angled hair glides over snow when pushed forward and grips snow when pulled back.)

driven home by a few "turtle-necked" changelings who took pleasure in mocking my pre-pubescent circumcised tackle, that's not what I recall hating most about the shower room. No. I reserved far greater contempt for the facility's substandard plumbing and its overseer, the shower captain charged with maintaining the open flow of an undersized floor drain that was constantly getting clogged.

Matron, 1972.

That seemingly minor design flaw triggered broad social consequences for the bathers of Belvedere. The younger boys were forced to wash downstream, in the brackish effluvia of their elders. My memories of showering at Aiglon mostly involve hopping from one foot to the other in a futile effort to avoid an ankle-deep stew of human grease. (And if that weren't bad enough, Cesar, in his capacity as said shower captain, could legitimately compel me to clear away the Brillo pads of pubic hair that continually blocked the drain.)

All my hopscotching in microbial gunk ultimately led to an appointment with Matron, the school nurse.

"Dirty little child," she scolded. "You've gone and gotten yourself verrucas."

I stared up uncomprehendingly. Matron had severe dark features and a starched white uniform reminiscent of a daguerreotype widow. Verrucas? The word puzzled me. Was she talking about Veruca Salt, the bratty girl in *Charlie and the Chocolate Factory*?

Without warning or anesthesia, Matron reached for a scalpel and hacked away at the mosaic of plantar warts that had colonized my feet. Because surgery failed to address the underlying cause of the

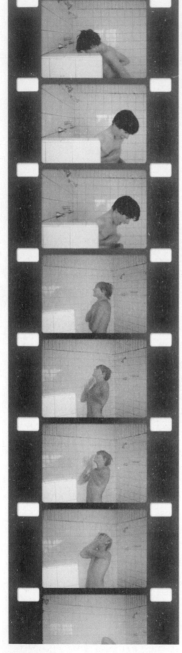

A 1971 film commissioned by the school highlighted a daily routine I hated: cold showers.

infection—namely, the toxic slurry of boy bilge into which I waded most afternoons—a fresh batch of warts sprouted soon thereafter. Matron attacked that second bloom by daubing my feet with pepper paste.

I didn't mind. In fact, I was grateful. My chronic outbreaks of *verruca plantaris* exempted me from PT and cold showers. So while my roommates submitted to jog trots and icy hosedowns, I was permitted to get dressed at a leisurely pace in a dorm room entirely free of menace.

FOOSBALL

And menace, after all, lurked everywhere. Despite our differing class schedules, Cesar and I often crossed paths. During daily meditation. At meals. In the alcove that housed the foosball table. That's where our mismatched rivalry found public expression most often.

Like most things at Aiglon, the Belvedere foosball table took a great deal of abuse. Its legs were scuffed, its bumpers shot, its rods misaligned. No amount of ski wax could silence the squeaky bearings, and the battered coin slot required a safecracker's touch (plus ten centimes) to release the pitted balls. Yet despite those blemishes, the table was a revered object. In pairs, and in pairs of pairs, the boys of Belvedere would bend over its scarred surface much the way the faithful bow before an altar. Unless one of the boys was Cesar.

Cesar approached foosball, as he did so many things, from a perspective all his own. When on defense, he would sometimes squat down behind his goalie and grip the backfield rods like the handlebars of the Harley in the *Easy Rider* poster taped to our dorm-room wall, an unorthodox crouch that provided an unobstructed sight line and which facilitated ramming the distal end of a metal rod into the groin of an inattentive foe.

In all fairness, Cesar rarely resorted to such dirty tricks. He didn't have to. He had near-total control over the actions of his men, whether formed from flesh and bone or from injection-molded plastic. His bank shots were especially lethal—they ricocheted off the walls with Euclidean precision—and his brush strokes imparted enough English to curve a ball *around* a player. And when he tired of finesse, or if the adversary appeared prepared for it, he could, in a pinch, fire off a torpedo. Or *begin* to fire, pause to ramp up the tension, and then gently pass the ball to a player better positioned to score. Beyond his extensive repertoire of throttles, feints, and pivots, Cesar possessed an unnerving ability to read his enemy, pinpoint weakness, and, whether by force or by sly misdirection, exploit that weakness to advantage. By the age of twelve, he was already a supremely gifted fake-out artist.

One last observation regarding Cesar's foosball technique requires mention. Whenever an especially difficult maneuver enabled him to score a goal, his mouth would curl in a grimace of pleasure. I recall that facial expression vividly because I associate it with his most deviant assault against me, an act of humiliation that, by Lady Forbes's logic, brought me face-to-face with God.

"The Thirty-nine Lashes"

As we were approaching the Christmas recess, Cesar decided to play a prank on me by paying homage to *Jesus Christ Superstar*, a wildly popular Andrew Lloyd Webber rock opera that our roommate Timothy, the lover of show tunes, played nonstop on his cassette recorder, a "compact" Philips the size of a shoe box.

One song, "Trial Before Pilate," caught Cesar's fancy more than all the rest. His devotion to it may have been partly narcissistic—the lyrics invoke Caesar by name—but I'm convinced he was also drawn in by the song's infamous interlude, "The Thirty-Nine Lashes." Whatever the reason, he decided to stage a dorm-room performance of the song during "close time," a late-afternoon recess reserved for indoor recreation.

This is what I remember. Cesar cast himself as Pilate and he gave Paul the part of the centurion, a part Paul was born to play, a part he had been playing since the start of school. Joseph, the kid from Kentucky, was cast as the rabble and Timothy handled sound.

That left only one major casting decision: Who should play Jesus Christ?

"Tie up his hands," Cesar declared.

Paul gleefully obeyed, securing my wrists to the metal crossbars of a bunk with a couple of towels. Timothy was then ordered to cue up the interlude,

Cesar, age eleven or twelve.   which comes halfway through

"Trial Before Pilate." While that was taking place, I said and did nothing. Resistance, I knew, would only prolong the performance.

When everything was set, Timothy hit PLAY, and Cesar began lip-syncing:

> *PILATE:*
> *I see no reason. I find no evil.*
> *This man is harmless, so why does he upset you?*
> *He's just misguided, thinks he's important,*
> *But to keep you vultures happy I shall flog him.*

Pilate's proposal—to whip the prisoner—fails to calm the bloodlust of the rabble, which demands nothing short of crucifixion:

> *THE MOB:*
> *Remember Caesar.*
> *You have a duty*
> *To keep the peace, so crucify him!*
> *Remember Caesar.*
> *You'll be demoted.*
> *You'll be deported. Crucify him!*

In the Broadway version of the scene, Pilate stands firm, if only temporarily, and has Jesus whipped with clockwork precision thirty-nine times. But in the Belvedere staging, Cesar, doubling as judge and whipmaster and brandishing a belt, took liberties.

> *One!—THWACK! . . . Two!—THWACK! . . .*
> *Three! . . . Four! . . . Five!—THWACK! . . .*
> *Six! . . . Seven!—THWACK! . . .*

Not every syncopated blow heard in the song yielded a correlative crack of the whip. Cesar often lifted his arm, advanced toward me as if to strike, and then stopped. Fake-outs were as much a part of the performance as those moments when the belt made contact. Introducing randomness into the rhythm of abuse appeared to delight Cesar as much as the abuse itself.

Once the interlude was over and I was released, I fled the room and, taking the stairs two at a time, found refuge in a dank corner of the basement filled with potatoes and mice. I stayed there until dinner, doing my best to stop crying by staring at the glowing face of my father's wristwatch.

THE FOUNTAIN PEN WARS

Although the origins of the Fountain Pen Wars remain murky, I am certain of this much: for a few months between late 1971 and early 1972, dozens of Belvedere boys turned writing instruments into semiautomatic weapons, in direct contravention of the *Rules*, which prohibited pupils below the rank of standard-bearer candidate from storing ink in the dorm. During a brief but exhilarating period of rebellion, the house was polka-dotted by fountain-pen-wielding lower-schoolers who could, with a simple flick, strafe a target fifteen feet away.

Group Captain Watts tried his best to quell our insurrection—tried his best and failed. Sure, Groupie had shot down Luftwaffe pilots during World War II, but those skills were useless when confronting a band of insurrectionists concealing improvised explosive devices in their pockets. Tally-board black marks and pensums, though well suited to the nature and color of our misbehavior, failed to stop the wars. Ink sales at the smoke shop soared.

Firing a fountain pen demands supple wrists and keen hand-eye coordination, the same skills required in foosball. So it should come as no surprise that Cesar was an accomplished sharpshooter, or that I was one of his regular targets. Of all our inky showdowns, only one leaves an indelible mark. Forty years on, I can still conjure up the scene in cinematic detail.

The setting is a Belvedere hallway. In the presence of half a dozen boys, a scrawny ten-year-old finds himself squaring off against a beefy enemy two years his senior. In my mind's eye, the camera travels over the face of the older kid—thick dark hair, beady black eyes, sly smile— before moving across the snow-white expanse of a freshly laundered No. 1 Dress shirt, the

Group Captain Watts.

pocket of which holsters an ebony-black Montblanc of German manufacture.

The twelve-year-old draws his weapon, unscrews the cap, and slips it over the barrel. He cocks his arm so that the gold nib of the pen hovers a few inches above his shoulder and then leans forward, poised to fire, while his rival bobs from side to side.

The twelve-year-old squints as he takes aim and, after a few feints, empties the Montblanc with a quick flick of the wrist.

Moments later, I look down to discover black spatter marks dotting the legs of my pants. A couple of bystanders, allies of Cesar, let out a round of cheers.

Okay, so you got me. But now it's Nosey's turn. I unholster my weapon, an American-made Parker 45. The Parker might lack the elegance of the Montblanc, but like the Colt .45 revolver after which it is named, it's sturdy and reliable.

As I take aim, anticipating the satisfaction of transforming my white-shirted adversary into a spotted dairy cow, Cesar serpentines with unexpected agility.

The tension mounts until I empty my chamber.

Flick!

A brief silence follows, during which I survey my target, my target surveys himself, and the onlookers survey us both.

"Blew it, Kikewheel!" Winn shouts when it becomes obvious that Cesar's shirt is as white as it was before I discharged my pen.

Cesar smiles and takes a bow.

How could I have missed? I was standing barely ten feet away.

"No, he didn't!" Woody suddenly yells.

All eyes turn toward Cesar, whose grimace of pleasure abruptly disappears. Confused, he again inspects himself and finds no black marks anywhere on his clothes. "What? Where?"

Woody points.

A wave of satisfaction flows through me once I realize that my shot has, in fact, hit its mark. A single blob of ink has smacked Cesar right in the kisser.

"What? Where?" Cesar says a second time.

His questions rupture the black globule. It spreads over his lips and teeth, then travels down his chin, where a subsidiary droplet begins to pool. Then, for what seems like an eternity, the secondary bead grows until it, too, bursts, and the ink, once more airborne, continues its descent until it strikes the breast pocket of Cesar's No. 1 Dress shirt.

My triumph was fleeting. But in that moment of intense joy, I felt as if I'd channeled the determination and achievement of a Swiss underdog marksman from an earlier time, William Tell.

"I SUPOSE MY INFERIORITY WILL LAST"

My reputation as an inkslinger might have been secure after the showdown with Cesar, but I was hopeless when it came to using pens as they were intended to be used. The *Rules* required me to write a letter home once a week. My mother, true to her archival tendencies, re-tained seven of those dispatches: six originals addressed to her plus a photocopy of an aerogram she forwarded on to my father's aunt, a Viennese émigré who ran a boardinghouse in South London.

None of the seven letters mentions Cesar. I only told my mother about him four or five years after I'd left the school. But the surviving correspondence does capture my loneliness, as well as some pretty shaky spelling:

> *Dear Mom,*
> *How are you? I am fine. I have recieved only one letter from you!*

> *Dear Tante Martha,*
> *I am feeling hungry at the moment . . . I have found out that people are aloud to have some of chocolate so you can send me a bar or two.*

> *Dear Mom,*
> *I am a little homesick . . . I haven't been hearing from you resently.*

> *Dear Mom,*
> *Mark reading is soon. (Gulp!)*

Mark reading was yet another source of stress. Every two weeks the Belvedere housemaster assembled his boys in the dining hall and, while consulting color-coded report cards that distinguished "effort" from "achievement," he would, with the tenderness of a drill sergeant, issue public appraisals of our intellectual and moral worth. One of his early assessments of my scholarship began with a single word.

"CARSWHEEL!" he bellowed.

Sniggers spread through the hall.

"CARSWHEEL!"

After a lengthy scolding for grades that put me at the very bottom of the first form, the British equivalent of sixth grade, the housemaster informed me (and everyone else) that my report card—he held the damning evidence high in the air—compelled him to compose a lengthy indictment, which he planned to send to "any school stupid enough to consider taking on Carswheel once we give him the boot!"

The longest of the seven letters my mother preserved is easier for me to quote than to analyze:

Dear Mom,

How are you? I am fine. When I look at the size of your letter and compare them with mine I feel very inferior, so today I plan to write a long letter. Last night I did not sleep well. I bet if I didn't have my Aiglon blankets (little that I get) I am sure my toes would have gotten frost-bitten and would have fallen off! Everything is O.K. on the Aiglon Campus (except for a little student unrest). Some one ran away from school and was found with his father in <u>London</u>*! I went on my second expedition with my warm sleeping bag. I went to Solalaix and farther. I am sorry I didn't write earlier. I supose my inferiority will last . . .*

Love, Allen xxxxxxxxxxx . . .

"Found with his father in <u>London</u>!" I underlined the name of the city, but the word I should have highlighted is *father*. That was the source of my awe, and behind the awe, the source of my unacknowledged longing.

TEMPUS FUGIT

When I was seven or eight, I found a box of Dad's stuff in the back of a dresser drawer. The keepsakes included a slipcased slide rule, a leather billfold, two pairs of silver cuff links, an ivory-handled shaving brush, and a wristwatch. *The* wristwatch. The one my father was wearing when he was wheeled out of my life. Except for the watch, none of the uncovered personal effects had much personal effect on me. But, man oh man, how I loved the watch! Whenever Mom let me wind it up—it was an "automatic," so all one had to do

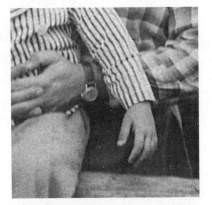

The long-lost Omega on the wrist of its original owner—my father.

was give the thing a few shakes—the ticking set in motion memories of Villars.

As soon as I learned I'd be attending Aiglon, I began pestering my mother to allow me to take the watch to school. She said absolutely not. It was way too precious. A huge fight ensued. In the end, my mother caved, and a good thing, too, I thought. Dad's watch, a stainless steel Omega Seamaster, became my talisman, my pacifier, my shield. Staring at its luminescent dial tempered homesickness, deferred bad dreams, and offset humiliation.

You'd think a watch bearing the name Seamaster would be waterproof. It wasn't. Steam had a way of fogging up the crystal. So to play it safe, when taking a shower, I would unstrap the watch from my wrist and hide it under my pillow.

A few months into the school year, I returned one day from the shower room, lifted my pillow, and discovered that Dad's watch was gone. My first reaction was disbelief. I put the pillow back down and counted to five with my eyes shut tight. I was breathing heavily when I removed the pillow and opened my eyes. The watch was still missing.

I searched under the bed. Nothing. I tore the sheets and blanket off my mattress. Nothing. I looked around the room, hoping some prankster had moved the watch from its usual resting place. It was nowhere to be found.

Even now I find it difficult to describe the queasiness that came over me as the consequences of the theft began to sink in. I begged my roommates to return the watch or at least help me identify the thief. Each one disavowed any role in or knowledge of the crime. That seemed extremely unlikely. I had no evidence of a conspiracy, but the more upset I became, the more Paul giggled and looked at Cesar.

The pair knew something. I was sure of it. I pleaded and pleaded until Cesar smiled and traced the curve of his nose with index finger and thumb. "Don't be so nosy, Nosey."

A few days later, Paul admitted that he had hurled Dad's watch from a balcony. When asked why, he explained he had been dared—*duped* is probably a better word—after being told this grade-school riddle:

Question: Why did the man throw his watch out the window?
Answer: He wanted to see time fly.

The identity of the riddler never surfaced. But rightly or wrongly, I felt in my bones Cesar had had a hand in the crime.

Knee-deep snow covered the ground, but that didn't stop me from combing the area where the watch might have fallen. I lasted outside about an hour before the cold forced me to suspend the search.

Two weeks after the crime, Mom drove up for a visit. "Where's Dad's watch?" she asked as we were sitting down for lunch at a local café. I tried changing the subject. She persisted. I told her that I'd forgotten the watch in my room. She knew I was lying and pressed further. "I dropped it out the window," I improvised. My powers of deception were no better than Paul's, and by the time dessert arrived, I had spilled the beans.

Over my protests, Mom did the unthinkable. She told. Group Captain Watts immediately commanded the Belvedere housemaster to undertake a search. The housemaster passed the order along to the house captain. The house captain responded by telling a prefect, and he in turn ordered a couple of subalterns to poke about in the snow with ski poles.

The watch never resurfaced. The loss left me bereft—more than bereft. I felt annihilated. I would have done anything—gulped down an entire bottle of Cesar's hot sauce or submitted to "The Thirty-Nine Lashes" thirty-nine times—if I'd thought it would return the watch to my wrist. (I still would.)

Yet oddly enough—there's no other way to put this—time began to fly soon after the Omega was launched from the tower. There were two reasons for this. First, Paul left the school. The watch incident, plus lapses in judgment that didn't implicate me, compelled Groupie to inform Paul's parents, the heiress and the huntsman, that their child required a degree of oversight Aiglon could not provide. (Paul eventually found his way to a Connecticut boarding school with a one-to-one student/teacher ratio.)

The second reason things improved was even more extraordinary: Cesar disappeared. From one day to the next—*poof!*—he just vanished.

He didn't get expelled. I was sure of that. His poster collection and knives remained in the room. At the time, I didn't initiate a full-scale investigation into his whereabouts—that would only come much later—but I did ask around. No one could explain his absence. Among the lower-school boys (at least the smaller ones) news of Cesar's departure provoked palpable relief.

For me, probably more than for anyone else, the payoff was immediate and wide-ranging. My mood improved dramatically, and so did my schoolwork. At one mark reading, I even managed to get the top grades in my class (of ten students), a turnaround that Belvedere's ill-tempered housemaster was forced to announce before a dining hall full of boys. I was repromoted to the rank of red badge. I learned to "wedel," a difficult and outmoded downhill maneuver requiring one to wiggle one's butt side to side while barreling down the slope. (Think Chubby Checker doing the Twist—on skis.) My exes grew

increasingly audacious. One hike included a near-vertical climb up
a succession of iron ladders bolted to a rock face, followed by a ten-
kilometer ridge walk to a stone hut perched some ten thousand feet
above sea level. Derek Berry, a mountain climber allergic to hype,
called the trek "fearsome" in his year-end expeditionary review.

By May 1972, the puncture wound on my left foot had closed, and
my verrucas had been eradicated. A star was added to my red badge.
My sleep improved, as did my bank shot, and thanks in large part to
Woody, I learned to slide down the full length of the Belvedere banister hands-free (though my dismount remained unsteady).

Graduation took place on the Fourth of July. The commencement
speaker, the widow of a distinguished American ambassador, offered
her audience some reflections on the nature of courage.

"Say NO to self-pity," she urged in a speech that drew a distinction
between anxiety and fear. "Fear has an object," she declared. "Anxiety does not."

That difference was lost on me back then, and even now I'm not
sure I buy it. Cesar had done a first-rate job fusing those two emotions into a general sense of dread. But where the widow's talk *did* hit
home was in its closing quotation, an apt, if now overused, line from
Nietzsche recently sampled in a ballad by pop singer Kelly Clarkson:
"What does not kill me makes me stronger."

I declared my independence from Aiglon by tearing my school
blazer to shreds. It turned out that the gesture of subversion was both
ineffectual and misdirected.

REMISSION

The same month I said my good-byes to Aiglon, my mother said hers
to the Marxist. I didn't know it at the time, but she had secretly married the man six months before, in the kitchen of Emily Dickinson's
house. (This was before the homestead was turned into a museum.)

Exchanging vows in the home of America's most celebrated spinster? What the hell was she thinking?

Mom must have had her doubts. She didn't tell me about the ill-fated union until after she had it annulled. Clearly, I wasn't the only one inclined to hide roommate problems.

In August 1972, the two of us returned to New York, where the plimsolls, anoraks, and rucksacks I wore at Aiglon reverted to sneakers, parkas, and backpacks. I no longer had to address my teachers as *sir* and *ma'am*. The crossbars disappeared from my sevens and I scuttled my schooner-sail fours, but memories of Cesar persisted.

He visited at night, in dreams of burning tree limbs and endless free falls, and by day, as well. A few months after leaving Aiglon, I had to sketch a map of Europe, circa 1648, for seventh-grade social studies. (We were finishing up a unit on the Thirty Years War.) To accommodate my completionist tendencies, and with an eye toward extra credit, I crammed as many territories as I could onto my map, no matter how small or remote: Iceland, Cherkassy, the Khanate of the Crimea. So it's curious that I left a penny-size area at the center of my map untouched and unlabeled. The very spot where I had been teased, burned, whipped, and robbed remained blank, an omis-sion that expressed graphically what I refused to say out loud. I wanted to wipe Cesar off the face of the earth. Hardly a practical solution. I ended up dealing with the lingering rage by transforming my memories into a series of amusing narratives.

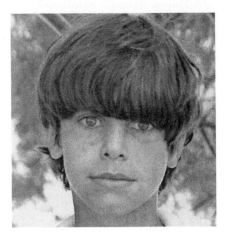

I recounted the whipping as if it were a comic pantomime and told tales of madcap expeditions free of adult supervision. When I revealed to my mother the stuff

Me, the year after my year at Aiglon.

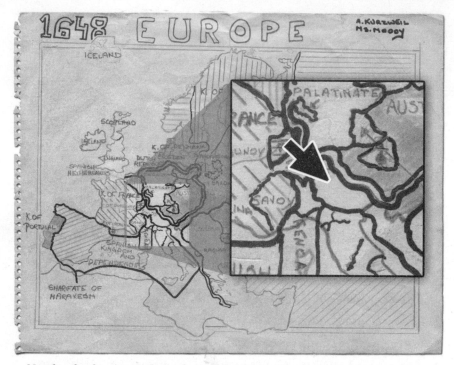

Months after leaving Aiglon, I drew a map for my seventh-grade history class that obliterated my boarding school and everyone in it.

Cesar did to me, she was horrified. Yet rather than endorse her distress and milk it for pity, I downplayed my humiliation and laughed off my pain. Doing otherwise would have forced me to confront feelings I preferred to forget.

When I graduated from high school, my mother unknowingly resurrected my boarding school anguish. "Remember how you tried to tell me Dad's watch had accidentally fallen out of the window? I knew immediately that wasn't possible. You would *never* have let that happen. You cried and cried when you finally admitted that one of your roommates, that tall troubled boy who lived in a château, had thrown it out the window. I was so annoyed at myself for having given it to you—that I hadn't been more firm. I should have kept it, despite your pleading. I should never have given in. Maybe this will make up for my mistake."

Mom handed me a box containing a brand-new Omega that she

hoped would serve as a worthy replacement for the one lost in the snowbank. It was a thoughtful and extravagant gift, and I had no right to be anything other than grateful. And I was, up to a point. But the watch never, not even for a day, left its velveteen cradle.

FRANÇOISE

I gave little thought to Cesar during my early twenties. He'd pop up in conversation now and then, the way bullies do, but when that happened, I continued to cover up the pain in diverting narratives of boarding school hijinks. Humor kept the sorrow at bay. I got through college, had my heart broken a few times, worked at a newspaper in Rome, toyed with the idea of graduate school, and then, in fits and starts, embarked on a career as a journalist. Eventually I found a few editors willing to accommodate a freelance writer whose obsessive research habits all too often got in the way of deadlines.

In mid-July 1985, I received an assignment from the *International Herald Tribune* to write about a television station launched by a group of Warlpiri Aborigines in Central Australia. Five hours after I drove into Yuendumu, a desert settlement three hundred kilometers northwest of Alice Springs, a French anthropologist named Françoise Dussart spotted me wandering toward a sacred site off-limits to visitors. Concerned for my safety, she drove up and warned me away. She was sitting in the cab of a Toyota Land Cruiser and cradling a baby kangaroo. How could I *not* fall in love?

After four months of courtship—a long-distance affair chronicled in correspondence that now fills a small file cabinet—we decided to live together.

Françoise packed up her field journals and reel-to-reel audiotapes. I packed up notes for a novel and a personal computer the size of a carry-on suitcase. She flew west, from Alice. I flew east, from New York. We met each other halfway, in Paris, broke and in love.

For more than a year we lived in penniless bliss. Our needs were minimal, our indulgences restricted. We rented a crêpe-sized fifth-floor Latin Quarter walk-up facing the exhaust vent of a Lebanese shawarma joint and buried ourselves in our work. Françoise had a thesis to write on the ritual life of Warlpiri elders. I had my novel. Once a week we'd either catch a film at the local revival house or share a mango.

A few months after moving to Paris, Françoise and I blew off work and spent the morning roaming the Louvre. Toward the end of our ramble, I stopped short in front of a fourteenth-century altar cloth depicting the Passion and Resurrection of Christ. Françoise caught me staring at one panel in particular, a gruesome scene of flagellation.

Her forehead wrinkled. "You like that?"

"No. It's just that it reminds me of something that happened at boarding school."

"*Ah, oui, le Cesar,*" Françoise said. She had heard my stories. "Do you ever wonder what became of him?

This was the first time anyone had asked me point-blank a question I often asked myself. "Of course."

"So, what do you think he's doing?"

"If I had to guess? Probably something in sales. He was always wheeling and dealing at Aiglon. He did a huge business selling posters."

"You're a journalist. Why don't you find out?"

I let out a laugh. "Fly to Manila to track down the kid

Françoise tending to Kirrkirr in Yuendumu, the Aboriginal settlement where, in 1985, we met.

who abused me when I was ten? Get me *that* assignment, and I'll catch the next plane."

I was joking. Françoise was not. She knew long before I did that there was darkness buried under the snowdrift of alpine anecdote.

The novel I started in Paris was published in 1991. By then Françoise and I were married and living in New York. The book was well received and translated into a dozen languages. European readers, in particular, responded to the tale, which I had set in the eighteenth century. By all outward appearances, *A Case of Curiosities* had nothing to do with my experiences in Villars. But strip away the period detail and certain parallels emerge. The story, which begins in an isolated part of Switzerland, records the struggles of a fatherless boy apprenticed to a watchmaker.

That same year, a foreign edition of the novel required a trip to Europe. I had some promotional obligations in Milan on a Tuesday and a few more the following Monday. Five days to kill. So on a whim (or what I convinced myself was a whim) I decided to visit Aiglon, with an eye toward answering the question Françoise had posed in the Louvre.

PART II

"WE HOPE TO MAKE YOUR JOURNEY UNFORGETTABLE"

What must you do, when you are afraid, to overcome your fear? Instead of rejecting, running away from the thing which you fear, you must, by means of an act of faith, go out to meet it, to embrace it, to draw it to you in confidence and affection; in other words you must love it.

John Corlette, "Meditation on Fear"

My very chains and I grew friends,
So much a long communion tends
To make us what we are:—even I
Regain'd my freedom with a sigh.

Lord Byron, "The Prisoner of Chillon"

BACK TO SCHOOL

During the train ride to Switzerland, I write the word *Cesar* on the cover of a new journal. How absurd it is to presume I will need forty-eight pages for the topic at hand. The blank notebook taunts me into writing down all sorts of nonsense. A sample entry: "The ashtrays glisten. The antimacassars are freshly ironed. Even the slots of the screws are all perfectly aligned. But I have to ask myself: Which is crazier, lining up screw slots so that they're all parallel? Or making a note about that fact in a journal?"

At each stop, a loudspeaker squawks, "We hope to make your journey unforgettable" in Italian, French, German, and English. I distract myself for much of the trip by leafing through an illustrated copy of the *Inferno*, a freebie from a Milanese publisher. As we cross into Switzerland, I assign Cesar to the Seventh Circle of Hell, a hot spot Dante reserves for sinners prone to violence.

When I reach Aigle, the end of the line, I catch a bus to Villars. After a nauseating series of hairpin curves, made all the worse by dense fog that blocks my view, the bus breaks through the cloud line and I'm smacked in the face by a breathtaking vista, a jagged snow-capped mountain chain wrapped in a tutu of mist. Until just then, I had completely forgotten the postcard splendor of the region.

The bus lets me off directly across from Belvedere. As I grab my backpack, I spot a boy, no more than twelve, standing inside a telephone booth. He appears nervous. He keeps glancing at his watch. As the bus pulls away, the phone rings and the boy lunges for the handset. He says a few words. Then, for a very long time, he listens.

I can't hear the exchange, but I get the gist of it: Stand tall, he's being told. Suck it up. You'll be fine.

But the boy is *not* fine. He slumps against the wall of the phone booth. His chin begins to quiver. He rubs his eyes with a knuckle and wipes his nose on a sleeve. Only after hanging up does he allow himself to cry. I consider approaching but sense it's best to leave the boy alone.

I register at a tiny hotel kept in business by visiting parents, and receive a key from a woman with a giant chin mole further embellished by a single black hair the length of an inchworm. That night I fall asleep thinking about the sobbing boy, wondering if I'd done the right thing keeping my distance.

The following morning, while walking to the school, I pass three Aiglon students loitering outside the smoke shop where Woody and I bought candy and ogled knives.

"Who has money?" one of them says.

"Ali, we all have money," his schoolmate replies. "It's just that none of us has any right now."

"Hold on. I have three francs," the third boy says.

"Right then, hand 'em over," Ali commands.

When the boy with the three francs balks, he is reprimanded. "Oh, don't be such a bloody Jew."

I arrive early for my ten a.m. appointment at a newly erected alumni center named after Lady Forbes, and take a seat below a portrait of my irrepressible elocution teacher. The painter, a former Aiglon art teacher, has draped a rope of pearls the size of grapes over his subject's daunting bosom and has blended her hair into the snowcapped mountains that frame her craggy face. It's a wonderful likeness. Still, the painting doesn't capture the retired opera diva as I remember her. Had I received the commission, she'd be wearing cat's-eye glasses and hiking boots, and nibbling on a centipede (a delicacy she had sampled during her travels through Mexico) while reading a chapbook of Sufi poetry.

A bit after ten, the school's director of alumni relations, a solicitous chain-smoking American woman, escorts me across campus to morning tea, where I meet a longtime housemaster named Teddy Senn.

"Caesar Augustus, you say the boy was called? How extraordinary. Awfully sorry, the name draws a total blank. You might consider talking to Mrs. Senn," Mr. Senn advises. "Mrs. Senn's memory is not nearly so shabby as mine."

The head of the school joins our conversation. "Did you distinguish yourself during your stay with us?" he asks.

"I was on the track team briefly, but was sidelined by an accident."

"What was your rank when you departed?"

"Red badge star."

"Oh, I see," he says coolly.

I ignore his imperious disappointment and stick to the subject at hand. "I'm hoping to locate one of my old roommates. Does the school keep up-to-date contact information about alums?"

"It should do," the headmaster sniffs. "Unfortunately, our database

I sent this postcard to my mother in 1991. On it I wrote, "Dear Mom, I've put a big circle (marked A) around the room where I was tortured. The smoke shop (marked B) is where I bought a switchblade after Dad's watch was stolen. Love, Allen."

is woefully inadequate. But if you wish, have a look in the archives. Such as they are."

The alumni director walks me back to Forbes House, where I spend a few hours sifting through photographs, pamphlets, and back issues of the *Aiglon Association News*. When I'm done, she kindly offers to photocopy the material I have set aside while I revisit my old dorm room.

As we're saying good-bye, I notice a flock of black birds with beaks the color of Swiss cheese circling overhead. "Crows?"

"No, mountain choughs. Disgusting little creatures. They raid the nests of songsters and eat their young."

Belvedere, the converted hotel that lodged me for a year, has undergone a face-lift. The scratchy sisal floor coverings are gone. The battered foosball table has been retired. The shower room has been renovated, so it's safe to assume the drains no longer clog with wads of pubic hair and human grease. Webs of nylon rope crisscross the stairwell. I suppose it's to prevent books and things from falling on the heads of passersby. Either that or to stop students from surfing the banister.

As I head up to the top of the tower, my breathing becomes erratic and I begin to sweat. It's as if I'm scaling the Matterhorn rather than a few sets of stairs. The symptoms intensify when I enter my dorm room and they blossom into a full-fledged panic attack while I'm standing at the balcony, taking in the view. I retreat to a bunk bed and, after a few minutes with my head between my knees, the anxiety subsides.

MRS. SENN REMEMBERS

The visit to Villars hasn't yielded much. No one recalls Cesar. I haven't even obtained a mailing address. I settle my bill with the mole lady and head off for one last rendezvous before calling it quits.

"Your husband thought you might recall a bit about the time I spent at the school," I tell Elizabeth Senn over a pot of tea at the café next to the smoke shop.

"Mr. Senn is quite the optimist. I fear I'm a bit dotty. I tend to remember only certain things and only certain years. Nineteen sixty-seven, for instance. I remember 1967 *very* clearly, like it was yesterday, in fact. And 1984. That year sticks with me, too. But the rest of the eighties?" Mrs. Senn shakes her head despairingly.

Elizabeth Senn, circa 1971.

"What about the early seventies? I was at Aiglon for just one school year, starting in September 1971."

"Oh, you're in luck, Allen." Mrs. Senn takes a moment to gather her thoughts. "Nineteen seventy-one. Nineteen seventy-one. Well, for starters, that was when students were wearing those frayed bell-bottoms and ratty sweaters. One boy, son of the king of Somaliland, insisted on sporting overalls like the local petrol station attendant. Can you imagine? And all the while his father is under house arrest, translating Shakespeare into, well, whatever language it is that they speak in Somaliland."

For the next ten minutes, Mrs. Senn details the fashion anomalies that marked my time at the school, then follows up with a similarly thorough catalog of student misfortune, circa 1971. I learn of the classmate whose brother died of a brain tumor; of the boy who lost his girlfriend in a raffle; of a youthful suicide; of the two students who burned down a shepherd's hut ("It was a relief when we saw *both* sets of footprints leaving the shelter"); of the governor's son expelled for possession of unauthorized funds ("Ten francs, I believe it was").

Her inventory continues: "There were quite a few injuries the year you attended the school. There was that fellow who put the gunpowder in the ski pole. The damage to his fingers was, if I recall correctly, permanent. And then there was that poor girl who raced for the school."

"What happened?"

"She took a pole too tightly during the slalom. This was when we had bamboo gates on the course. Her parents hired the very best surgeons, but the poor girl's nose? Well, it was never quite the same after that."

"That's horrible!"

"Not so horrible as what happened to young Scurlock. Suffered frostbite during a long ex and lost two of his toes straight up to the first joint. I believe it was the first joint. It may have been up to the second. Anyway, Docteur Méan took care of it as best he could and Scurlock was back at school by the end of the year. And then of course there was poor Woody Anderson. Poor, *poor* Woody."

"What happened to Woody? He was a very close friend."

"You don't know?"

"Know what?"

"It must have happened just after you left."

"*What?*"

"Did you notice the net stretched across the Belvedere stairwell? Why do you think it's there?"

"To stop boys from sliding down the handrail?"

Mrs. Senn shakes her head. "It's because of what happened to poor Woody. He was sitting on the banister, at the very top of the stairs."

"And?"

"And somehow he managed to tip backward and fall head over heels."

"No!"

"Or would that be heels over head? Anyway, the point is, he hit his neck on the second floor and then again on the first. Poor dear. He was dead by the time he hit the ground."

"Oh my God!"

"I know. Tragic." Mrs. Senn describes the grief that spread through the school in the weeks and months after the accident. "There's a little plaque in his memory, and his father donated some lovely marine biology books to the library."

The news leaves me reeling. I barely have the energy to bring up the purpose of my visit. But I eventually mumble forlornly that Woody and I had bonded, in part, while trying to avoid Cesar.

The news startles Mrs. Senn. "Trying to avoid a seizure?"

"No, Cesar."

"Pardon?"

"The boy's name was '*Say-CZAR.*' As in the emperor."

Mrs. Senn gives me a puzzled look and, echoing her husband's reflection, says, "You'd think I'd remember a name like that."

But she doesn't, much to her regret and mine.

The trip turns out to be a total bust. I arrived at Aiglon hoping to find an enemy and leave learning I had lost a friend.

THE REALISTIC INSTITUTE

Back in New York, I go through the annual reports photocopied by the alumni officer. They're mostly given over to lists of teachers and students, broken down by seniority, honors, and rank, and detailed accounts of long and short expeditions. The report covering the year after my residency includes a half-page obituary for Woody, an otherwise tender tribute marred by an inept remark from our housemaster. Surely he could have avoided the phrase "*bouncing* personality" to describe a boy who died by tumbling down a stairwell.

While scanning a directory at the back of the report, I find my first genuine lead. It's a small one, a tiny one, in fact: the 1973 mailing address for my former roommate. Just seeing his name in print gives me the willies: "Viana, Cesar. Mr. and Mrs. Cesar A Viana,

Realistic Institute, Quiapo Shopping Center, Barbosa Street, Manila, Philippines."

The institutional affiliation is curious—Cesar having ties to something called the Realistic Institute is like Genghis Khan operating the Mongol Empire Charm School—but invigorating. The address, outdated though it is, gives the search newfound purpose and focus.

No phone number is listed, so I head down to the New York Public Library and spend a few hours in a giant hall packed with telephone directories from all over the world. While nearby researchers are looking up numbers in Madrid and Detroit and Caracas, I thumb through tattered copies of the *Philippine Long Distance Telephone Directory*. One of them yields a phone number and clears up a minor mystery. The Kissingerian-sounding Realistic Institute is, in point of fact, a "vocational school for hair and beauty culture."

Over dinner that night, I ask Françoise, "How do I start up a conversation with a bully I haven't seen in twenty years?"

"What do you want to say?"

"I'm not sure."

"What do you want *him* to say?"

"I don't know."

"Well, that's a problem."

"I know."

For more than a week I drag my feet about making the call. Ultimately I muster up the courage to dial the number, but hang up before anyone answers.

"What's the matter?" Françoise asks.

"I can't decide whether to sound lighthearted or prosecutorial. Do I say, 'Hi, Cesar. Guess who! It's Nosey!' Come out guns blazing: 'Did you dupe Paul into launching my father's watch out the window?' Maybe I should just play 'The Thirty-Nine Lashes' into the receiver and wait for a reaction."

"What time is it in Manila?"

"About nine at night."

"Perfect. Stop overthinking and call him."

As I reach for the phone my stomach is in knots. I dial the number and take a deep breath. I hear a couple of feeble long-distance chirps, the crackle of static, another few chirps, and then, a few seconds later, the dull unchanging buzz of a connection that's gone dead.

I hang up.

Françoise gives me a look.

"Disconnected," I say, trying to hide my relief. "I guess that's that."

But we both know I'm full of shit. We both know the boy I can't get a hold of still has a hold on me.

DARWIN AND DICKENS

After deadending in Switzerland and New York, I suspended the hunt. That was in 1991, when professional and personal commitments were keeping Françoise and me on the move. Fieldwork, magazine assignments, teaching gigs, residential fellowships, Aboriginal land claims, conferences (literary and anthropological), book tours, workshops, and family holidays—the Jewish ones in America, the Catholic ones in France—demanded ceaseless relocation.

In 1994, Françoise gave birth to our son, Max. We traveled light during his infancy, jerry-rigging suitcases into bassinets, discarding research files after wrapping up assignments. Yet wherever we went, I carried along the Cesar journal. Just because I wasn't actively looking for him doesn't mean he was absent from my thoughts. Reminders popped up in the most unexpected places. At the back of a dingy bar in Alice Springs, a pair of drunks playing foosball recalled my ex-roommate's unstoppable bank shot. In Vienna, hanging on the wall of the Kunsthistorisches Museum, a *Flagellation of Christ* reinvoked the musical whipping. Hot sauce, Andrew Lloyd Webber tunes, Ferdinand Marcos, Montblanc fountain pens, and, more than anything else, vintage Omegas had me reaching for the journal.

Over time, the nature of my note taking underwent a change. Rather than waiting to be waylaid by memories of Switzerland, I began to build on them. When, for example, I noticed that many of the British writers I admired had been victimized by boarding school thugs, I investigated the connections between their educational struggles and the books they produced as adults. Were Darwin's theories of natural selection inspired by the adversity he faced at Dr. Butler's school? Were the sour educators in the works of Charles Dickens an indictment of the churlish instructors the novelist endured at the Wellington House Academy? Would George Orwell's worldview have been so Orwellian had the headmaster of St. Cyprian's resisted the impulse to break a bone-handled riding crop on the buttocks of the young bed wetter and future author of *1984*? And what about the atavistic boys who knock each other off in *Lord of the Flies*? Could their behavior have been captured with such merciless authority if William Golding hadn't attended, and later taught, at residential grammar schools? Maybe boarding school misery nourishes later achievement. Wouldn't *that* be reassuring!

The Belvedere foosball table provided a similar chance to procrastinate. I spent the better part of a week researching the biometric development of the foosball figurine from the mid- to late twentieth century.

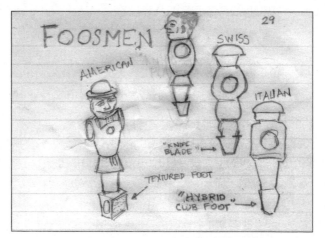

Table soccer players from the '70s. A detail from my journal.

Françoise tolerated my detours but refused to endorse them. "Where is Cesar in all this?" she protested. "Where are you?"

She had a point. Obsessively charting the physical and material evolution of four-inch figurines kept me from digging into more consequential matters. I had cast my net so far beyond the terror of the tower that I'd forgotten what I was fishing for. The distractions might have dulled the pain, but they would never fully dispel it. All forms of anesthesia eventually wear off.

THE TANK

When my son turned five—this was in 1999—he had a series of run-ins with a seven-year-old known around the jungle gym as Thomas the Tank Engine. Because the boy failed to get the hang of kindergarten, he had been held back. It was during his do-over year that the Tank shunted into Max's life. Although most of the skirmishes between the two were minor, the kind of playground dustups quickly remedied by a time-out, one incident had more serious repercussions. During the annual Christmas pageant, the Tank settled a property dispute over a Pokémon card by throttling my son with a necktie. Max had a red ring around his neck for a few days, but the psychological impact lasted a good deal longer. School suddenly became scary. On more than one occasion Françoise had to pick Max up early because he felt menaced by his archenemy.

"Did you ever have a bully?" our son asked me soon after the necktie incident.

"I did."

"What did you do?"

I had no ready or reassuring response. "I tried to avoid him," I said unhelpfully.

"Did it work?"

"No, not really," I acknowledged, giving Max a hug that probably offered more comfort to me than it did to him.

I was in way over my head. Max was asking for the kind of counsel I had never received. It made me reflect on what my father would have said or done had I had the chance to tell him about Cesar.

I wanted to protect Max—I wanted him to protect himself—but was at a total loss about what to say or do. He was still too young to hear about the tower.

Four years later, Max again confronted a nemesis, a beefy third-grader requiring no moniker. (His surname, poor little guy, was Hogg.) This time around Max gave as good as he got.

Once more, we had the bully talk. Now nine, Max was old enough for a PG version of the Cesar narrative. It came as a relief to be able to share those ancient memories, even if I did have to sugarcoat the details.

Like most kids that age, Max was full of questions. "How hot was the hot sauce Cesar made you eat? How does foosball work? Did you get wedgies?"

"I don't think wedgies had made it to Aiglon."*

"Did you get him back?"

"Once," I said. "I smacked him in the mouth with a blob of ink from a fountain pen."

"A fountain pen?" Max was puzzled and unimpressed until I told him in greater detail about the hallway showdown.

The last year my son believed in Santa, he insisted that we set out a snack of carrots and cookies and (at the urging of his aunt and uncle) a bottle of single malt Scotch. Father Christmas proved grateful. Max got what he'd asked for: a foosball table.

"I gather your chimney prevented Santa from delivering the

---

*My memory is faulty. Subsequent interviews with housemates reveal that wedgies were, on occasion, dispensed during my time at Aiglon.

bloody thing *assembled*," my British brother-in-law groused as we worked our way through the instructions (and a bottle of eighteen-year-old Laphroaig).

Max's training began on Christmas morning. Smacking around a cork ball, we traded bully tales, offering each other counsel and consolation. Those father–son foosball talks constituted some of our most heartfelt exchanges. In fact, they resonated so strongly that I ended up writing a children's book featuring an amalgam of the bullies Max and I discussed.

My two previous novels, both written for adults, had included antiheroes inspired by people in my life. The cranky pornographic bookseller who spits and coughs his way through *A Case of Curiosities* relied heavily on the respiratory challenges of my mother's fourth husband, and the anachronistic bibliophile in my second novel, *The Grand Complication*, emerged from a friendship struck up during the year Françoise and I lived in Paris. But the youthful villain in *Leon and the Spitting Image* mined a deeper vein of personal history. Although the bully in the tale was named Hank the Tank, a nod to the seven-year-old who had garroted my son, I drew much more heavily on my own memories of childhood cruelty.

When I submitted the manuscript to my editor, she raised the possibility of rehabilitating the bully at the end of the story.

"Don't do it, Dad!" Max pleaded. "Don't change the Tank. Some kids are evil. Period."

I sided with Max and told my editor the Tank would not be mending his ways. After which, the gloves came off. Thanks, in part, to my son's unwavering conviction, the bully ends up receiving a giant helping of whoop-ass. Vengeance may be the Lord's, but in His infinite wisdom, He sometimes outsources order fulfillment to mere mortals.

FALSE POSITIVES

Leon and the Spitting Image was released in 2003. The publisher dispatched me to classrooms and multifunction "cafetoriums" all around the country to give readings, sign books, and answer questions: How many words do you have to write a day? What time do you have to start working? How much money do you get to make? Does your editor fix all your mistakes? Do you know J. K. Rowling?

Invariably, the Q&As zeroed in on the Tank. Was he based on a real person? What was the worst thing he did? Did you tell on him? Did you really get to cover him in ice cream and hot fudge? What happened to him? Where is he now? What would you do if you saw him again?

I started carrying around a photograph of the boys of Belvedere, circa 1972, so that school kids could compare Cesar's face to the fictional bully smirking on the jacket flap of the book. It was a pretty good likeness—a lot more accurate than the preliminary sketches. (At my urging, the illustrator had curved the Tank's mouth downward, narrowed the eyes, and added some flesh to the cheeks.) After most presentations, a small knot of students would surround me, eager to compare notes. So many of them, I discovered, had Cesars in their lives.

The unexpected and uncompromising cross-examinations reawakened my fixation. Questions I thought I had laid to rest suddenly felt more pressing than ever. It couldn't have come at a more opportune time. I was just getting the hang of a newfangled search engine called Google. Suddenly here was no need to fly to Switzerland or the Philippines to hunt down an ex-roommate; I could pursue him far more effectively with laptop and modem.

Within seconds of Googling Cesar's name, I got a hit. It turned out Cesar Viana was *not* working in sales, as I'd casually speculated when

Françoise first raised the matter in Paris, nor was he living in Manila.

Cesar Viana was a *professor extraordinário* with an endowed chair in electrochemical engineering at the University of Lisbon, as well as the international president of the Society of St. Vincent de Paul, the respected Catholic aid organization devoted to helping the poor.

The news pissed me off. It was hard—no, not hard, it was impossible—to reconcile the Cesar I knew with the four core beliefs of

The character Hank the Tank was inspired, in part, by memories of Cesar.

the global nonprofit: charity, friendship, community, simplicity.

Maybe my editor had been right and Max and I had been wrong. Maybe the once-a-bully, always-a-bully hypothesis that legitimated the vengeful finale of *Leon and the Spitting Image* had unfairly pigeonholed the character of the Tank and, by implication, Cesar.

My irritation and dismay lasted about a week. Follow-up web searches revealed that even though my former roommate and the extraordinary professor shared an uncommon name, they were different people. Portuguese Cesar was too old to have been my roommate.

I tweaked the search terms by adding the initial *A*. Doing so netted half a dozen new matches, including a musical director living in Belgium. That made a little more sense. Cesar's boarding school production of *Jesus Christ Superstar* might well have presaged a career in the performing arts. But further digging revealed that Belgian Cesar, like Portuguese Cesar, was a false positive; he was too *young* to have been my roommate.

In quick succession, I vetted and rejected two more like-named Cesars. The first was the coauthor of "Human Saliva as a Cleaning Agent for Dirty Surfaces," a technical report that quantified what my grandmother Wilhelmina proved every time she saw me—namely, that spit on a hankie works wonders for removing schmutz. The second near miss was a flute player living in Spain.

A few days later, I broadened the search by adding *Aiglon* to my list of key words. All that did was grow the grim inventory of alumni tragedy started by Mrs. Senn. The web alerted me to a Belvedere boy who had drowned in a yachting accident off the Florida coast and the avalanche death of the son of the ski instructor who had taught me how to wedel.

Some nonfatal updates proved equally disturbing. A sexual predator sneaked into the school, anesthetized three girls, and raped them; a chemistry teacher was relieved of his duties after posting a series of homoerotic fantasies online; an Aiglon headmaster spent two years in a Swiss prison cell after his wife accused him—wrongfully, it later emerged—of abusing the younger of their two sons.

Much to my regret, Cesar Augustus steered clear of such tawdry misfortune. As far as the Internet was concerned, he didn't even exist. While that frustrated me, it also offered some comfort. It suggested that Cesar Augustus Viana was venturing through life without distinction.

THE MANILA FOLDER

Although the web failed to locate Cesar, it did provide an update on the beauty school where Cesar had previously received his mail. According to a site devoted to Filipino jurisprudence, the Realistic Institute was entangled in a protracted civil lawsuit stemming from a tragic accident. Records revealed that on October 24, 1955—in other words, a few years before Cesar was born—a fire had broken out in a downtown Manila warehouse near the beauty school where my future roommate would later receive his mail. Panicked by the ensuing smoke and flames, some 180 cosmetologists-in-training charged toward the institute's only exit. That stampede resulted in four deaths.

Relatives of one of the four victims sued the institute's owner, a woman named Mercedes Teague. The case dragged on until 1973, when the Supreme Court of the Philippines ruled in favor of the plaintiffs. Try as I might, I was unable to establish an explicit connection between Mercedes Teague and Cesar Augustus Viana (beyond the mailing address).

The case popped up while I was investigating Cesar's family background and, more specifically, his father's rumored ties to Ferdinand Marcos, the longtime president of the Philippines. The unverified connection made sense to me now, in a way that it hadn't as a child. The temperament of the Filipino strongman meshed nicely with Cesar's martial sensibilities. Still, I wanted proof.

When the web failed to corroborate the hearsay, I contacted an Australian friend who worked for the United Nations. The same day I sent him a note, he emailed an American colleague based in Manila.

"I have a cryptic request for you," he told his associate:

> *A very old friend of mine periodically sends me very odd emails asking for obscure information. His latest request sets a new standard, and I am going to pass it on to you for a quick bit of local research. In a nutshell, Allen needs to confirm whether the father of some kid who beat him up in a Swiss boarding school (1971–72) was (or was not) head of security under Marcos?! (I have learnt not to ask too many questions BTW). I will let Allen give you more information on surnames etc. . . . and am copying him on this email.*

Another dead end: Fabian Ver was not Cesar's father.

Matt Sherwin, the young foreign service intern on the receiving end of the email, also responded promptly: "Ha, yes that *is* a pretty cryptic request, but I'm glad to help. Allen—do you have a name that I could try to track down?"

I sent the information he requested and, for good measure, attached a PDF of *Teague v. Fernandez, et al.* Matt promptly contacted various Filipino politicians, historians, and journalists. He also checked half a dozen Southeast Asian databases. Cesar's surname didn't come up.

"A number of people have asked if I meant *Virata*, who was Finance Minister under Marcos and PM from '81–'86," Matt wrote back.

No, I assured him. It's not Virata.

"What about Gen. Fabian C. Ver, who was in charge of security of Marcos (Presidential Security Command)?"

No, it wasn't Ver, either.

"I think this confirms that the Marcos claims were fictitious," I informed Matt in an email thanking him for his help, adding in a post-script: "If business ever takes you near the building where the four girls perished, I'd love to get a JPEG, but don't put yourself out."

As I hoped, Matt ignored my feigned discouragement. A few days later, he sent me thirteen JPEGs and the following reconnaissance report:

> *Allen, I couldn't find a Barbosa Street in Quiapo.*
> *The court opinion mentions the corner of Quezon*
> *Blvd. and Soler St. as the location of the Realistic*
> *Institute. Quezon Blvd. is a main thoroughfare,*
> *Soler St. a side street that runs perpendicular to*

*Quezon, but, at least as of today, does not intersect
with it. Soler intersects Evangelista (parallel to
Quezon) about 70 meters short of Quezon, where
it turns into Florante. Florante is a tight alley
of crammed living spaces on one side and an
abandoned building on the other. It does not intersect
with Quezon; the alley ends with more of these
"homes," on the other side of which is Quezon.*

It pleased me to learn I wasn't the only one who took research way too seriously. Surveying the photographs Matt attached to his email, I was struck by the squalor. It was hard to connect Cesar to the seedy locale. Geographically and economically, Quiapo was a world away from Aiglon. No hay fields, no milk cows, no aristocrats. And it wasn't the Alps that loomed in the background. It was the faded facade of the Philippine College of Criminology.

The location, in Manila, of the defunct Realistic Institute.

WHITE OWL CIGAR BOX

A few months after the search hit an impasse for the umpteenth time, it was revived by Max while we were visiting my mother at her summerhouse on Cape Cod. He approached me as I wrestling with a rope of bittersweet, an invasive vine that has killed off much of the Cape's native flora.

"Hey, Dad, check this out!"

I took a look. He was holding a battered White Owl cigar box he'd discovered in the bottom of a trunk. I put down my loppers and pulled off my gloves. As soon as I opened the lid, I was transported back in time.

The cigar box was full of Swiss memorabilia: ski patches and postage stamps, a wooden match safe encased in a tiny ski boot, a dried-up sea horse. (How *that* found its way into the box, I can't say.) A small pink object the size of a Scrabble tile caught Max's attention. "What *is* that?"

"A Sugus. Your grandfather introduced me to them. They're like Starburst, only better."

"No way!"

"Yes way."*

Max held up a small Swiss coin. "How much is this worth?"

"Ten centimes? It would have paid for a game of foosball."

"What's this?" Max produced a rusty red disk of metal.

"My rank badge."

I was holding the patch I had torn from my Aiglon blazer on July 4, 1972, running my fingers over the motto ("God Is My Strength"), when Max produced the tape cassette.

---

*My son and I later settled our confectionary dispute by purchasing a large tin of Sugus from an eBay vendor in Thailand. After a series of blind taste tests, Max grudgingly acknowledged the incontrovertible: Sugus is *vastly* superior to Starburst.

The Swiss time capsule Max found in the bottom of a trunk.

"Jesus Christ!" I blurted out. I couldn't have cursed more relevantly if I'd chosen my words with care. What the hell was *that* doing in the box?

"Uh, Dad?"

Did I swipe it to stop the performances?

"Dad?"

Was it given to me as a sadistic going-away present?

"Yoo-hoo. Earth to Dad."

Did I buy it, like a brainwashed hostage who forms a pathological attachment to his abductors?

"Dad? You okay? You look funny."

Max was around twelve—old enough to receive an unedited account of my alpine terrors.

As usual, he was full of questions. "Did Cesar really whip you, or was it just pretend?"

"A bit of both."

"What kind of belt did he use?"

"A normal belt."

"Did you tell?"

"Kids didn't tell back then. Not at that school."

"That sucks."

"Not as much as when he and another kid swiped my dad's—your grandfather's—watch."

"What a douche!"

A few days later, I decided to play the ancient tape. In the graveyard of electronics that clutters our attic, I found a cassette player minus its power cord. After a futile attempt to match some dozen adaptors to the obsolete device, I pried open the battery compartment, removed the leaky C-cells, cleaned the heads, popped in three new batteries, reinserted the audiotape, and pressed PLAY.

I barely made it through the overture before I was overcome by nausea and hit STOP. I tried more than once that day to listen to "The Thirty-Nine Lashes." I couldn't. I tried a week later and failed that time, too.

Despite my persistence certain stuff remained off-limits. Why was that? What caused me to swing between compulsion and revulsion? It was hard enough to ask questions like that. Finding answers was all but impossible.

PART III

"A LIE, A CONTRIVANCE, A FICTION"

I like treachery, but I cannot say anything good of traitors.
Caesar Augustus,
in Plutarch's *Life of Romulus*

If you have the ambition to become a villain, the first thing you should do is learn to be impenetrable. Don't act like Blofeld—monocled and ostentatious. We journalists love writing about eccentrics. We hate writing about impenetrable, boring people. It makes us look bad: the duller the interviewee, the duller the prose. If you want to get away with wielding true, malevolent power, be boring.
Jon Ronson, *The Psychopath Test*

"Throne for a Loop"

Until Max found the cigar box, evidence relating to my search fit comfortably in the slim journal bearing Cesar's name and a couple of manila folders. (Given the subject's birthplace, manila folders seemed an appropriate storage solution.) The new cache of materials demanded a bigger container, so I consolidated the materials and placed them in a document box, which I labeled the Cesareum.

The title was wishful. Although I had surveyed an impressive pantheon of imperial impostors, my ex-roommate—the *real* Cesar—remained at large, his whereabouts and personal history a complete and total mystery.

Once more I was standing at a crossroads: abandon the inquiry or pull out all the stops. The choice was obvious.

My revived efforts began in 2005 at a major research institution that subscribed to a broad range of licensed news sources. When I explained at the reference desk what I was after, a sympathetic librarian overlooked the institution's user restrictions and slipped me a password that allowed access to dozens of proprietary databases. When I thanked him, he said, "No problem. I had a Cesar when I was growing up."

Most of the digital records proved useless. They either duplicated material I had already obtained or supplemented information about irrelevant Cesars. Only one fresh lead emerged, but boy, was it a doozy! A passing reference to a new Cesar appeared in a 2001 *New York Post* article bearing the headline: 'KNIGHT FALLS' AS FEDS BUST UP A ROYAL RIPOFF. Here's how the story began:

*A trio of American fraudsters posing as fake European royalty
were busted on charges they swindled more than $1 million out
of unsuspecting investors, authorities said yesterday.*

*The three allegedly posed as a British knight, a Serbian prince
and a German prince to pitch bogus "medium-term notes" to investors in a scheme dating back to 1997.*

The article went on to allege that the three con men duped dozens
of sophisticated investors into entering loan agreements with the
Badische Trust Consortium, a sham investment house claiming to
manage some $60 billion. According to the *Post*, the fake financiers
rented suites in Switzerland, traveled on diplomatic passports issued
by the Knights of Malta, and adhered to a fourteen-point dress code
that required the use of walking sticks, homburg hats, and Montblanc
fountain pens.

The names of the crooks were equally preposterous. The chairman
of the bank was identified as Prince Robert von Badische (rhymes with
baddish), his chief lieutenant called himself the Baron Moncrieffe, and
their youthful "administrator" was known as Colonel Sherry. And how
did the man whose name matched my roommate's figure into the cock-
amamie con? "Cesar A. Viana" was one of two so-called independent
project consultants who, according to a federal prosecutor, "lured [the
victims] in with false promises of big money."

It's my guy! I told myself. *It's* got *to be!*

The Badische fraud, with its reliance on theatricality, manipula-
tion, and misdirection, was a perfect sequel to the juvenile spectacles
Cesar staged in the tower. In fact, it was the apotheosis of all things
Cesarean, even going so far as to exploit my nemesis's preferred brand
of fountain pen. Never in my wildest dreams had I expected to un-
earth such exquisite corroboration of childhood villainy. Max had
been right all along. Once a bully, always a bully.

For the next five hours, I sat glued in front of the library computer,
greedily downloading every reference to the crime I could find. The

pinch-me feeling only grew when I learned that all the defendants (except for Prince Robert, who only eluded prosecution by skipping town) were tried, convicted, and sent to federal prison.

Given the outlandish nature of the fraud, it was puzzling that the news coverage hadn't spread much beyond New York. (The AP, for example, limited its reporting to a brief arrest bulletin.) Still, the local tabloids had a field day with the headlines. The *Daily News* was partial to forced rhyme (41 MOS. IN SLAMMER FOR PRINCELY SCAMMER and PRISON FOR SCAMMIN' BARON), whereas the *Post* had a weakness for puns: THRONE FOR A LOOP and ROYAL FLUSHED.

The reporting itself was pretty perfunctory. I did, however, pull up one lengthy piece about the crime, but it was written in Dutch. I forwarded the story to a translator I'd met years before at a literary festival, along with this melodramatic note:

> *Nadine, I'm contacting you with a sense of dire*
> *(but thrilling) urgency. I believe I've located a*
> *despicable boy who tormented me during a miserable*
> *year (1971) at an English boarding school in*
> *Switzerland. . . . Details of his postgraduate crime*
> *spree are (in part) chronicled in an article I cannot*
> *read. Do you think you could supply a translation?*
> *(See attachment.)*

I was on a high, confident that the Dutch article would amplify the perfunctory local coverage. But that *Gotcha!* feeling vaporized when I came across a photograph of the criminals in a *New York Post* article headlined CON JOB "KINGDOM"—EX-GI ON TRIAL IN $50B FANTASY-NATION SCAM.

None of the men in the group portrait resembled my former roommate, which raised doubts I was trying to ignore: How could I be sure the convicted shill was my childhood bully? Maybe I had stumbled upon another false positive.

Only two concrete biographical details about Cesar the shill emerged from the news reports: (1) he resided in San Francisco, and (2) he was forty-four years old at the time of trial, in 2002.

The first fact was of little significance. Although a quick search confirmed that nearly one in five residents of San Francisco claim Filipino ancestry, that hardly explained how a Manila-born kid educated in Switzerland had relocated to the Bay Area.

The second fact was more encouraging. The ages of the two Cesars matched. The forty-four-year-old criminal would have been twelve when I was ten.

So where did that leave things? Was I confident *my* Cesar was the San Francisco con man? Yes. Was I certain? No.

FEAR

I told Max about the scam.

"Cesar's a crook? Cool!"

"He *might* be a crook. I'm not a hundred percent sure."

"Same first and last name? Same age? What are the chances?"

I pulled out the Belvedere house photo. "Compare this kid"—I tapped the face of a frowning schoolboy—"to the guys in the newspaper photo. None of the con men have the kid's eyes or nose. And the smile is *completely* different."

"Where is he now?" Max asked.

"In prison."

"Forever?"

"No, not forever, kiddo. He got thirty-seven months."

"That's all? When will he be out?"

"I'm guessing in about a year."

"What happens then? What if he tracks us down? What if he steals all our money like he did those other people's?" Max was no longer young enough to believe that his father was invincible. The prospect of facing a *real* criminal who had stolen *real* money from *real* people made my son anxious. Hell, it made me anxious. All the more so when I realized Max was the age I had been when the Cesar saga began.

"Don't worry," I told him. "It's probably not the same guy. And even if it is, the guy knows nothing about us, and there's no reason he ever will."

"So you won't try beating him up?"

"I have no interest in beating him up," I assured my son. But

CON JOB 'KINGDOM'

Ex-GI on trial in $50B fantasy-nation scam

The photo in the New York Post *identified only Colonel Sherry (seen standing on the left) by name. Was the fellow on the far right my former roommate?*

Max's question raised a deeper issue. What *would* I do if I ever crossed paths with Cesar? I had invested so much energy looking for him, and yet neglected to consider the consequences of actually finding him. In fact, I had actively *avoided* confronting the consequences of confronting Cesar. Doing otherwise would have forced me to face feelings of vengeance and anguish roiling just below the surface of the search.

Max's concerns were echoed by Françoise. "What do we know about him?" she said. "Maybe he is violent."

I tell her what I told Max. "It's probably not even the same person."

"Whether he is or isn't, promise me you won't make contact."

I felt torn. Françoise was right to worry. Still, I wasn't willing to abandon the search. Not now. Not before confirming that I'd found my fugitive. "You're the one who first pushed me to look for Cesar, remember?"

"That was before I knew he was dangerous."

"*Might* be dangerous," I corrected before adding, foolishly, that the criminal revelations only made the search *more* compelling.

"You find danger compelling?"

"Part of me does," I acknowledged.

Two weeks after receiving my translation request, Nadine replied. In my giddy haste to learn what the article said, I had misremembered her nationality. Nadine is Belgian, not Dutch. Graciously overlooking my stupidity, she fed the story through a virtual translator and emailed back the results. The computerized conversion wasn't entirely coherent, but fluent enough to amplify the charges mentioned in the New York tabloids. It turned out that some Badische associates were tied to acts of "deception, forgery, fraud, and assassination." Assassination?

The Dutch update prompted me to conduct a criminal background check on the San Francisco Cesar, a decision I didn't reach lightly. It's one thing to Google a long-lost roommate. It's another to pay a website to tap into law enforcement databases. It felt slimy. I knew what my former roommate would have said had he known: "Don't be so nosy, Nosey."

Even after I overcame my moral misgivings, I still faced some practical obstacles. Criminal background checks, to be done thoroughly, require the subject's date of birth and a social security number. I had neither. That meant the search results would omit information from all California archives, as well as most federal databases. Given those limitations, it seemed unlikely that I'd get much on a *San Francisco* con man prosecuted by the *United States* Department of Justice. Still, the report would, at a strict minimum, provide basic data on everyone in the country who shared Cesar's first, middle, and last name.

My $9.95 investment generated nine matches. Of those, four Florida Cesars, two New Jersey Cesars, and a Cesar living in Texas went straight to the trash folder; their ages didn't jibe with my ex-roommate's. That left two viable candidates: one from San Francisco and another living in New York on a fancy stretch of Fifth

Avenue. More likely than not, the San Francisco Cesar was the criminal mentioned in the *Post*. But what about the other guy? If Fifth Avenue Cesar turned out to be my guy it might alleviate Max and Françoise's fears. But I couldn't help feeling that it would really suck to learn that my long-lost nemesis was an upstanding citizen and, worse still, stinking rich.

In addition to the nine exact matches, there was a tenth with the same mailing address as the San Francisco Cesar but a slightly different surname. Two guys named Cesar living in the same building? That seemed odd. Odder still was that the tenth Cesar had a double-barreled last name that combined my roommate's surname, Viana, with Teague, the name of the owner of the Realistic Institute. What were the chances?

Still, residential coincidence could hardly be taken as proof. If only I had a mug shot. I felt sure a recent picture would clear things up.

Realizing my amateur efforts weren't getting me very far, I asked for the help of a high school buddy named Paul Hechinger. A producer at Court TV, Paul had been covering criminal matters for years.

"Who was the arresting agency?" he asked when I told him I was trying to get my hands on a mug shot.

"I have no clue."

"That's going to be a problem."

He explained some sixty federal agencies are sanctioned to make arrests. "They're *supposed* to network their crime data. That doesn't always happen." Paul agreed to walk my request down the hall to the Smoking Gun, a Court TV affiliate with extensive law enforcement contacts and a vast archive of arrest photos.

A few days later, he called me back. "Struck out. The guys at the Smoking Gun don't have anything. Short of filing a FOIA, it'll be tough to get your hands on the guy's mug shot."

"FOIA?"

"Freedom of Information Act."

"Are FOIAs hard to file?"

"Not hard. But you need to know the name of the arresting agency."

"Wonderful."

"If I were you, I'd review the court filings. They're bound to contain a lead."

"Done that. I can't make head or tails out of the legalese. 'Admission of a Codefendant's Self-Inculpatory Plea Allocution to Prove the Existence of a Charged Conspiracy.' What the hell does that mean?"

Paul commiserated. "You could try cold-calling the FBI. They might have a bulletin or wanted poster."

I followed his advice and left messages at bureau field offices in New York and San Francisco. No one got back to me. Apparently, twelve-year-old bullies aren't a federal law enforcement priority.

KISMET ON JEBEL HAROUN

Once more, the inquiry had stalled out. I had a search without a solution and a story without an ending. Or rather, I now had *two* stories without endings—one about a bully and one about a fraud. And the only possible link between them was extremely tenuous: a double-barreled surname connecting a boarding school bully and a hairdresser from Manila. I had exhausted all leads and, in the process, exhausted myself. And my family. All of us were more than a little weary of the search for Cesar.

A few weeks after the FBI blew me off, the mother of my godson proposed we join them on an archaeological tour of Jordan. I jumped at the chance.

"The trip will be great," I told Françoise. "It'll put some distance between me and you-know-who."

"My eye," she said. Her skepticism was understandable. Françoise saw Cesar for what he was: the symptom of a chronic condition that might go into remission for months or even years but that would never disappear for good.

Few places match the visual splendor of the Swiss Alps, but as we hiked from Petra (the ancient Jordanian city that hides the Holy Grail in *Indiana Jones and the Last Crusade*) to the summit of Jebel Haroun (a sacred site where the prophet Aaron is said to be buried), I have to admit the arid beauty of the Ma'an came pretty damn close. There were a dozen parents and children in our expedition, plus four Bedouin guides and their flatulent pack animals. After dinner, the adults gathered around a campfire, sipped whiskey, watched the sun set below the sandstone hills, and swapped stories. I told the group about Cesar. That led to a heated debate about whether or not my bête noire was the guy the feds had sent to prison. The most vocal skeptic was a man named John Hall, senior partner at the New York law firm of Debevoise & Plimpton. Fascinated though he was by my inquiry, he was unswayed by the evidence linking my Cesar to the San Francisco con man. Before turning in for the night, he took me aside and, after gently correcting certain technical errors in my account that touched on matters of law—for instance, I had conflated the roles of district and US attorneys—he offered to help review the specifics of the case when we returned to the United States.

"Thanks," I said. "That's really generous."

"Generosity has nothing to do with it. I want to know how this all plays out."

THREE EMAILS

A few months after the trip to Jordan, I turned again to Cesar. It was the Sunday before Thanksgiving. I was in my office reviewing yet another batch of court documents, trying once more to establish a link between my roommate and the Bay Area swindler. While I was skimming an "appeal from a judgment of conviction for mail fraud, wire fraud, and conspiracy to commit wire fraud," something caught my eye. One of the defendants cited in the brief, the Baron Moncrieffe, had apparently received pro bono representation from a law firm with a name that rang a bell. I checked my address book.

Son of a bitch!

I immediately fired off an email to John. After a few pleasantries, I cut to the chase:

> *. . . Do you happen to recall my account of a bully named Cesar, whose anti-Semitic attentions I endured at a boarding school back in 1971?*
>
> *I discovered, in a file transcript of the Appeal made in the Second Circuit, that one of the defendants (not Cesar) was represented by Mark P. Goodman, a lawyer at your firm.*
>
> *Do you think I might be able to speak with Mr. Goodman? I'm guessing he'd be able to help me establish whether or not [his client's] codefendant was the same guy I knew thirty-plus years ago.*
>
> *I'm attaching the two PDF files about this case. Any guidance you might provide would be greatly appreciated.*

John emailed back in under an hour:

> *Allen,*
>
> *I will talk with Mark Goodman on Monday. He is a former assistant US attorney and regularly takes pro bono cases for indigents. I assume [his client] is such an assignment. Although it is possible that there are some restrictions on what Mark can tell you about [Cesar] (because he learned them*

in connection with a confidential relationship or
because of some sort of joint defense arrangement),
I am sure that he will be quite willing to talk with
you and tell you whatever his ethical responsibilities
permit. And I would think that general biographical
information would be fair ground and should
answer the identity question.

John

"These Guys Conned Everybody"

Before placing the call, I spend a few hours Googling Goodman and his firm. The results are intimidating. *American Lawyer* ranked Debevoise & Plimpton the number one firm in the nation and singled out Goodman by name for building a practice devoted both to lucrative "big mess" corporate cases and to unpaid pro bono work. (He reportedly provides some 250 hours of uncompensated representation each year—five times the standard recommended by the American Bar Association.) A hotshot litigator at a firm where partners receive upward of $2 million a year probably has better things to do than help a colleague's vacation companion chase down a former roommate. I tell myself, *Don't waste his time.*

"I'm bound by ethical limitations," Goodman informs me as soon as he picks up the phone. "There are some things I cannot discuss. Understood?"

"Understood."

"But this much I can say. Everything these guys touched, promised, concocted, represented, and did was a lie, a contrivance, a fiction. I've been around a lot of con artists. I handle a ton of white-collar crime. A ton. This was the most massive fraud I have *ever* come across. *Massive*. Fake knights. False banks. Imaginary kingdoms. Are you getting the picture?"

"Very clearly, yes."

"These guys traveled on bogus passports. They hosted lavish dinner parties at five-star hotels. They performed knighting ceremonies." Goodman chuckles. "All the movie stars they scammed. There's a file somewhere around here. Letters, photos. Liza Minnelli, Dionne Warwick, Gene Kelly."

Gene Kelly! Temping though it is, I resist pressing for details. "It's not the victims who interest me. It's one of the con men."

"Which one? The prince? My guy the baron? The colonel?"

"No. Cesar Augustus."

The name confuses Goodman.

"He's identified as Cesar A. Viana in the court records."

"Oh," says Goodman. "The shill."

"That's right."

I provide a succinct account of my time at Aiglon.

"And you think the kid who tormented you in 1971 is the same guy who worked for Badische thirty years later?"

"I hope so."

Goodman is silent for a moment before he says, "What do you want to know?"

"Well, for starters, do you recall if Cesar was Filipino?"

"I believe all the defendants were American. But I didn't deal with Cesar directly. Hold on. There might be something in the files."

I hear the rustle of paper. "You still have the files?"

"Only the recent briefs. Most of the stuff is in storage or with associates."

"Other lawyers were involved?"

"It was a full-court press," Goodman says. "That's how it works here, even pro bono. We never cut corners. The point is to win. It's a shame we pled out. I was all set to argue." He explains he had little choice. A week before trial, the prosecution produced irrefutable proof that the Baron Moncrieffe had filed a false financial affidavit to obtain court-appointed counsel.

"If the baron had assets, how did he end up getting free representation from your firm?"

The question prompts another chuckle out of Goodman. "Like I said, these guys conned *everybody*. It's all in the record. If you want, you can come down and have a look."

It takes me a moment to absorb the magnitude of the proposal. "That'd be great," I say, trying very hard to remain calm.

Seventy-two hours after Goodman's invitation, I send him the following email:

> *Dear Mark,*
>
> *I can't thank you enough for the kind offer to allow me to look over the files that touch on Cesar (the coconspirator in the Badische affair). It should quickly become apparent if "my" Cesar is the same one currently serving time.*
>
> *I've looked at my calendar, and find that the second half of December is chock-full of obligations. I can, however, come down on any of the following dates: Monday, Tuesday or Wednesday (November 28th, 29th or 30th) or the following Monday, Tuesday or Wednesday (December 5th, 6th or 7th).*
>
> *Cordially,*
> *Allen*

I spend the rest of the day clicking the GET MAIL button. By the time Goodman's reply arrives, five days later, I'm a wreck.

Dear Allen,

*The Badische files will be available for you to review
in our offices next Tuesday, December 6. I will
arrange for a conference room.*

m

The next week is even more maddening. The Tuesday meeting
is rescheduled to Thursday. Then the Thursday meeting is post-
poned until Friday. I keep myself busy composing long lists of questions about the scope and scale of the fraud. But only one question
truly matters: Is the sadist from Switzerland the shill from San
Francisco?

THUNDERSNOW

It's five a.m., two hours before I have to catch the train to New York.
I'm standing in front of a full-length mirror, adjusting the knot on my
tie. I feel like I'm in high school primping for the senior prom, and I
am just as uncomfortable in my blue blazer and oxfords as I was in the
tan three-piece corduroy Brooks Brothers suit and almost matching
suede Wallabees I wore in 1978.

On the walk to the Providence train station, my foot begins throbbing where Docteur Méan stitched me up, a sure sign that the weather
is about to change. While waiting for the Acela to arrive from Boston,
I pick up a copy of the *New York Post*, the paper that revitalized the
search. Flipping through the tabloid's dependable mix of sex scandal,
drug crime, and institutional corruption—topics efficiently consolidated in today's lead story, FDNY FLOOZY A "WHACK WHORE"—a quotation, in a gossip column of all places, grabs my attention: "Almost
without fail, lawsuits are about revenge!" The line makes me wonder:

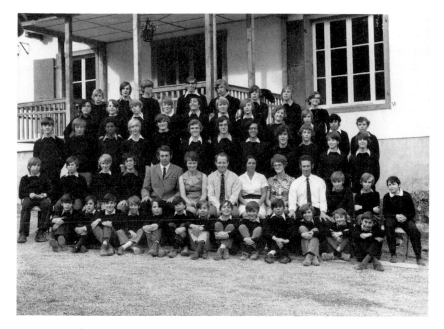

The boys of Belvedere, 1972. I'm seated on the ground, far left.
Cesar looms directly above me, fourth row from the bottom.

The Dents du Midi, as seen from Aiglon. I spent every winter of my early childhood in this Alpine wonderland, then returned, as a ten-year-old, for a fateful year at the unconventional boarding school that introduced me to Cesar.

*Robert Kurzweil, my
father, hiked the Alps
in good weather and in
bad. He was twenty-
three when these photos
were taken.*

Another picture of us in Villars. At least, I'd like to think I'm standing with my father. (The hiking boots on the unidentified polar bear appear to match Dad's.)

Robert Kurzweil, thirty years later, in Villars with his youngest child—me, age three. My father died two years after this photo was taken, at the age of fifty-five.

Gravestones make me queasy. The clinical term for this aversion, taphephobia, *is commonly tied to a fear of being buried alive. My anxiety, however, has never focused on internment. On the contrary, I avoid cemeteries because of the loss they resurrect. For the longest time, I was incapable of approaching my father's headstone, seen on left, or the marker in the Villars cemetery honoring my Belvedere buddy Woody Anderson (1959–1972). While I have subdued my dread of cemeteries, these images will always fill me with sorrow. I find my father's epitaph, a lamentation pulled from the Psalms, especially grim.*

John Corlette ("JC"), the founder of Aiglon
(second from left), often took his charges on
"expeditions." This photo was taken along
the Côte d'Azur during one such trip.

The year I attended Aiglon, JC
undertook a yearlong, around-the-
world voyage of personal discovery,
and placed his school in the care of
Group Captain Watts, a decorated
World War II fighter pilot, who
walked about campus with a chunk
of shrapnel in his shoulder.

Luia Forbes, my beloved elocution teacher,
was a retired opera diva who shared JC's
passion for Eastern mysticism. Lady Forbes
taugh me to ee-NUN-see-ate even though
her own diction was compromised by loose-
fitting dentures.

Jacques Stump, my ski
instructor, started the first
independent ski school
in Switzerland the year I
attended Aiglon.

Aiglon's founding headmaster, a chronic asthmatic, put great stock in physical training and manual labor. On the left, morning PT. On the right, Cesar mugs for the camera as one of our housemates shovels.

Punishment Runs

5	Loutish behavior	JS
3) 3) 3)	Lentitude in the run	RB
2) 2) 2) 2) 2) 2) 2)	Late for class	DRcl
3) 3) 3)	Wearing tennis shoes	CB
5	Wolf whistling during meditation	RB
5	Being slimy	JX
5	Falsifying log sheet	JX
5	Chewing after warning	JX
3	Salad dressing in water	AFH
3) 3) 3) 3) 3) 3) 3)	Missing meditation	BF
5	Using Belvedere/24 door	GLR
5	Has no option	RB

Misbehavior at Aiglon often led to "laps," known more formally as punishment runs. The numbers to the left of the listed offenses indicate how many mile-long circuits the malefactor was required to complete.

*Many of my happiest memories of Aiglon
are tied to all manner of Alpine adventure.*

Dear Mom

16 ₧ 44

16/X/71

How are you? I am fine. When I look at the size of your letter and compare them with mine I feel very inferior, so today I plan to write a long letter. Last night I did not sleep well. I bet if I didn't have my Aiglon blankets (little that I get) I am sure my toes would not have gotten frost-bitten and would have fallen off! Everthing is O.K. on the Aiglon campus (exept for a little student unrest). Someone ran away from school and twas found with his father in London! I went on my second expedition with my warm sleepingbag. I went to Sololaix and further. I am sorry I didn't write earlier, I so supose my inferiority will last in writing letters.

Love,
Allen
xxxxxxxxxxxxxx 11..!

One of my weekly letters home.

Is the search for Cesar an act of prosecution or a hunt for some deeper verdict about myself?

Near the Rhode Island–Connecticut border, a heavy snow, coupled with lightning and thunder, coincides with a flurry of phone calls. "Canceled?" the guy next to me says. "What do you mean canceled?" "The shovel?" says another commuter. "How do I know? Check in the basement. And try to get Manuela to at least stay until noon."

My mother contributes to the electronic birdsong. "I'm watching CNN," she informs me breathlessly from the comfort of her over-heated Manhattan apartment. "A blizzard is hitting the city!"

"I know, Mom. I'm in it." The weather app on my phone informs me the Northeast is under assault by a meteorological anomaly called thundersnow.

When the train reaches Penn Station, I call to reconfirm my appointment with Goodman. No one picks up. I catch a subway anyway, make it uptown with forty minutes to spare, and bide the time by devouring a large tub of rice pudding at a deli across from Goodman's firm.

Shortly before my ten a.m. meeting, I finagle two plastic bags from a cashier, tie them over my oxfords, and brave the winter squall. The knee-deep snow makes it nearly impossible to cross Third Avenue. My pants are soaked, my hair is dripping, and my toes are throbbing by the time I enter the reception area of Debevoise & Plimpton. The rice pudding starts to rebel as I take a seat.

I try to hide my discomfort by bending over the Cesareum, which I've lugged into the city to confirm, if confirmation becomes necessary, the legitimacy of my inquiry. Ten minutes go by before I notice something that ratchets up my self-consciousness: I'm guessing very few visitors enter the number one law firm in the nation wearing white plastic bags on their feet.

At ten thirty, I'm still cooling my heels, now liberated from their makeshift galoshes, and wondering if Goodman is blowing me off.

The receptionist can't (or won't) say. She can't (or won't) even tell me if he is in the building. Maybe he's spending the morning sledding with his kids. Or maybe he's decided that attorney-client privilege precludes granting me access to the files. Every time the receptionist talks into her headset, I imagine Goodman on the other end telling her, "I don't *care*. Just get rid of the guy."

At ten forty, a compact woman approaches and introduces herself. "Diane. Mark's assistant. Mark's in the middle of a big report. He can't get away right now."

"I can wait."

"No, that's not going to happen," Diane informs me brusquely. Before I have a chance to protest, she says, "Come."

I follow her down a long corridor, up an internal staircase, down another long corridor, and into a room dominated by a conference table rimmed by a dozen chairs. Plate-glass windows on the far side of the room offer up a tempestuous view of the Manhattan skyline intermittently accentuated by lightning bolts. My focus, however, locks onto an even more electrifying prospect: a ziggurat of document boxes stacked at one end of the table.

"I've set out the chron logs," Diane says, pointing to a pile of binders. "You may want to start there. Then, if I were you, I'd work through the Redwelds."

Chron logs? Redwelds? Now's not the time to ask questions. I nod and say, "Great."

"Okay then," she says. "Knock yourself out." And without another word, she leaves.

THIRTY-TWO NORTH

The moment I'm alone, I begin my excavations. As instructed, I start with the "chron logs"—chronologically arranged lists of every memo, order, judgment, motion, declaration, decision, petition, and letter that has flowed in and out of the law firm regarding the matter of "George R. Englert, a/k/a 'George Crombie Moncrieffe,' a/k/a 'Dr. Moncrieffe,' a/k/a 'Baron Moncrieffe,' a/k/a 'Prince George.'"

Because Cesar rates barely a mention, I get through the registers swiftly. I then turn to the Redweld folders—so named, it only dawns on me much later, because of their color (red) and the brass rivets that reinforce the seams. The Redwelds contain dozens of briefs, some of which are typeset and bound like paperbacks. Given my allergy to legal papers, they quickly join the chron logs at the far end of the conference table.

That leaves the ziggurat itself—fourteen cartons of documents relating to the prosecution of the Badische Trust Consortium. The outside markings do nothing to clarify the contents. I grab the carton at the peak of the pyramid and pop the lid. Inside, I find copies of bank records, subpoenas, phone bills, business plans, canceled checks, and monthly credit card statements. There is no order to the stuff; everything appears to have been dumped into the carton higgledy-piggledy. (I guess that's what happens when a client pleads guilty and trial prep comes to a halt.)

It's almost noon by the time I get through the first box. Since I have a lunch date with John scheduled for twelve thirty p.m., even a perfunctory review of the remaining material is impossible. I disassemble the pyramid, arrange the cartons in a single row, and remove the lids. My worst fears are confirmed. The uninspected cartons are every bit as jumbled as the one I've just examined.

Fourteen cartons. Each one is roughly the size of a five-thousand-sheet box of photocopy paper. That means—I make a quick calculation—seventy thousand documents!

Diane reappears to let me know that John is heading over. "So? Find what you were looking for?"

"Nope. Barely made a dent."

"Well, come back after lunch if you want."

"Thanks," I say. "I will." I could have kissed her.

Lunch with John is brief. Over crab cakes and iced tea, we reminisce about hiking in Jordan. John is gracious and attentive. I am distracted and rude. All I can think about is the cache of material still awaiting inspection.

By two p.m., I'm back upstairs, excavating the residue of a fraud that may or may not implicate my nemesis. Around two thirty p.m., I find a file of AmEx receipts for purchases made by the Cesar of San Francisco in his capacity as managing director of the Barclay Consulting Group. The charges confirm that the cardholder has ties to Switzerland—there's an invoice for a weekend at the Dolder Grand hotel in Zurich ($18,598)—and that he likes Southeast Asian food. Those two details hardly constitute irrefutable proof of a link. Still, they're circumstantially encouraging.

Around five p.m., bundled-up paralegals begin passing by the conference room. The workweek appears to be over. I hunt down Diane before she, too, heads home.

"How'd we make out?" she asks from a cubicle facing Goodman's corner office.

"Not great. All that paper. It's a bit overwhelming."

"Welcome to my world."

"I was hoping to schedule a time when I might come back."

"Leaving already?"

"It's past five, it's Friday, and the city's a mess. I figured everyone would be heading out."

"Not everyone," Diane says, nodding at the closed door across from her sentry post. "*Someone* has to hand in a big report on Monday. In fact, *someone*, and that someone's assistant, will be working all weekend. You're welcome to join us."

Once more, I'm tempted to give her a kiss.

"Oh, and here, take these," she adds. "Mark thought you might find them interesting." Diane places two more bulging Redwelds on the parapet of her workstation.

I carry the files back to the conference room, plop into a chair, and put my feet up on the table. *Two more days!* The extension comes as a huge relief. I call Françoise. "Just letting you know, I'll be down here all weekend. I'll sleep at my mom's."

"Find something?"

"No, but there's still tons to go through."

I anticipate a mild reproach, maybe something as subtle as a sigh.

"*Bon courage*," she says. Her support catches me off guard, uplifts me, reminds me why I love my wife.

I skip dinner and leave the law firm sometime after nine none the wiser. The thundersnow has stopped, but the effects linger. Everything is white. The parked cars. The trash cans. The streets. The signs. Everything. As I walk west toward my mother's place, I pass a man pulling his son on a sled. I follow the pair for half a block even though it's out of my way. The scene, of son and father tethered to each other, hits me with a vague sense of longing.

Near Fifth Avenue, I manage to hail a cab. The ride crosstown is slow and silent. Snowdrifts muffle the din of the city. Sledders and cross-country skiers transform Central Park into a winter scene reminiscent of Villars. My wistfulness grows. I lower the cab window and breathe in the smell of fresh snow and for the first time in a long while, I think about my father. I miss him.

THE RAISED-LETTER CARTE DE VISITE

I sleep poorly that night. The uninspected cartons, the creaky Murphy bed in my mother's study, and the beeping of snowplows make it impossible to nod off. I find myself checking the time on my cell phone, a gesture that recalls the sleepless nights in Belvedere before my father's wristwatch disappeared.

By nine the next morning, I'm back at the law firm. Diane greets me at the guard station. In the elevator, she asks about my interest in the fraud. I tell her about Cesar.

"You were ten, and he did that to you? What a little shit!"

"No argument there."

"And you think he's one of the crooks who worked with the baron?"

"I'm not sure, but I think so."

"Well, *I'm* sure," she says.

"You sound like my son. He's positive the two Cesars are the same guy."

"Smart kid. You know what they say. What goes around comes around."

I have two days to work through the rest of the discovery materials. The task is so daunting that I make a pledge to myself: If a document doesn't concern Cesar, it won't concern me.

By noon, I manage to polish off two cartons. No smoking gun. At this rate, I'll be able to survey all the files before I have to catch the train back to Providence on Sunday. But around two o'clock, a folder full of black-and-white celebrity photographs slows my pace. "The [Badische] Chairman with his wife and Pope Paul during the bestowal of decorations at the Vatican," reads one caption. "The Chairman and the Administrator presenting the President of Malta with a donation for the disabled children at the Presidential Palace," reads another. "The executive committee director with British Prime Minister Sir Winston Churchill and General (later U.S. President) Eisenhower," reads a third. Many of the photos feature Prince Robert tapping a ceremonial sword on the shoulders of movie stars: Anthony Quinn, Sammy Davis Jr., Liza Minnelli, Ernest Borgnine.

I'm hoping to find a picture of Cesar. No such luck. Soon after I force myself to set aside the photo file, I uncover another possible clue. It takes the form of a raised-letter carte de visite bearing the House of Badische coat of arms: a golden eagle with outstretched wings and a pair of lions standing on their hind legs, front paws raised as if ready to strike.

I've seen a crest just like it, but I can't recall where.

With a growing sense of déjà vu, I reach for the Cesareum. It doesn't take long to locate what I'm looking for. Eagle with outstretched wings? Check. Lion rampant with paws extended? Check. The heraldic symbols on the Badische calling card are uncannily similar to the ones on my Aiglon blazer patch. The correspondence suggests yet another. A crazy image pops into my head: Cesar sketching the Badische coat of arms with his Aiglon blazer close at hand.

I take a break to inform Goodman and Diane of the graphic connections.

"Case closed," Diane says, delicately touching my tattered school patch as if it were the Shroud of Turin.

"Not so fast," Goodman interjects. He asks if I have further proof.

I run through the rest of the corroborating evidence.

"That's it?" he says. "Sounds like a stretch."

His doubts don't surprise me. He's a lawyer. He's paid to be skeptical. I return to the conference room and continue to dig. By midnight, I have worked through the last of the fourteen boxes. Seventy thousand documents and not one of them, not a damn one, provides the proof I'm looking for.

Did the Aiglon crest inspire the logo of the Badische Trust Consortium?

Defendant's Memorandum in Aid
of Sentencing

By the time I arrive at the law firm Sunday morning, Goodman and Diane are already at work, fine-tuning a seventeen-hundred-page report for a drug manufacturer fending off a multibillion-dollar class action suit. I say a quick hello before returning to the conference room. Documents blanket the full length of the table. It's as if the Friday blizzard has moved inside.

Cesar, you son of a bitch, where are you?

Beleaguered by the mess, I barely have the energy to reach for the Redwelds Diane furnished late Friday. But hours before I'm scheduled to return home, while forcing myself to leaf through the supplemental index to a "Defendant's Memorandum in Aid of Sentencing," I come across a short declarative sentence that raises the hairs on the back of my neck: "Cesar A. Viana was born on April 24, 1958 in Manila, Philippines."

Bingo! After unleashing a string of curses and completing a fist-pumping victory lap around the conference table, I call Françoise.

"Listen to this!" I read her the incriminating line.

"*Merde!* What else does it say?"

"That he's upper-middle-class. That his mother ran the family business, the Realistic Beauty Institute, and that his father was an inventor."

"Like your father," Françoise interjects.

"I know. Eerie."

"So I guess Cesar's father didn't torture people for a living."

"Guess not. He left that to his son. It also says the dad was a severe alcoholic and that he died of a heart attack when Cesar was nineteen." I read Françoise a key paragraph:

Although the defendant suffered no physical abuse or neglect at the hands of his father, the emotional impact of his father's deterioration was crushing to him. . . . Cesar "has spent much of his life seeking appropriate male role models to fill the void left by his father's illness and eventual passing," as his sister documents in her letter to the Court. See letter annexed hereto as Exhibit C.

I flip to Exhibit C, the letter from Cesar's sister, and read part of that submission to Françoise as well:

Cesar's school, Aiglon, was a mountain away from my school, and essentially he was all on his own through puberty. I imagine he must have been quite lonely, and this and the lack of a male parental role model made him unusually susceptible to peer pressure from his male classmates . . . he would go to great lengths to have his schoolmates like him, doing their work for them, despite my phone calls to him to be his own person.

    This was a pattern that I believe caused his present difficulties and if he has one fault it has been to not possess a proper sense of discrimination. . . . In his desire to belong to this present group of people with whom he was charged he showed poor judgment and I believe they took advantage of him. To my knowledge, in the over 40 years I have known him, Cesar has never knowingly taken advantage of any individual, although he suffered many incidents of being on the receiving end of abuse.

"*C'est pas possible!* She's saying *he's* the victim?"
"Yup, that's *exactly* what she's saying."
Françoise's shock pales in comparison to mine. The bizarre professional overlap between our fathers—that they were both inventors—is mildly annoying. Far worse is the suggestion that Cesar is a blameless casualty of the boarding school that brought us together. But the detail that *really* kneecaps me, the thing that hits way too

close to home, is that all of Cesar's problems are tied to the absence of his father. *Join the club, buddy.*

With time to kill before heading to Penn Station, I gather together the most compelling discovery documents and arrange them in nine discrete piles: SWINDLERS, VICTIMS, BADISCHE BANK DOCS, LAWYERS, KNIGHTS OF MALTA, TRANSCRIPT, CELEBS, and (the biggest pile) CESAR/BARCLAY. Then I take a few pictures of the reconstructed ziggurat before dialing Diane's extension to say that I'm done with the files, at least for now.

"Mark wants to know if you found your smoking gun," she says.

"I did."

"We'll be right over."

A few minutes later, the pair enters the conference room to review the newly uncovered evidence. I show them the relevant sections of the sentencing memo.

"See, I told you," Diane tells her boss. "What goes around comes around."

Goodman leafs through the brief. "This *is* more convincing," he acknowledges.

I could have ended my search there and then. After all, I had proved, beyond all reasonable doubt, that "my" Cesar was a convicted felon. Yet the notion of wrapping things up never occurred to me. Over the course of the weekend the focus of my obsession had broadened to include the fraud that had put my ex-roommate behind bars. The completionist in me needed to know a little more about the Badische Trust Consortium. No, that's not accurate. The completionist in me needed to know *everything* about the Badische Trust Consortium.

Which explains why I turn to Goodman and Diane and say, "I'm hoping I can come back and review some of these files more closely."

Diane frowns. "Does that sound convenient, Mark?"

"During the holidays?" Goodman shakes his head. "*Way* too much of a hassle."

Their rebuff unsettles me. What if I can't return to the firm? Over the last three days, documents have been passing through my hands like envelopes through an optical mail sorter. There's no way I'll remember what I've looked at.

"Is that the stuff you're hoping to go through?" Goodman asks, motioning to the nine stacks of paper.

"That, plus the trial transcript and some briefs."

Goodman thumbs through the documents, pausing occasionally to pull an item. He says nothing as he conducts his review.

"I could come back at the beginning of the year," I say, doing my best not to sound desperate.

"No, I don't think so."

"Or maybe I—"

Goodman raises his hand like a cop halting traffic.

In the silence that follows, I find myself wondering once again why I'm so intent on looking through the trial documents. I know for

I snapped this picture an hour after I found proof that my roommate worked for the Badische Trust Consortium.

certain that Cesar is a crook. Isn't that enough? Not by a long shot. The bank fraud that landed him in jail remains a total mystery. Ditto his role in the crime. The journalist in me can't let go of the story. At least that's what I tell myself.

"You really need to review all these documents?" Goodman asks after completing his examination.

"I really do."

"Then we'll just have to send you duplicates."

"Excuse me?"

"Merry Christmas."

I look over at Diane. She says nothing, but the smile stretching across her face betrays what she's thinking: *What goes around comes around.* *

Ten Thousand Documents Lost
in the Mail

The night before the night before Christmas, I have dream in which the Badische files get lost en route to Providence. The mix-up compels me to return to the law firm, where a mailroom clerk informs me that my shipment has been dispatched to Bermuda. While he's detailing the weight limits of parcels posted to US protectorates, the law firm is bombed, and I find myself plunging down a stairwell under a shower of construction debris.

I don't need help unpacking the significance of the stairwell tumble. It seems pretty obvious that I have linked the fraud to memories of Aiglon, although the nature of the connection remains vague.

---

*Years later, I asked Goodman why he had been so forthcoming. After noting that he'd removed all privileged material from the files and had checked with his client the baron before granting me with access, he added, "It's simple, Allen. We've all had bullies. Helping you seemed the right thing to do."

Christmas arrives. I make out like a bandit. Max has put a copy of *How to Be a Villain* in my stocking. Françoise has wrapped up a printer/scanner in anticipation of the care package I'm expecting from New York. My sister and brother-in-law present me with a first edition of *Forty Years a Gambler*, the late-nineteenth-century memoir of a notorious flimflam man named George H. Devol.

It's a bit unnerving to receive so many gifts tied to a kid I haven't seen since I was eleven, especially since they call attention to the undelivered gift I want most of all: the legal files from New York. I spend much of Christmas day moping about like an ungrateful brat.

On December 26, my sister and her husband, Max, and I drive to Vermont, for three days of skiing. (Françoise, a devotee of the desert, forgoes all winter sports.) Perfect conditions on the slopes improve my mood. When not skiing just a little faster than I'd like (in a futile effort to keep up with my daredevil son), I immerse myself in the hotel pool, after which I immerse myself in free nachos, after which I immerse myself in the ostentatious reflections of George H. Devol, who, the title page of his memoir proclaims, cheated at cards by the time he was eleven, stacked decks by fourteen, "bested soldiers on the Rio Grande during the Mexican War; won hundreds of thousands from paymasters, cotton buyers, defaulters, and thieves; fought more rough-and-tumble fights than any man in America; and was the most daring gambler in the world."

On the last day of the ski trip, while stuck with Max on a stalled chairlift, I feel my chest start to tingle. At first I assume it's some midstation chili con carne asserting itself. Only when the tingle returns do I realize my cell phone is

This memoir of a riverboat cheat was one of the fraud-themed gifts I received for Christmas.

vibrating. I extract the device from the inner pocket of my parka—no easy matter when one is wearing mittens and holding ski poles—to check the incoming messages.

"They arrived!" I shout.

The pronoun needs no clarification. Max holds out a clenched glove, and we fist-bump while rocking back and forth twenty feet in the air.

That night we decide to eat at a steak joint halfway down the Killington access road. The guy taking reservations informs us there's a forty-minute wait. We don't care. We're in no hurry. After Max puts our name down, we head over to a nearby sports bar in search of a foosball table and return to the restaurant just as the maître d' is calling out, "Cesar, party of four? Cesar, party of four? We're ready for you."

"Very funny, Max."

Very funny and also very true. I don't know it at the time, but Cesar is about to be served.

PRINTS OF THE CITY

On December 30, 2005, I lug the two heavy cartons Françoise has parked under the Christmas tree to my third-floor office, and slice through a thick skin of reinforced packing tape. I spread the contents of the cartons—the handiwork of a duplicating service called Prints of the City—on the carpet next to my desk. Amazingly, every item I set aside at the law firm, right down to the Post-its, has been perfectly reproduced and placed in labeled folders. This makes it a snap to replicate the organizational logic I applied to the documents during my frenzied weekend of triage. Yet I soon realize there's no point in rebuilding the nine paper piles. Doing so obliterates the chronology of the scam, thus making it impossible for me to figure out who did what when. Plus, the categories are way too broad. The LAWYERS stack, for instance, lumps together documents produced by the corporate attorneys who worked for the "bankers" when they appeared to be legit with memos generated by criminal defense attorneys working for the indicted con men.

Only one of the stacks is worth preserving: TRANSCRIPT. The twenty-four hundred pages of trial testimony, though reduced to four hundred double-sided sheets of paper, are so unwieldy that I make a trip to Staples and buy the fattest three-ring binder I can find. While I'm there, I splurge on a box of tab folders, some hanging files, and four interlocking milk crates complete with carpet-friendly casters.

Back in my office, I hole-punch the transcript and feed it into the oversized binder and arrange the rest of the papers in the milk crates. I

Christmas came a little late for me in 2005.

set the massive transcript binder on one side of a comfy reading chair and roll the freight train of discovery materials to the other.

Across the hall, Françoise and Max are starting a project of their own—a James Bond marathon.

"Come on, Dad," Max shouts. "*Dr. No* is about to start."

It's tough to say no to *Dr. No*—it's my favorite Bond film—but I stay put. And long after Max and Françoise have turned off the TV, I'm still reading. I'm not sure when I get to bed that first night—I'm guessing sometime after three a.m.—but I do know I'm back upstairs a few hours later.

Around ten the following evening, Françoise and Max try once more to coax me across the hall, this time to watch the New Year's Eve fireworks.

I shout over that I'll be right there, but I never make it. The spectacle arranged by the city of Providence can't compete with the pyrotechnics of the royal bankers and their principal shill.

PART IV

SUBMISSION

Yes, as through this world I've wandered
I've seen lots of funny men;
Some will rob you with a six-gun,
And some with a fountain pen.
                Woody Guthrie, "Pretty Boy Floyd"

Evil is fiendish. Evil is malevolent. Evil is wicked. But isn't there more to it than that? Yes, what the dictionary cleverly leaves out is for an elect few to know: Evil is fun.
                Neil Zawacki, How to Be a Villain

The Mark

Not since I plowed through *Crime and Punishment* has the printed word packed this kind of unremitting wallop. I can't stop reading. I end up devouring the entire transcript, all twenty-four hundred pages, twice. The court record plunges me into a narrative of fraud and humiliation that's impossible to fully believe. Or fully understand. Because no evidentiary material accompanies the testimony, it sometimes feels as if I'm reading a graphic novel without the graphics. The omission of the exhibits requires me to move back and forth between the bindered transcript and the milk crates in an attempt, often unsuccessful, to match citations to evidence. And there's another frustration. The voices of the felons never surface since none of them testified.

Still, it's possible to conclude this much: The Badische fraud, for all its five-star frills, was a basic advance-fee scheme. Cesar would induce his clients into signing contracts for loans of between one-hundred- and five-hundred-million dollars. But there was a catch. Before the lender—a one-hundred-and-fifty-year-old German bank—would hand over the funds, the borrower had to furnish all sorts of advance fees, including a so-called performance guaranty—one percent of one percent of the face value of the loan. That obligation cost Cesar's ill-fated clients anywhere between one-hundred- and five-hundred-thousand dollars a pop. Oh, and there was another catch. The bank wasn't a bank, and the bankers weren't bankers. Badische (the word was pronounced *BAD-ish* by the con men) was a variant of the Nigerian 419 scams clogging junk folders the world over. With one big difference. The officers of the Trust apparently transacted their deals live and in person.

The dossiers of Cesar's clients occupy one entire milk crate. Even with my overwrought sense of purpose, I know it will be impossible to contact every one of the victims. It's essential to narrow the scope of the inquiry.

Of the five Badische "borrowers" who testified at trial, one stands out: a television executive named Barbara Laurence. It was Laurence who first brought the dubious practices of the royal bankers to the attention of the federal prosecutors. Absent her complaint there would have been no investigation, no trial, no convictions.

I reread her testimony and, not without difficulty, connect the statements she made on the witness stand with the materials in the milk crates. Then, hoping to add a little context and color to the written record of the fraud, I give Barbara Laurence a call.

"You'll never believe it," she says with a chuckle the first time I reach her. "You've caught me at the Waldorf of all places—where Cesar and I first met."

I'm relieved by her good-natured response to the cold call. But my relief doesn't last. As soon as I clarify that I'm a writer researching a story, she shuts down.

"I have deals I'm doing," she says. "I don't want them jeopardized by the crap Cesar and the other guys pulled. They made me look like such a fool."

"But you took the case to the feds. You testified in open court using your name. Why not take credit for that?"

Laurence isn't interested in being memorialized as a whistle-blower, but after considerable back-and-forth, she warms up to the prospect of revisiting the scam. "I hate what happened to me, but I love the story, so sure, go ahead, ask me anything you want."

"How did you and Cesar first make contact?"

"Same way you and I did," Laurence tells me. "By phone. He was expecting my call. He'd been prepped about my project by a mutual acquaintance. He already knew I was looking for $50 million to launch a television network."

Cesar also knew that Laurence's business plan had received the thumbs-down from a slew of investment banks and venture firms specializing in media financing. No one could make the numbers work.

"Cesar wasn't fazed," Laurence tells me. Quite the contrary. Where others hit roadblocks, Cesar built on-ramps. "He said he'd done deals similar to mine as a managing director at Barclays."

Barbara Laurence.

Their first conversation took place in April 1999, while Cesar was in Las Vegas. "He told me he was wrapping up a $6 billion casino deal," Laurence remembers. "When I wondered out loud if the deal involved the Venetian"—a resort complex scheduled to open the following month—"he told me his negotiations were *highly* confidential and turned the discussion back to my project."

Laurence made her pitch: "I explained I was putting together a home shopping network targeted at the Spanish-language market. I had already lined up purchase-and-sale agreements with ten TV stations, and had two more deals in the works. Cuchifritos—that was the name of my start-up—would eventually require some $350 million in long-term financing, but my immediate needs were more limited. Fifty million would get things going."

"What was his reaction?"

"He liked what he heard. He told me one of his principal partners, the Badische Trust Consortium, might be willing to review my business plan. I knew of Barclays obviously. But Badische? Who the hell was Badische?"

Cesar explained the Trust kept a *very* low profile. That it served high-wealth clients demanding complete anonymity.

"I asked about the firm's investment strategy."

"What did he tell you?"

"Not much. He kept saying nondisclosure agreements prevented him from mentioning specifics."

But this much Cesar could say: The Badische bankers were European aristocrats capable of underwriting loans from $10 million to $500 million. "And he said the Trust was keen to help minorities, which sounded perfect since my business was targeted at Spanish speakers."

"Had Cesar done business with Badische before?"

"I asked the same question. As I said in court, he told me he had. In fact, he boasted he was the Trust's exclusive liaison."

By the end of their first call, Cesar had agreed to shepherd Laurence through the complexities of the Badische loan process, which started with a two-page request for financing. "Cesar reviewed the form, then forwarded it to some division of the Trust, I can't remember which."

I check the milk crates. "It was called the 'cabinet fiduciary.'"

"That sounds right. Anyway, a few days later, Cesar calls with good news. The Trust has fast-tracked my proposal. He needs to know if I can meet the Badische board in New York the following week. I told him I thrived on deadlines. That it wouldn't be a problem."

After setting up the appointment, Cesar sent Laurence a memo stating: "You should have liquid capital facilities able to be accessed by you at short notice to cover any expenses related to the transaction such as documentation preparation requirements, travel, legal expenses, bank fees, performance guaranties, collateral expenses, accounting studies, etc."

"I took that as a boilerplate warning," Laurence recalls. "I'd closed enough deals to know it takes a lot of money to make money and that it takes even more money to borrow it."

She and her team met Cesar, as planned, in the lobby of the Waldorf Astoria.

"So that was the first time you actually saw him?"

"That's right."

"What did he look like? I couldn't find any pictures of him on the web."

"Around forty. Six feet tall. Spanish. Maybe Asian. I'm not sure."

"And your impression of him as a businessman?"

"Very slick. Armani suit. Designer glasses. Shiny hair. Cuff links. He was extremely polished. Overly polished."

"Overly? How so?"

"He was like a cheap version of Richard Gere in *American Gigolo*. He wore all sorts of accessories like they were armor. To protect himself. To hide something."

"What do you think he was hiding?"

"In retrospect I'd say everything. But again, that's looking at things in hindsight. Back then he was much harder to read. I had no idea about his background, and there was something distinctly androgynous about him. I couldn't tell if he was straight or gay. I never did find out. But it was very clear from the beginning that he had strong ties to one of the lead bankers, a guy named Colonel Sherry."

"Anything else?"

"His belt."

"Sorry?"

"Cesar wore this amazing belt. Hermès, Gucci—I don't remember the brand. All I can tell you is it was striking."

A *striking* belt? The phrase distracts me, recalling as it does another kind of striking belt Cesar once possessed.

"What happened next? After you met?"

"We waited in the lobby together. For hours."

Eventually, a Badische representative escorted Cesar, Laurence, and her team—an accountant, a merchandising expert, and a former television president—to a suite on a high floor of the Waldorf Towers,

Colonel Brian Sherry, the administrator of the Badische Trust Consortium.

an exclusive residential section of the Park Avenue hotel.

"As soon as we got into the suite, Cesar parked himself off to the side while the officers of the Trust introduced themselves. It was a crazy scene. A room full of old guys all wearing matching silk cravats, fancy lapel pins, medals. A receiving line formed so I could meet each of the kooks one by one."

First up was Colonel Sherry, the thirty-nine-year-old administrator of the Badische Trust Consortium. "He told me he was a distinguished, decorated war veteran," Laurence recalls, a boast even then she found hard to fathom. "He was very thin and very pale. He didn't look like a war hero."

"What *did* he look like?

"Like Young Dracula waiting for his next infusion."

Next in the receiving line was the Baron Moncrieffe, at the time the Trust's septuagenarian vice chairman. "He was the one who always wore spats. After kissing my hand, he tried to put me at ease by telling me to call him George."

Then came the Trust's executive committee director, Duke Eric Henri Alba-Teran d'Antin. "He said he was a nephew to the king of Spain." The duke's piercing blue eyes mesmerized Laurence almost as much as the grapefruit-sized goiter veiled by a loose-fitting ascot. "It was growing out of his neck like an elbow."

At a certain point a door at the far end of the suite opened to reveal a tiny man covered in ribbons and medallions. "That's when someone announced—I think it was the colonel—'Prince Robert von Badische,

Seventy-Fourth Grand Master of the Knights of Malta, Chairman of the House of Badische.' The only thing missing were the trumpets."

The men in the room bowed and averted their eyes. Laurence did the exact opposite; she gave Prince Robert the once-over. "He must have been pushing ninety. He wore a tailcoat, a sash, ribbons, pins, and a giant Maltese cross. I know this sounds hard to believe, but he was clenching a gold monocle in his eye, and every finger on both of his hands had rings. One ring had an emerald-colored stone the size of a doorknob. I have paperweights that are smaller than that thing!"

The Baron Moncrieffe, vice chairman of the Badische Trust Consortium.

To counteract the burdens of old age (and, quite possibly, the weight of the decorations), Prince Robert relied on an intricately carved gold-handled walking stick to remain upright as he made his way across the room.

As the prince shuffled forward, Colonel Sherry directed Cesar and his clients to the distant side of a long gilded table. The Badische executives arranged themselves on the near side.

"What was Cesar doing while all this was taking place?" I ask.

"Nothing. He was the lure. I was the fish. He had brought me to the shark tank. At that point, his job was pretty much done."

The news disappoints me. I so wanted him to be the mastermind behind the whole operation. I keep the unfulfilled hopes to myself and let Laurence continue to describe the scheme.

"Everyone remained standing until Winky sat down in this ornate chair set up at one end of the table."

"Winky?"

"Sorry. That's what I called the prince. Because of the monocle." I chuckle.

"Yeah, I suppose it does sound funny when I tell it now. But it wasn't funny while I was living through it."

"I'm sure."

Once seated, Prince Robert asked the colonel to present a brief overview of the investment strategy governing the charitable trust bearing his family name. The colonel dutifully explained that the House of Badische, also known as the Trust, was a 150-year-old bank founded in Baden, Germany, and now based in Switzerland. It managed some $60 billion in assets that were invested in a wide range of sophisticated financial instruments: "structured finance, collateral guaranties, nonrecourse loans." Sherry corroborated the claim by handing Laurence a one-page document titled "Transaction Experience" that listed some dozen Badische deals. The largest, a railroad contract connected to the Bechtel Corporation, had a stated value of €3.7 billion. Smaller transactions included a €29 million "supertanker sale" and €10 million in "French film financing."

The colonel noted that the Trust's "scope of interests" extended far beyond the itemized list. "At one point he said that the Badische's timber holdings included all the trees in the Black Forest and that the Trust could easily finance my start-up ten times over."

"How did you react?"

"I asked the colonel the same question I asked Cesar: 'Where do you get your money?'"

"What did the colonel say?"

"He told us most of the Trust's assets originated in Africa and Saudi Arabia and that a smaller percentage came from Europe. That's when the duke chimed in that the Trust handled *all* of his funds, as well as the investments of his wife, Michaela von Habsburg, the archduchess of Austria."

After Sherry gave his brief overview, it was Laurence's turn to perform.

"I began my presentation with a broad analysis of the Latino television market, then bullet-pointed my way through the specifics of the Cuchifritos business plan."

Asked by the Trust's in-house counsel, a man named Richard Zeif, about her professional qualifications, Laurence informed the gathering that she had previously served as the president of a home shopping

TRANSACTION EXPERIENCE

The record below indicates the scope of interests and modern focus of Badische's Finance Committee, and illustrates the diverse experience of its Members in transactions in which they participated. All figures are in *Euro* for uniformity.

INDUSTRY TYPE	DESCRIPTION	SIZE (000,000)
Railroad	Development in Brazil with Bechtel	3,700
Construction (project incomplete)	Enlargement of Panama's Culebra passage – negotiation role	300
Investment bank	Liquidation of foreign currency position	110
Export / technology	Transfer management	100
Shipping	Vessel Acquisition	70
Real Estate	Acquisition	50
Ski resort	Equity financing	30
Shipping	Super-tanker sale	29
Aircraft	Sale of aircraft to Mexican airline	27
Telecom	Refinancing	18
Foundation	Seed capital for new foundation	12
Government	High security trade	12
Film	French film financing	10

A summary of Badische business ventures presented to potential borrowers.

H.R.H. Prince Robert von Badische, Seventy-fourth
Grand Master of the Knights of Malta and Chair-
man of the Badische Trust Consortium.

network with 159 full-time employees. Asked about the name of the
new venture, Laurence said, "Cuchifritos is a cute Hispanic term for
a small fried food."

"I fielded softballs for a half hour before Winky wrapped up the
meeting by saying, 'Let's have cake.' And the next thing I know we're
sharing a loveseat, eating room-service pastries, and leafing through
a scrapbook."

"Containing . . . ?"

"Yellowed newspaper clippings. Old black-and-white photos. Pictures documenting the prince's charitable work. Images of flood victims. Photo ops with celebrities. There was one picture of Anthony
Quinn wearing a robe. There was another with Steven Seagal wearing a similar robe. There was an article from a Palm Springs paper
about the prince walking his Maltese dogs. There was a picture of Dr.

Moncrieffe with the Queen Mum. There was even one of Winky with the pope. It was pretty impressive."

Colonel Sherry eventually approached the pair and informed his boss that other loan candidates were waiting for an audience. "Basically, my time was up."

"At that point, what did Cesar do?"

"He escorted me and my team out of the suite and said, 'I'll be in touch if you've presented an acceptable deal and if the Trust deigns to fund your venture.' I don't know if that's the exact word he used—*deigns*—but that was his general tone. Badische were royals, and I was a commoner."

A few days later, Cesar stoked Laurence's hopes by requesting her "bona fide financials." If the documents she provided checked out, contracts could be drawn up and a signing ceremony could be scheduled. Almost as an afterthought, Cesar noted that in order to receive funding, Laurence would be required to establish a small number of offshore bank accounts through which the loan would flow.

"Why was that necessary?" I ask.

"Cesar said it was to preserve the anonymity of the people whose assets Badische managed."

"Did that shock you?"

"No, not really. American companies regularly do that kind of thing. What *did* surprise me was the price tag. Cesar told me Barclays charged a flat fee of $9,000 per offshore account, and that my deal would require six such entities."

"So $54,000?"

"Correct. I said I'd like to use my own lawyer. That I could get the accounts set up a lot more cheaply." Her counterproposal was summarily rejected. "Sherry called me and said the involvement of outside attorneys at this stage would be looked upon in a very disfavorable manner." Badische would be "gratified and pleased" if Cesar's firm handled the preliminary paperwork. Laurence would be allowed, indeed *expected*, to bring legal representation to the final contract negotiations and signing.

"That didn't make me happy. I knew Cesar was gouging me. But I wasn't about to jeopardize the deal just to save a few thousand dollars."

Laurence supplied the requested documents and half the $54,000 fee. Cesar immediately called and inquired about the remainder. "He was very upset. I could hear the desperation in his voice, though I didn't think much of it at the time."

Laurence explained she needed a few days to shift funds before she could wire the outstanding balance. That precipitated another call from the colonel. "He was very imperious. He told me I was taking advantage of both Badische and Barclays." The rebuke rattled Laurence. Within forty-eight hours, she transferred the second half of the fee. Ruffled feathers smoothed, Cesar set up six accounts in the British Virgin Islands tax haven of Tortola, and informed Laurence that the loan closing would take place in Zurich on June 17.

"I was thrilled. Despite the payment hiccup, everything was on track." And it remained so until a few days before the scheduled signing, when, without warning, Laurence's maternal grandmother passed away. The funeral services conflicted with the meetings in Zurich. Laurence called Cesar and requested a postponement. "He said, 'Too late. Everyone is already in transit.'"

Laurence asked her mother what to do. "My mother told me, Grandmom Rose would have wanted you to go. Grandmom Rose would have said, 'Go and be successful.' So I left my family to meet up with Cesar in Switzerland."

GREEN FINGERS

To meet up with Cesar in Switzerland.

For obvious reasons, the phrase resonates. So does the helplessness

Laurence invokes. I find myself making all sorts of connections between her narrative of alpine humiliation and my own.

Some parallels are more consequential than others. At one point I find myself wondering if the Trust's devotion to uniforms, titles, and symbols of privilege can be traced back to Cesar's boarding school experiences. The speculation isn't nearly so far-fetched as it sounds. After all, Aiglon, with its contingent of royal residents, its No. 1 Dress uniforms and rank pins, its "Bouquetin badges," "Colours Awards," "Five Star" certificates, merit cups, and trophies, reveled in the kind of ornamentalism later deployed by the Badische boys. And there's something else worth mentioning. While we were at Aiglon, Cesar and I were shown a movie called *The Captain from Koepenick*, an obscure 1956 tale of imposture chronicling the exploits of an indigent shoemaker who pulls the wool over the eyes of an entire town after purchasing a captain's dress uniform from a secondhand shop. The authority that the self-styled "captain" accrues by wearing a gold-braided outfit is a lot like the legitimacy that "Prince" Robert acquired by donning a Maltese cross and a medallion-studded sash. Isn't it possible our rank-obsessed boarding school inspired the paraphernalia on show at the Waldorf? If so, that would give Cesar a much bigger role in the scam than the trial testimony indicates.

I present my theory to Laurence.

"Seems like a stretch," she says.

Her skepticism does little to dilute my conviction. The penchant for Montblanc fountain pens, the parallels between the blazer patch and the carte de visite, and now this. The overlaps make me all the more determined to clarify Cesar's role in the fraud. Was he, as his

The Captain from Koepenick, *screened at Aiglon in 1972, anticipated the sartorial embellishments of the Badische boys.*

sister argued, a victim? Or, as his felony conviction and my experiences in Switzerland suggested, a masterful fake-out artist with a knack for misdirection? Or—a third option—a small-time roper with a minor role in an elaborate fraud? It's impossible to tell given how little I know.

The Captain from Koepenick concludes on a cheery note both for its lead character and the community he dupes. The submission of Barbara Laurence did not end so happily.

Laurence flew to Zurich on June 15, 1999, checked into a downtown hotel, and waited for Cesar's call. When he made contact the following morning, he told her to join him at the Dolder Grand, a hotel spa on the outskirts of the city, and await further instructions. After yet another lengthy delay in the lobby of yet another five-star hotel, a Badische lackey guided Cesar and his client to a suite that managed to outdo the gilded splendor of the Waldorf, enlivened, as it was, by panoramic views of Zurich and the Alps.

"They told me it was the Presidential Suite and that Clinton had stayed in the rooms the night before. They made a big deal of that. It could have been true. The setting was pretty amazing."

"Did you go to the meeting alone?"

"No. I brought three colleagues along. My attorney, a Wall Street go-between, and Victor Benetar, my merchandizing expert."

The Badische roster was substantially larger. Nine men, representing three branches of the Trust, were on hand: the prince, the colonel, and the baron; three members of the Trust's finance committee; and Badische lawyers based in New York, London, and Zurich. "There were also a couple of bodyguards and Winky's 'private nurse,' who I'm now convinced was a hooker hired for the evening."

After twenty minutes of chitchat focused on the fragile health of Prince Robert's Maltese lapdog—like its owner, small, old, unstable, incontinent, and pedigreed—the borrowers and lenders again arranged themselves on opposite sides of a long conference table.

Once Prince Robert was ensconced "in another one of his thrones," Colonel Sherry announced that the Badische Trust Consortium had formally approved the Cuchifritos proposal. Laurence recalls he then said, "His Highness is now prepared to sign a funding agreement in the amount of $500 million."

The sum shocked Laurence. "Five hundred million dollars?" she remembers blurting out. "I came here for *fifty*!"

"Where did the extra zero come from?" I ask.

"I wondered the same thing. The way the deal worked was I was to receive $500 million in 'collateral instruments' that would be used to purchase medium-term notes with an average yield of 7.5 percent and a maturity of ten years. My $50 million would come from the 'spread'—that was the colonel's term—between the discounted purchase price of the notes and their face value at maturity."

"Sorry. I'm not following you."

"Basically, I'd be getting my money from interest spun off the larger sum."

"What were the repayment terms?"

"There were none," Laurence says.

"Excuse me?"

"Badische said they'd put up half a billion dollars so that I could buy discounted notes on their behalf for $450 million, and that I could retain the prepaid interest—$50 million—free and clear."

"You didn't have to pay them back?"

"That's what they said. At which point I asked the obvious: 'Why the hell would anyone do that?' It sounded too good to be true, which I later learned was the case."

"How did the Trust respond?"

"The colonel explained that the prince regularly signed loan agreements on behalf of individuals with too much cash on hand." The loans were designed to preserve capital *and* confidentiality. "That's why the anonymous lenders were willing to pay $50 million. It was considered a parking fee."

Laurence discussed the proposal with the lawyer she flew in from Washington. He said he would need to review the contract before endorsing its legality. "That's when Colonel Sherry told us that wouldn't be possible. That my lawyer would not be allowed to read the actual contract."

"Seriously?"

"Seriously. A Badische representative would read the loan agreement out loud." If the terms, as presented orally, were deemed acceptable, Laurence and the prince would sign a "principal-to-principal" agreement. Once she satisfied certain prerequisites detailed in the contract, the prince would dispatch, by courier, a fully executed agreement, along with a confidential "transaction code" authorizing the transfer of $500 million in Badische funds to the offshore companies Cesar had set up in Tortola.

When the lawyer representing Laurence questioned this unusual protocol, the colonel shut him down. "Sherry told me, 'This is a principal-to-principal transaction. Your attorney cannot ask questions.'"

He then instructed Robert Gurland, the Trust's London lawyer, to begin reading aloud the twelve-page agreement. In a plummy British public school accent, the dapper sixty-eight-year-old obliged: "'It is hereby agreed between the parties as follows . . .'"

"It was a crazy contract," Laurence now acknowledges. Much of the language was impenetrable and imprecise. Periodically, her lawyer, prevented from raising objections directly, would whisper a concern to his client so that she could request clarification.

Two clauses proved particularly problematic. The first, Clause Three ("Banks and Venues"), imposed seemingly insurmountable geographical constraints by prohibiting Laurence from using financial institutions based in the United States, Great Britain, Australia, New Zealand, France, Spain, Switzerland, Italy, or Mexico. Also banned: all nationalized, state, or central banks, all Eastern-bloc banks, and all banks in "any Middle Eastern, Latin American or otherwise 'Third World' countries." In addition, Clause Three entitled the prince to reject, without explanation, any bank "not of satisfactory status or reputation acceptable to 'THE LENDER.'"

"That didn't leave you with too many options, did it?"

"No, it didn't," Laurence says. "But I came up with what I thought was a pretty clever work-around. I asked to use the offshore branch of a US bank."

The colonel discussed her request with his colleagues. After considerable debate, the Trust gave its approval, with the caveat that the offshore American branch had to be both exempt from US banking law and willing to receive what the contract identified as "clean good funds" no questions asked.

That concession removed the first sticking point.

Robert Gurland continued the legal recitals, with the colonel and the Trust's in-house counsel, Richard Zeif, taking over whenever the Londoner's voice grew hoarse. At eleven p.m., the second nettlesome issue surfaced: Clause Seven ("Performance Guaranty").

"Before receiving funding, I was required to put in escrow a tenth of 1 percent of the total loan. Badische called it a performance guaranty."

One tenth of 1 percent didn't sound like much until Laurence did the math.

"I lost it when I realized what that meant. I said, 'You're asking for another $500,000? On top of the $54,000 I've already paid to Cesar? But I came here to *borrow* money!'"

"What did Cesar say while all this was happening?"

"Nothing. Like I told you, once he handed me over to Winky and Young Dracula, his job was done."

Colonel Sherry tried to placate Laurence, explaining that the performance guaranty was *not* "a processing fee, retainer, or advance fee." It was simply a deposit required, as the contract stated, to verify "the borrower's bona fides, good intentions, and serious ability to fulfill the terms and conditions of the agreement."

"The colonel said, 'We have to know that you can afford to travel and pay your lawyers and your accountants, and that you will be able to complete this transaction. Once the deal is closed, the $500,000 will be returned. There is really no risk if you feel you can perform.'"

"*Perform*? That's the word he used?"

"It was," Laurence says. "I know it almost sounds sexual. Maybe it was for Sherry. One giant perverse performance."

"What did you say when they shanghaied you with that upfront fee?"

"I said, 'What happens if *you* guys can't perform? What happens to my security deposit?'"

The colonel assured her that the funds would be returned, minus "10 percent in consideration of legal costs and professional expenses."

But that reassurance was moot. "I didn't have $500,000 to tie up," Laurence later testified.

Tensions mounted until Victor Benetar, the Cuchifritos merchandising expert, intervened. "Victor stood up and said, 'Hey look. Her grandmother just died. She should be sitting shivah. Go easy on her.' One of Winky's helpers gave me some bottled water, and I took a few minutes to compose myself."

When the talks resumed, Laurence tried to remove the fee clause from the contract. The colonel wouldn't budge. "He said, 'Sorry. That condition is written in stone.'"

From the head of the table, Winky summed up the stalemate succinctly when he told Laurence: "'Sometimes, dear, it comes down to cold hard cash.'"

With the negotiations at an impasse, the two teams agreed to adjourn until the following day. Once outside the suite, Laurence and her partners did what executives often do when a deal collapses. "We ordered a pizza."

The postmortem that accompanied the late-night snack focused on the $500,000 performance guaranty—the one stumbling block separating Laurence from the $50 million she needed to launch Cuchifritos. The prince's remarks about "cold hard cash" apparently resonated with Victor Benetar. He offered to front the fee.

The proposal wasn't exactly selfless. It was tied to a side agreement granting Benetar one third of the funding Laurence was expecting from the Trust. As the merchandizing expert saw it, scoring one third of $50 million—almost $17 million—by fronting $500,000, represented a healthy return on investment, certainly better than the profits he made on the steeply marked-up consumer electronics he sold at his Times Square enterprise, Broadway Video and Computer.

Laurence agreed to his terms. "I chalked it up to the cost of doing business."

Negotiations with the bankers were supposed to continue the following afternoon. "But when Cesar greeted us at the entrance of the Dolder, he said things were delayed. Then I saw him scurry off to handle some other clients. It was a repeat of the Waldorf experience. Hurry up and wait. We ended up sitting in the lobby for hours and hours."

Late that evening, well past midnight, Laurence was granted another audience with the prince. "I told Winky, 'I have the money. Let's do a deal.'"

The news so pleased Prince Robert that he ordered champagne and asked for his "laptop"—an antique escritoire containing, Laurence recalls, "a bottle of green ink, a very large Montblanc pen, and some sort of thing you make a seal with."

After a round of toasts, everything was set. Under the watchful gaze of some dozen Cuchifritos and Badische executives, lawyers from three countries, an ailing lapdog, a couple of bodyguards, the prince's private nurse ("Like I said, I think she was a call girl"), and Cesar Augustus, Barbara Laurence and "Prince Robert von Badische" began signing their $500 million principal-to-principal loan agreement.

They didn't get very far. Things hit a snag when Laurence, agitated by the promise of her hard-won $50 million (minus Benetar's cut),

Cesar witnessed the Zurich loan agreement between Prince Robert and Barbara Laurence.

knocked over the ink bottle. Green ink stained the wooden laptop, Laurence's hands and dress, and—most problematically—the loan papers. New contracts had to be rustled up before the transaction could continue. The two principals completed their deal just before dawn, signing their names and initials more than a hundred times on three duplicate contracts using a fountain pen the size of a large cigar.

"And guess who served as witness?" Laurence says coyly.

I fish out a copy of the loan agreement from one of the milk crates. The very bottom of the last page bears the name of Cesar Augustus Viana, the managing director of the Barclay Consulting Group and exclusive liaison to the Badische Trust Consortium.

As I'm staring at the signature, I imagine Cesar in Switzerland, signing his name with a flick of a Montblanc fountain pen. Okay, okay. Technically, it wouldn't have been a *flick*. Still. What are the chances that the twelve-year-old kid I nailed with a Parker 45 in 1972 would return to Switzerland, Montblanc in hand, thirty years later?

I ask Laurence what she thinks Cesar was thinking about when he helped close the deal.

"In a word? Same thing all those guys were. *Ka-ching.*"

THE PERFORMANCE GUARANTY

Barbara Laurence left Zurich empty-handed (and green-fingered). To secure the loan for her cable network, she needed to do two things.

First, she was contractually required to wire $500,000 to the Trust's London counsel, Robert Gurland, by "16:00 hours, Greenwich Mean Time, the 25th day of June, 1999." That gave her a week. Second, she had to furnish a so-called bank letter from a Badische-approved financial institution willing to handle $500 million no questions asked. Under the terms hammered out at the Dolder, the bank letter had to be presented *in person* within thirty days of the signing.

Laurence satisfied the first requirement—payment of the performance guaranty—in the time allotted, thanks to Victor Benetar's pre-dawn pizza pledge. Doing so triggered a reciprocal obligation from the prince. He had three days to deliver a copy of the loan agreement, complete with transaction code.

"*His* deadline came and went, and guess what? No contract."

Only on July 6, two weeks after she posted the performance guaranty, did Laurence receive the paperwork. "It was *supposed* to be hand-delivered by courier." It wasn't. "It was tossed like it was a newspaper. I spotted a package in the bushes beside the front door."

Laurence tore open the envelope and began reading. "All at once I started to panic. The confidential transaction code Winky promised wasn't on the contact."

"What did you do?"

"I called Sherry."

The colonel apologized for the oversight and agreed to provide the code over the phone. But before he did, he swore Laurence to secrecy. "He told me the confidential password would reveal the identities of the people whose assets were involved. By this point, I was so agitated I could barely hold a pen. I kept getting the numbers wrong."

In the end, the colonel sidestepped Badische protocol and faxed Laurence the password: Allied-GMTC-Merrill-Abboud/GPB320-304M=MTN500MU.S.D-7.5%-10YR/180699/BA-ZIH. "When I saw the code, I felt a huge sense of relief."

"Why? What calmed you down?"

"Two of the names. Merrill suggested a link to Merrill Lynch.

Abboud is the name of a wealthy Lebanese family." Laurence still rues her lapse of judgment. "I know what I'm telling you makes me sound like a complete idiot. But while all this was taking place, the names made things seem on the up-and-up."

THE BANK LETTER

Contract in hand, Laurence focused her attentions on the second of the two loan requirements—the bank letter. She had thirty days to secure the all-important document. After a few false starts, she obtained a letter from the Dublin branch of Bank of America affirming its willingness to receive the "clean good funds" no questions asked. When, as the loan contract dictated, Laurence requested a face-to-face meeting with the officers of the Trust, she learned that Badische had a policy of conducting all contract negotiations outside the United States.

"That's when the colonel informed me that he had authorized the Trust's in-house lawyer, Richard Zeif, to use his diplomatic clout to arrange a meeting at the United Nations. They told me the UN was neutral territory exempt from US law."

"Did Cesar join you?"

"I don't think you're getting it, Allen. Cesar was the shill. Once he delivered me to the Badische boys, his job was over. He moved on. He was looking for the next Barbara Laurence. And he found plenty of them."

"So I guess my image of Cesar Augustus as an International Man of Mystery is a little off the mark."

"Just a little. Cesar was more intelligent than some of the other members of the Trust and often better dressed, but I wouldn't call him an International Man of Mystery."

"No?"

"No. I think a more accurate description would be"—Laurence

takes a moment to choose her words—"a schmucky, nebbishy lying sack of shit."

Laurence presented her bank letter to the Badische board in the Delegates Dining Room of the United Nations. Careful to preserve the "comfort level" of the prince, Laurence listened "like a good little girl" as he digressed about his philanthropic work.

"He made a big deal about heading up an order of the Knights of Malta. He said his organization gave big donations to Jewish charities and Catholic causes. Disaster relief. Flood victims. He made it sound like he did something for everyone. Finally, at the end of the meal, I handed the colonel my bank letter. I was hoping to get it approved there and then."

"I'm guessing that didn't happen."

"Good guess. The colonel scolded me for being pushy and rude. But that was nothing new. He humiliated me constantly during the negotiations. He criticized the things I said. The things I did. The clothes I wore. He told me I was too flamboyant, too brash. Well, all I can say is guilty as charged."

A few days after the UN lunch, Laurence received unsettling news. "Colonel Sherry called and said he was embarrassed by how poorly my bank letter was written."

The assessment shocked Laurence, particularly since so much of the language had been lifted verbatim from the Badische loan agreement. Undeterred, she contacted the bank officers in Dublin and requested a rewrite. They obliged her promptly but not promptly enough, for now a new problem arose: the thirty-day submission deadline had come and gone. Colonel Sherry remedied the situation by authorizing an extension and waiving the usual penalty.

"He told me he'd forgo the $15,000-per-day late fee the Trust charged delinquent applicants. Then he made me fly to Toronto to deliver the revised bank letter in person."

"Why Toronto?"

"That's where he was doing business. He said come to Toronto, so I came to Toronto. I had no choice."

Laurence met up with the colonel, prince, and baron in the dining room of the King Edward Hotel, yet another five-star landmark. Her second petition for funding repeated the pattern of the first: lengthy meal filled with rambling royal pronouncements followed by formal submission.

A SPANKING

The Trust was nothing if not thorough. Colonel Sherry had Laurence's second bank letter vetted by attorneys at firms in the United Kingdom, the United States, and Switzerland. He then used their legal reservations to downgrade her contract to "nonperformance status."

"When I got that news, it was worse than passing a kidney stone," Laurence recalls. But pass it she did, and a few days later she petitioned for another extension. This time the colonel informed her, by fax, that Badische would only reinstate the contract and grant a thirty-day extension upon receipt of £100,000.

"One hundred thousand pounds! I was furious. All these hidden expenses were leaving me with very little breathing room." After much discussion, Laurence negotiated less onerous terms: £10,000 up front, with the balance due two weeks after the $500 million deal closed.

But the late fee constituted only one part of her penalty. "Colonel Sherry said something to me I will never forget. He said, 'When my little girl does something wrong, I spank her. What kind of spanking should I give you?'"

"What did *that* mean?"

"I was required to submit a handwritten apology to the board of the Trust."

"You're kidding."

"No. And what's worse, Sherry kept forcing me to rewrite the thing. It was like I was back in grade school."

The punishment reminds me of the Aiglon pensums, but I keep that thought to myself. "How many times did you revise the apology?"

"I can't remember. All I can tell you is each rewrite was like pouring salt in a wound. Eventually, Sherry dictated what he wanted me to say word for word."

I quote back to Laurence a large chunk of the mea culpa she was forced to submit to the Badische board:

In all of our meetings, you've exhibited the highest level of integrity and good will towards me and my endeavor. I hope that you can find it in your hearts to accept my most sincere apologies for this delay and unintentional indiscretion, and consider granting my request for an additional extension of time.

Your continued belief in my project, and the care and caution taken by you and your council, is of great comfort to me. I look to you and your esteemed colleagues for direction.

I hope this correspondence in some way conveys to you my deepest feelings of regret for causing any discomfort or hardship. If given the chance, I am sure that you will not be disappointed by my continued efforts.

"They certainly weren't disappointed by my continued efforts," Laurence says. "Not at that point anyway," she adds. "The apology letter and late fee bought me another month."

With the clock reset, Laurence hopped a plane to Paris to consult a corporate lawyer with ties to ING. "The Dutch bank was one of the few specifically endorsed by the Trust." Laurence spelled out her predicament to the French attorney. "He was super well connected and wrangled an appointment for me with senior executives at ING in Amsterdam."

The prospect of a half-billion-dollar deposit, as well as the reputation of the Paris advocate, made the Dutch bankers receptive. "They even put a rush on the background checks." Two weeks ahead of deadline, Laurence had yet another bank letter in hand. "And this one was bulletproof. I faxed a request for a face-to-face meeting with the Badische board that same day."

"And what happened?"

"Nothing. I never got a response."

"IN DEFAULT"

Laurence waited three days before sending another fax. It, too, went unanswered.

"Why the silence?" I ask.

"That's what I wanted to know. I called Gurland in London to find out what was going on. He said the colonel was incommunicado. Something about hush-hush business at the Vatican. I couldn't learn more. Finally, on the day of deadline, I got a reply."

More precisely, Laurence received *two* replies, neither of which came from Sherry. The first, a fax transmitted by Robert Gurland, informed Laurence that she was "in default" and that Badische would be returning her £10,000 late fee. The second notice, also sent by fax, and bearing the armorial shield of the House of Badische (spread eagle and lions rampant), was less terminal in tone than the legal communiqué:

> *Dear Ms. Laurence,*
> *By the time you receive this, you have had other*
> *communications, which are self-explanatory. I suggest*
> *that in order to proceed with our mutual aims, we*
> *meet once again. Perhaps between us we can find a*
> *solution that would be reciprocally beneficial.*
> *Most sincerely yours,*
> *Dr. G. Moncrieffe*

The baron insisted Laurence meet him in Liechtenstein.

"I said, '*Liechtenstein?* Where the hell is Liechtenstein? Who wants to schlep to a place you can't even find on a map?' The baron told me, 'Hey, look, I could have made you to come to China!'"

Desperation again rendered Laurence submissive. She flew to Zurich and hired a chauffeur to take her to Vaduz, the capital city of the tiny, hard-to-locate tax haven. On the way, her limo blew a tire. "To make the appointment, I had to help the driver fix the flat. In the rain!"

Things went from bad to worse once the meeting started. It wasn't long before the baron, the colonel, and Richard Zeif, the Trust's in-house counsel, began interrogating Laurence about her professional ties to a disgraced rabbi named Rachamim Anatian.

"They were super aggressive. I told them I was his former employee. That he owned GSN, a television shopping network that was on the air for two years before filing for Chapter 11. I told them I was the network's president. But they knew all of that from the meeting at the Waldorf and from information I gave to Cesar during the vetting process.

"Zeif kept pressing me. He said, 'Isn't the rabbi in question the subject of a ninety-six-count indictment? And didn't you conspire with him?'"

Laurence acknowledged that her former boss had acted in a "disreputable manner" and that he had fled to Israel to avoid prosecution. But she expressed outrage at the suggestion that his improprieties in any way tarnished her reputation. "I had provided Cesar with documents, signed by a judge, releasing me from all wrongdoing associated with the bankruptcy."

That might be, Zeif countered, but Badische wasn't about to risk its good name by conducting business with someone who conducted business with an alleged felon.

Once more, the long-suffering TV executive was given her marching orders. "They told me, 'Get us evidence that that you're not a criminal.' That's like asking someone when he stopped beating his wife."

Laurence persevered. "I went to visit—this is so *embarrassing*—all these people and had them write character references. I had background checks done stating that I had no judgments against me. That I was never convicted of a crime."

"What happened after that?"

"I delivered my 'honesty package' and never heard another word from the Badische boys. That's when I decided it was time to cut my losses."

Laurence contacted Gurland and demanded the return of the $500,000 performance guaranty wired to a bank account he managed on behalf of Badische. His assistant dispatched a terse reply: "All communication with regard to the transaction with Badische must be done through Colonel Sherry as Robert Gurland has no official position or authority in this matter."

"I'm not the type of person who likes being blown off."

"I'm getting that impression."

"I contacted the colonel while he was supposedly conducting loan negotiations in the Far East and made it clear that if Badische failed to return my escrowed deposit, I would go to the authorities. Sherry lost his cool. He said, 'I don't know how you can talk to me that way! Haven't we had a wonderful relationship? I'm *really* hurt!' He acted like *he* was the victim."

Unmoved by the histrionic deflections, Laurence petitioned the baron for the half million dollars. He proved more receptive. "Boy, did he change his tune once I started threatening to make a stink. He said he'd meet anywhere I wanted to remedy the misunderstanding. So I said Bermuda. I was going there anyway for my anniversary."

The final showdown between the Baron Moncrieffe and Barbara Laurence (before their three-week reunion in federal court) took place at the Ariel Sands, a beachfront resort owned in part by the family of actor Michael Douglas. Laurence wore sandals to the rendezvous. "The baron wore Ferragamos and spats."

Some ten years later, Laurence still remembers their exchange:

"He was extraordinarily nervous. Running off at the mouth. He confessed that he had never wanted to go into banking. That for much of his life he had resisted the profession, even though the Moncrieffe clan had been in banking since before there was a Wall Street. He confessed that he much preferred attending the Paris collections with his mother and the knighting ceremonies overseen by his two mentors, King Peter II of Yugoslavia and Prince Robert."

Laurence tolerated the baron's digressions but refused to be distracted by them. "I told him, 'I want my money back.'"

The baron said he appreciated her position, and apologized for the indignities she had suffered, admitting that he didn't always see "eye to eye" with the methods of the colonel. He went on to say that the bond market had changed significantly and that fluctuating interest rates and the volatility of treasury offerings would make it difficult to execute the loan under the original terms. Difficult but not impossible. He assured Laurence that if Badische couldn't fund the transaction, he would underwrite the $500 million loan personally. "I said, forget the $500 million. All I want is my $500,000." Laurence added that if Badische didn't make her whole, she would take legal action. The baron promised her that the performance guaranty would be returned. After all, he noted, "attorney bickering" was the last thing anyone wanted.

"HERE'S A PIECE OF FREE ADVICE"

When the baron failed to keep his promise, Laurence made good on hers. She put the contract dispute in the hands of the Washington lawyer present during the loan discussions in Zurich. He petitioned Robert Gurland for the funds placed in his care. Correspondence between the two attorneys remained amicable (and mutually remunerative) for a few months before negotiations broke down.

"At that point, I considered suing," Laurence tells me. "But the litigators I consulted all said forget it. I'd be throwing good money after bad." Already out $54,000 to Cesar, hundreds of thousands of dollars in legal costs, and nearly $100,000 in travel expenses (in addition to the $500,000 staked by Victor Benetar), Laurence heeded their advice. But while restitution was off the table, retribution was not.

"I made an appointment with the New York District Attorney's Office."

For some two hours she detailed an improbable tale of an international bank fraud operated by a trio of self-styled nobles and a shill named after a Roman emperor.

"The DA's office thought I was nuts. They looked at me like I had three heads. The whole story sounded so crazy. Then I showed them my files."

Laurence substantiated her complaint with faxes, emails, personal correspondence, financial statements, wire transfer records, canceled checks, loan contracts, legal memos, airline tickets, hotel bills, gold-embossed visiting cards, rejected bank letters, drafts of handwritten mea culpas, and website bios of the Barclay and Badische executives.

"They kept asking me, 'How could a savvy businesswoman like yourself get duped by guys playing dress-up?'"

I tell Laurence it's a fair question.

"I know," she acknowledges. "I've asked myself the same thing a thousand times since that first phone call with Cesar."

"And what's your answer?"

"The best I can come up with is that I was ripped off by a bunch of low-class bullies who figured out how to prey on ambition and dreams."

After reviewing her evidence, the DA's office declined to take the case. "They said, sorry, you may have been a victim of international fraud, but that's outside our jurisdiction. We don't have the authority or the resources to pursue the matter. Try the US Attorney. So I gathered up all my stuff and schlepped it a few blocks south."

Specifically, Laurence presented her dossier to a criminal investigator at the Southern District of New York headquarters of the US Attorney's Office.

"That's where my luck began to turn."

"What made you do it?" I ask. "Cesar fleeced I don't know how many victims, but you're the one who stepped up."

"You want to know the thing that really pushed me over the edge?"

"I do."

"It wasn't the money."

"No?"

"No. It was missing my grandmother's funeral. I'll never forgive those creeps for that. I'll never forgive myself. I wasn't there for my mother when she needed me most. And why? Because I was in Zurich getting ripped off by a bunch of pretend businessmen. So, sure, I can play nice, and I can jump through hoops. But in the end, here's a piece of free advice. Don't *ever* fuck with me."

PART V

WINDOW DRESSING

But what is truth?
Is truth a changing law?
We both have truths.
Are mine the same as yours?
Jesus Christ Superstar,
"Trial Before Pilate"

When one lies, one should lie big, and stick
to it . . . even at the risk of looking ridiculous.
Joseph Goebbels,
"Churchill's Lie Factory"

Before talking with Barbara Laurence, I had viewed the swindle in comic terms, taking my cue from the jokey headlines cooked up by the New York tabloids. But that lighthearted reading was insensitive. It overlooked the malevolence that infused the crime. I could tell that for all her good-natured self-mockery, Laurence still suffered the consequences of the abuse dispensed by the Badische boys.

We weren't the only two Cesar put through the wringer. As an exclusive liaison to the Badische Trust Consortium, he tried to broker at least a dozen dead-end deals. Besides Laurence's ill-fated loan, there was the $200 million agreement for a hundred-bed charity hospital in Belize. The $400 million for an oceanfront development in North Carolina. The "irrevocable $100 million funding commitment" intended to transform a derelict Long Island scrapyard into a tire-recycling facility.

Cesar helped the prince sign agreements with an Arizona real estate developer, a German plastics manufacturer, and a Japanese inventor of an underwater bonding agent similar to Krazy Glue.

The more I studied the dossiers, the more I came to realize that the spanking Barbara Laurence received was neither the cruelest nor the most enduring dispensed by the Trust. The file on another would-be borrower, a telemarketing executive named John Kearns, was far more sinister.

Kearns, a sixty-seven-year-old entrepreneur seeking $30 million for a web-based technology that promised to improve the performance of hotel switchboards, contacted the Trust around the same time Laurence did. (In fact, the two were ensnared at the Dolder

Grand the same weekend, and with the same ceremonial flourish: wooden laptop; green-ink, supersized fountain pen; champagne; etc.)

To set up the prerequisite offshore accounts, Kearns borrowed $30,000 from the friend of a friend, a pilot with Northwest Airlines. For the $120,000 performance guaranty paid to the trust he hit up his eighty-six-year-old mother-in-law; she took out a loan against her home in San Jose. And to cover travel expenses, Kearns borrowed $25,000 from his daughter's mother-in-law and another $40,000 from a bank in Costa Rica.

The international snipe hunt Kearns undertook was so extensive that federal prosecutors, at trial, charted his itinerary on a giant Styrofoam-backed map of the world, marking each fruitless stopover with a bright yellow star. New York received the first. Zurich the next. After that came Costa Rica and then Guam. From Guam, Kearns traveled to Hong Kong, then back to New York, where he attended a meeting with the Badische finance committee in the boardroom of Clifford Chance ("the largest law firm in the world"), followed by "a private luncheon in the Delegates Dining Room at the United Nations." He then rushed home to Lake Tahoe, California, to care for his wife, who was battling stage III multiple myeloma, an incurable cancer of the bone marrow.

But no sooner had he put down his bags than he was forced to pick them back up. Contractual deadlines imposed by the colonel compelled him to quit his wife's bedside and fly to Toronto, Halifax, New York, London, and Hong Kong. The Trust rejected every one of the banks Kearns hoped to use.

Government prosecutors never put a star on Bad Heilbrunn, Germany, but they could have. Kearns was in the tiny German village, overseeing his wife's cancer treatments at a renowned clinic, when Colonel Sherry showed up to declare that his loan was "in limbo" and that his performance guaranty had been forfeited. To temper the grim news, Sherry offered to cover Barbara Kearns's medical expenses and to underwrite a second loan, this one for a patented "hair augmentation product" that Kearns was keen to bring to market. The colonel assured the "nonperforming" borrower that Badische would invest $10 million in the new venture, which exploited recent break-throughs in fetal stem cell research.

Back in Lake Tahoe, Kearns tried to follow up on the commitments Sherry had made at the Bavarian cancer clinic. His efforts were stymied by the colonel's abrupt and unexplained disappearance.

Desperation made Kearns tenacious. "Our lives are on the line," he wrote in one of the many emails the colonel failed to answer. "The delays and unknowns have cost us to the point we have had to discontinue all of [my wife's cancer] treatments. It adds to our stress that we hear nothing from anyone and can only conclude the worst."

He was right to do so.

Badische wiped Kearns out financially. At trial, he estimated he lost "close to six hundred and fifty thousand dollars." But his testimony indicates that the Trust stole a great deal more than money. Like Laurence, Kearns was regularly chastised during the loan proceedings, both for what he said ("There was [to be] no 'John' or 'Brian.' It was all 'Mr.' and 'Mrs.' and 'Doctor.'") and what he wore ("They told me suit and tie. California Casual was *not* acceptable."). Like Laurence, he was punished for his contractual derelictions, forced to submit handwritten pensums apologizing for failing to present his bank letters in what Sherry called a "timeous" manner. And like Laurence, he might have overcome his bitterness more quickly if the

John and Barbara Kearns shortly before they were introduced to the Badische Trust Consortium.

bankers hadn't deprived him of something more valuable than dignity or dollars.

He told me tearfully: "Here's what I can't forgive. They stole the last months of my wife's life."

Reconstituting the plight of Barbara Laurence and John Kearns sidelined Cesar. That was to be expected. The job of the shill requires that he withdraw from the scene once his confederates take the stage. I didn't mind. On the contrary. The fraud was so alien to my own experiences I wanted to learn as much as I could about it. But there were other reasons, beyond curiosity, for my tenacity—reasons of temperament that had nothing to do with the crime.

Obsessives tend to have obsessions. Cesar wasn't my first fixation, and I'm sure he won't be the last. Baseball cards, Matchbox cars, Pez dispensers—I've always been a collector. From the age of seven until I left for Aiglon, I had an unquenchable interest in coins. I made regular trips to the local bank to exchange my allowance for rolls of pennies that I'd scrutinize, triage, and reroll while watching TV. I still have a blue Whitman coin holder with a single vacant slot—I never managed to harvest a 1909-S VDB—and a forty-pound box of duplicate wheaties rerolled by year of minting.* My point? I tend to go overboard. I investigated Cesar and Badische the same way I collected Lincoln pennies—intent on filling every void.

"THE LARGEST LAW FIRM IN THE WORLD"

During one of my conversations with Barbara Laurence I asked her: "What caused you to lower your guard?"

---

*The term *wheatie* is derived from the sheaves of grain on the reverse side of Lincoln pennies minted between 1909 and 1958.

"If I had to choose one thing that made me stupid, I'd say the lawyers. It never occurred to me that a distinguished Park Avenue law firm could be tied to a scam."

John Kearns echoed that sentiment when called to testify: "If the largest law firm in the world was working for Badische, how could it *not* be legit?"

I'd been asking myself the same question ever since I first started sifting through the discovery materials. It was nearly impossible to reconcile the memorandums generated by so many legitimate lawyers with the illegal shenanigans of the ersatz royals. The Trust's genius in this regard was most obvious in its sustained manipulations of Rogers & Wells, a Park Avenue law firm absorbed, in January 2000, by Clifford Chance, the London-based multinational behemoth.

Casual ties between the Trust and Rogers & Wells stretched back nearly twenty years, but the relationship was only formalized in 1998, when Colonel Sherry presented the firm with a $10,000 retainer. Soon after his check cleared, Rogers & Wells tapped a recently hired bank and regulatory law specialist named David L. Glass to serve as their "lead attorney" and liaison to the Trust.

"I was new to the firm and eager to build a client base," Glass later recalled. "I was told the Badische bankers were existing clients so I was only too happy to oblige them."

And oblige them he did.

Glass first helped the Trust, in August 1999, by drafting a regulatory memo that Colonel Sherry (unbeknownst to its author) deployed to reject Barbara Laurence's initial bank letter.

"After that, he latched on to me," Glass would later remember. Early on, the lawyer produced, again at the colonel's request, a series of "attestation letters" on Clifford Chance letterhead that served no obvious legal purpose. The first such document recorded the removal of Prince Robert as head of the Trust. As Sherry explained to Glass, the prince had begun behaving erratically in early 2000, soon after his wife, the self-styled Princess Audrey Khimchiachvili, fell ill.* The chairman's grief—which routinely expressed itself in drunkenness, self-directed monologues, slurred speech, and alarming lapses in personal hygiene necessitating the intervention of professional upholstery cleaners—made it impossible to keep him at the helm of the Trust, so Colonel Sherry asked that Glass memorialize, in writing, the promotion of the Baron Moncrieffe as interim chairman.

Glass considered the request unusual. None of his clients had ever asked for a so-called attestation. Then again, none of his clients controlled $60 billion in assets. Glass provided the letter. No sooner had he done so than Colonel Sherry asked him to affirm that Badische was "a client in good standing" of Rogers & Wells *before* it merged with Clifford Chance. The colonel supplied the following rationale: he feared potential clients might wrongly assume that Badische had "hired Clifford Chance just because it was a famous, worldwide global law firm."

Once again, Glass obliged.

Sherry's requests grew incrementally bolder. Could Badische receive its business correspondence at the firm? Doing so would allow the Trust to consolidate business plans and other confidential materials in a single location, a tremendous convenience for the globe-trotting bankers. Additionally, the impeccable reputation of Clifford Chance, Glass was informed, "would discourage people who were

---

*Princess Audrey died in late February 2000. A world authority on the history of miniature doll costumes—an expertise that informed her unique sense of fashion and, in particular, a lifelong passion for exotic feathers and lace—she was also a pioneer in the field of "psychic dentistry," a branch of oral medicine specializing in the telepathic transformation of base-metal dental fillings into gold. (Her motto: "Gold-mine yourself!") Later in life, Audrey extended her medical practice to include chromotherapy. Working out of an office above Carnegie Hall, "Dr. Audrey Kargere, PhD, of Stockholm, Sweden" treated all manner of illness—congestion, ulcers, anemia, chronic flatulence, etc.—by the application of colored lenses and lights. In 1949, she documented her breakthroughs as a "color healer" in *Color and Personality*. The monograph is still in print.

not serious from making idle inquiries." The Trust wanted to keep
scoundrels and swindlers at bay.

Glass conferred with his colleagues and, receiving no objection, approved the request. It was quickly followed by another: Could Badische
receive their clients at the law firm? A Waldorf Towers suite, for all its
gilded extravagance, lacked the gravitas of an international law firm.

Glass again checked with his colleagues and again gave the okay.

By the end of February, the offices of Clifford Chance, located at
the very top of the MetLife Building, the historic landmark straddling
Grand Central Terminal, became the de facto boiler room for a band
of make-believe bankers. There were some days when Cesar shepherded as many as six groups of Barclay clients in and out of the firm.
For major assemblies—gatherings that could include some dozen
Badische representatives and prospective borrowers—Glass had his
assistant reserve a vast conference room on the fifty-third floor. More
intimate meetings of the finance and executive committees were generally conducted in the firm's mahogany-paneled boardroom, a sumptuous venue more in keeping with the Baron Moncrieffe's Old World
aesthetic. Cesar, present at most of the loan meetings, remained aloof
during the negotiations. "He stuck to the sidelines," Glass later remembered. "He ushered people in and ushered people out, but it was
never very clear what role he had."

When it came to the prep work for the loan meetings, no detail, no
matter how minor, escaped Glass's attention, as the following email
exchange suggests:

> COLONEL SHERRY: *We will be eight on one side (incl.
> you) and eight on the other (for visiting clients) with
> one for the acting Chairman. Therefore, we would
> need 17 chairs. . . . We may also put one of our people
> at the foot of the table. This would decrease it to 7 on
> each side and one at each end, being 16 chairs total.
> Please advise.*

DAVID GLASS: I am pleased to inform you that we have
a room that should work for our meeting. It is room
K on the 53rd floor. It has a long conference table . . .

Glass did more than oversee the seating arrangements. He made introductions. When Badische asked for help developing an anti-money-laundering policy, Glass brought in a partner experienced in "international regulatory matters." When Badische expressed a desire to issue collateralized bonds tied to its African assets, Glass put the Trust's in-house lawyer Richard Zeif in touch with a Clifford Chance partner specializing in "securitization transactions."

All these efforts did not go unrewarded. In mid-July 2000, Badische named David Glass its "Honourary Avocat Generale." Colonel Sherry reinforced the symbolic appointment by sending the CEO of Clifford Chance an unsolicited reference letter. ("We have found David Glass of your New York office to be honest, sincere, diligent, accurate, respectful, resourceful, knowledgeable, pleasant and helpful in all matters of our business needs.")

Glass appreciated the framed commendation and the letter of support, but it was an altogether different expression of "confidence" (that's the word he would later testify Colonel Sherry employed) that left the most lasting impression.

The same week he doled out kudos, the colonel presented Glass with a sealed manila envelope and a one-page "tally" listing the investors bankrolling the House of Badische loan program. He then asked Glass to affirm the dollar values listed on the tally sheet by comparing them to confidential asset letters contained in the envelope.

Glass considered the request unusual but not unreasonable, and whatever qualms he might have had were trumped by his interest in learning the source of the Badische billions.

What the lawyer discovered, upon reviewing the contents of the envelope, shocked him. "The floor opened up from under me," he later recalled. The nine putative funding commitments included: an

CLIFFORD CHANCE
ROGERS & WELLS LLP

BADISCHE'S ASSETS TO FINANCE DEALS

1. CAPITAL FACILITIES:

A) MERRILL LYNCH   100. MILLION USD   (PER DE
B) HANOVER HOLDINGS   006. BILLION USD
C) MER DU NORD Coll. 001. BILLION USD
D) G.M.T. CORP.   010. BILLION USD
E) HABS BURG FOUNDATION 100. MILLION USD (PER DEA
F) ABBOUD FAMILY TRUST 005. BILLION USD
G) ABILAMP'S GENEVA INV. TRUST 030. MILLION USD (PER DE.
TOTAL: 22 BILLION, 230 MILLION USD
               $ 22,230,000,000. USD

2. AFRICAN TIMBER + MINERAL ASSETS BY MANDATE:

A) REGAL INVESTMENT HOLDINGS   17.9 BILLION USD
B) MOMBESSA KINGDOM   50. BILLION USD

TOTAL: 67.9 BILLION USD

3. COMBINED CAPITAL FACILITIES + ASSETS:

CAPITAL FACILITIES: $ 22,230,000,000. USD
AFRICAN ASSETS: $ 67,900,000,000. USD

TOTALS: $ 90,130,000,000. USD

US 007811

CC 009122

The tally Colonel Sherry provided attorney David Glass.

offering from a "high yield investment program" promising dividends of 50 percent a month; a generic solicitation letter from Merrill Lynch ("It was basically a sales document that in no way presented a commitment of funds"); an unsubstantiated promise of funds from Duke d'Antin's Habsburg Foundation; and a $1 billion loan proposal from a company that, a quick web search confirmed, shared space with a "scuzzy" used-car dealer in a California strip mall.

The most preposterous of the "assets" was this special deed of trust from the Kingdom of Mombessa:

Kingdom of Mombessa

Special Deed of Trust

We, His Majesty King Henri Francois Mazzamba, Sovereign Ruler of the Kingdom of Mombessa, situated in the Republic of the Congo (formerly known as Zaire), do hereby appoint Babische Anlage Treuhand, A.G., this Third day of July, 1997 to serve as Trustee and Administrator of the great wealth and resources of my Kingdom, in accordance with the objectives hereinafter set forth:

Whereas, the Kingdom contains great wealth in the form of such resources as its land, timber gold, diamonds, and other assets within and upon the earth, and

Whereas, those resources have a fair market value currently estimated to be in excess of fifty billion USD, and

Whereas, it is our desire to utilize those resources for humanitarian and commercial purposes both within and beyond the realm of the Kingdom, and

Whereas, we require certain assistance in the development of co-ventures, financial relationships and projects in order to generate maximum profit and utility through these resources.

Now, therefore, we do hereby instruct custodial care and management of these resources to Babische Anlage Treuhand, A.G., which entity shall, in its capacity as Trustee and Administrator to this Kingdom have discretionary authority, in its good faith and wisdom, to pledge or otherwise utilize those resources as they shall deem appropriate, and in the best interests of the Kingdom. Further Babische Anlage Treuhand, A.G. shall have, and is hereby granted, power of attorney and full authority to enter into and execute all of such agreements and other documents as may be reasonably required on behalf of the Kingdom toward the attainment of the objectives of the King, and as set forth above.

His Majesty King Henri-Francois Mazzamba
Sovereign Ruler of Mombessa

[Stamp: MOMBESSA KINGDOM · CITY OF MONDIMBI · THE KING LISUMBAYAKA II]

GOVERNMENT EXHIBIT 120 (ID)

All of the foregoing terms agreed to and accepted on this Third day of July, 1997 by:

Babische Anlage Treuhand, A.G.

US 014064

Dr. Robert von Babische
Chairman of the Board

Col. Brian Sherry-Berwick
Managing Director

In the presence of Financial Consultant, Margaret Nardus Merrill Lynch

CC 007957

USA 018759

The blatant illegitimacy of the deed devastated Glass. On the stand, he maintained a measured tone when asked to describe how he felt when he reviewed the alleged asset: "My immediate reaction was that this was not by any means a commitment of funds." (Years later, asked the same question, his response was more vivid: "When I perused those letters, I felt all of a sudden as if I was looking down into my open grave.")

Glass found himself in a quandary. Refusing to validate the declared value of the assets would undermine months of negotiations between Badische and their loan applicants. Yet endorsing the bogus documents might render his clients susceptible to civil or criminal action. Glass toted up the dollar figures cited in the letters and compared them to the figures on the one-page tally. The sums matched. At least the math was sound. That persuaded him to set aside his legal concerns, if only temporarily, and provide the colonel with the requested attestation. None of which resolved the bigger problem facing David Glass: how to tell a colonel (who he would soon learn wasn't a colonel), a baron (who wasn't a baron), and a prince (who wasn't a prince) that they might be the victims of an international fraud?

THE COLONEL IN THE BOARDROOM
WITH THE FOUNTAIN PEN

David Glass attempted to alert the Trust about the iffy nature of their assets, but each time he tried, something seemed to get in the way. First it was back-to-back loan conferences with Cesar and his clients. Then it was the alleged disappearance of a cherished object belonging to a Badische executive. That loss, spelled out in an email sent to every employee in the New York offices of Clifford Chance, caught my attention:

From: David Glass
To: #NYC: All Staff
Subject: Missing Pen—Reward

On Wednesday, July 12, a Montblanc fountain pen
belonging to a client of the Firm disappeared from
Conference Room 52-J some time between 1 PM
and 2:30 PM. The pen has sentimental value to the
client, who is offering a reward for its return. Please
reply in confidence . . . No questions will be asked
and all replies will be kept confidential. Thank you.

No questions asked? That may have been Glass's position. It wasn't mine.

I had nothing *but* questions: Was Cesar present at the time and location of the pen's disappearance? (Yes.) Did Cesar have an appreciation for Montblanc fountain pens stretching back to 1972? (Absolutely.) Was there any proof that the pen in question was Cesar's? (None at all. In fact, the memo notes the pen belonged "to a client of the Firm"; i.e., a member of the Badische board.) Was it possible that the disappearance was nothing more than a ruse designed to distract Glass from his concerns about the dubious asset letters? (Of course.) And assuming the pen's alleged disappearance *was* a ploy, could Cesar have masterminded its execution? (Sure, it's possible.) Was there any proof to justify that speculation? (No, unfortunately not. But that didn't stop me from connecting the petty crime to my fountain-pen triumph in the hallway of Belvedere.)

Glass eventually managed to express his apprehensions about the funding sources. He later recalled telling the colonel that even if, for argument's sake, the valuation of the Mombessa deed was "entirely valid, one couldn't assume [it] could be fully collateralized for the loan program."

The colonel dismissed his lawyer's misgivings. Hadn't a Clifford

Chance attorney already detailed how "nonliquid African assets" might be profitably exploited by means of a "securitization transaction"?

"That doesn't mean there is $50 billion available today for investment," Glass remembers countering. He advised the Trust to "proceed with caution." To that end, he and one of his London-based colleagues redrafted the Badische loan agreements "from scratch." The new contract, for which Clifford Chance billed Badische £16,000, was radically different from the ones signed by Laurence and Kearns. However, at the insistence of the Trust, two provisions from the original agreement remained: the performance guaranty and the bank letter.

ULTIMATUM

In August of 2000, a month after David Glass reviewed its asset tally, Badische decided to launch a $100 million private equity fund based in Luxembourg, a tax haven known for stringent bank secrecy laws. The offering required local legal representation, so Glass, ever obliging, arranged for the colonel and the baron to meet with attorneys at a highly regarded law firm headquartered in the tiny grand duchy.

The conference did not go well. The self-styled aristocrats put noses out of joint by presenting cartes de visite lacking addresses and phone numbers, a faux pas the colonel compounded when he provided, as a reference, the name of a local criminal.

The Luxembourgian lawyers decided they "did not wish to go forward" with Glass's clients, a snub that raised alarm bells among his colleagues in New York. They asked Glass to reconfirm the legitimacy of the Trust's financial representations. With that in mind, he

The visiting card that gave the lawyers from Luxembourg pause.

invited the baron to lunch in a private club at the top of the MetLife building. The baron tried to neutralize the law firm's concerns by noting that Prince Robert had ties to the largest chemical company in the world. "The *B* in BASF stands for Badische," he confided.

Glass informed the baron that anecdotal declarations wouldn't satisfy his bosses. They wanted an *independent* accounting of the bank's holdings. Reluctantly, Moncrieffe produced a financial statement for a Badische account managed by Robert Gurland in London. It showed a balance of £1 million. Glass speculated, correctly, that the £1 million represented *liquid* assets, the money required to run the day-to-day operations of the lending program. But what about the Trust's *investment* capital—the billions needed to underwrite the loans promised to Laurence, Kearns, and all the other borrowers? Glass was blunt. He asked the baron: "Is there capital *beyond* that million pounds?"

When the response he received proved unsatisfactory, Glass presented a four-point ultimatum. To continue to retain the services of Clifford Chance, Badische would have to deliver: a verified list of all loan transactions; two years of financials; indemnification of the attorneys doing work for Badische; and a list of the Trust's banking relationships.

Two days later, the name of Clifford Chance disappeared from the contact page of the Badische website. All ties between the law firm and the Trust were severed.

"Inconvenience" and "Misunderstandings"

David Glass and his colleagues weren't the only attorneys bamboozled by Badische. Documents in the milk crates indicate that the Trust also misled law firms in Zurich, Hong Kong, Vienna, London, Panama City, and Monte Carlo. The volume of the paperwork the various attorneys generated suggests it takes almost as many lawyers to start a fake bank as it does a real one. For the fraud to succeed, dummy companies had to be incorporated. Bogus prospectuses had to be generated.

Phantom partnerships had to be formed and dissolved. Websites had to be purged of actionable language. (There's a fine line between *eliciting* loans, which is legal, and *soliciting* loans, which is not.) Funding agreements for nonexistent mutual funds had to be written and revised. Default memos had to be composed and delivered when—not *if*—potential borrowers failed to meet their time-bound obligations.

David Glass later testified that he had no sense of the scale or scope of the fraud he had helped Badische pull off. He acknowledged he had been "snookered," but could not differentiate all the chiselers from those who were chiseled.

I wasn't entirely clear about that myself.

The bankers were obviously ne'er-do-wells. But what about the duke who claimed to be married to the archduchess of Austria? Or the retired UN ambassador who drafted the asset tally on behalf of the Trust's finance committee? Or the Merrill Lynch financial consultant who witnessed the signing of the special deed from the Kingdom of Mombessa? Were they dupes or deceivers? Fools or felons?

And what about *my* guy? Would the managing director of an august London bank knowingly broker deals with small-time con men? To quote my Belvedere housemaster: Not bloody likely!

Cesar never testified during the trial, and his lawyer called no witnesses on his behalf. Yet his voice did surface, if only briefly, after the jury reached its verdict. This is what Cesar told Federal Judge Shira Scheindlin moments before she pronounced sentence:

> THE DEFENDANT: *Your Honor, respected members of the government, thank you for allowing me to share my thoughts and feelings about the situation with the Badische group.*
>
> *I very much regret all the inconvenience and suffering that has occurred due to my actions and inactions. I hope and trust that all the people, whether I knew them or not, that were harmed and did lose time and money can be compensated for their losses and are able to recover from any misunderstandings.*

I feel naïve and incompetent about not being able to discern the real aspects from the illegitimate parts of the transaction. I did not do my duties as a broker and assist clients with overseas company formation work intending to harm or hurt anyone. I still believe that the transaction was a viable one, that some of the key people I was introduced to—the VPs of the banks, different advisers to the lenders, the Knights of Malta, the clients and their own attorneys—were all impressive, real, professional, and credible.

I must say that I myself have been suffering mentally, emotionally, and financially since this all started two and a half years ago. However, I have been trying to find meaning in all of this, to learn more about myself and how to be less trusting and more discerning. My various volunteer work, therapies, and spiritual study has been helping me to find a deeper meaning in life, to use this as a positive learning experience, while allowing me to have the strength to continue helping my mother and my sister with their challenges.

I hope and pray that everyone that has suffered can forgive me and find peace. I only beg for your understanding with what I knew at the time and for your forgiveness.

Thank you very much for your time.

It was strange to "hear" Cesar's voice, as set down in pages of the sentencing record. I found it more than a little irritating. *Situation, inconvenience, misunderstandings*—those aren't words I would have used to describe a multiyear, multinational, multiplayer, multimillion-dollar, and, while we're at it, multifarious fraud. His tone reminded me of the dismay Colonel Sherry expressed when Barbara Laurence confronted him: "Haven't we had a wonderful relationship? I'm *really* hurt!" Except Cesar wasn't trying to shoo away a pesky mark. He was standing before a federal judge.

I later learned that Cesar's presentencing testimony was excerpted from a much longer six-page letter submitted into evidence. The unredacted statement, though too long to reproduce in toto, warrants generous quotation. Here's a hefty portion of that written declaration:

> *It is my hope that you can realize my deeds were [done] with good intentions. I am truly sorry that the effects have not turned out that way.*
>
> *I do not make empty promises. I am a person of my word and follow through on what I do promise. If I am guilty of anything, it is primarily of not checking things out better. If my naiveté prompted me to participate in something less than legitimate and caused other people harm, I am truly sorry.*
>
> *I am a trusting person. This is my nature and I will die being this way . . . I relied wholeheartedly on people's word. In this particular situation, I relied mostly on Prince Robert of Badische & George Moncrieffe (the impressive chairmen), as well as Brian Sherry with whom I worked in order to properly prepare clients for their meetings. I was so impressed and honored by their supremacy that this impaired my judgment and ability to assess them.*
>
> *Prince Robert, Dr. Moncrieffe and other advisers . . . like Duke d'Antin . . . were part of [the Knights of Malta] order and I felt I was in the presence of credible, experienced people held in high regard. Even the largest law firm in the world, Clifford Chance, was involved, where we would have meetings with the clients and attorneys. Who am I to question their credibility?*
>
> *I still to this day believe that they were all real and that their contacts and interests were bona fide.*
>
> *You can imagine my frustration over the past 2 years. Emotionally & psychologically, I almost lost it but have been continually trying to take care of myself with Biofeedback/cognitive*

therapy and regular prayers. Physically I was in pain, and fi-nancially, I already have lost it. I've spent a lot of time over the last 2 years in spiritual study. This was further speeded up due to my Achilles tendon tear injury immediately after this whole investigation started.

I've been trying to use this as a positive learning and growing experience. It hasn't been easy with all the frustrations and let down feelings I have had.

As a spiritual teacher also taught me, there are no Justified Resentments. Since there are no justified resentments, I accept being here in this position, due to the choices I have made and have no blame towards anyone. The fault may not be entirely mine, however, I have no ill will towards anyone. Why? Because if I think that someone else cause[d] this, then I may have to wait forever for it to be resolve[d] by that someone else!

I humbly beg for your understanding of me, an appreciation for my actions taken at the time with what I knew and thought to be credible, and insight into my circumstances that brought me here, pleading not guilty, with all my heart and soul.

I'm no lawyer, but it seems pretty dopey to plead *not guilty after* you've been convicted—unless the appearance of dopiness is a ruse. Cesar's testimony raised a few questions. Actually, more than a few. Were the feelings expressed in his wishy-washy mea culpa heartfelt or fake? Did he truly consider himself guilty of being an innocent? Did he really imagine himself to be on the receiving end of abuse? Did he perceive his "deeds" to be undertaken with "good intentions"? How could anyone in his right mind serve up a plea so clotted with self-pity, wounded pride, insubstantial introspection, self-justification, and dubious assertion? And equally preposterous, how could so many entrepreneurs put their faith in a self-declared patsy claiming to be the managing director of the Barclay Consulting Group?

PART VI

"WHAT LIES WITHIN US"

There is a saying that we learn most about ourselves from our enemies. This I have truly been trying to do. I have learned how I was manipulated, and in a way, how to manipulate others as well.

Cesar Viana,
Memorandum in Aid of Sentencing

Many of the clues to the tectonic puzzle lie high up in the face of almost inaccessible precipices.

Leon W. Collet, *The Structure of the Alps*

Before I started digging into the mechanics of the fraud, I doubted that a San Francisco branch of Barclays could be large enough to handle the kind of casino financing that Cesar had mentioned when he first spoke to Barbara Laurence. I was mistaken.

Barclays' West Coast outpost could have easily underwritten a $6 billion hotel deal. While the Badische loan program was in full swing, Barclays Global Investors, a San Francisco–based subsidiary of the famous London bank, administered assets of $1.4 *trillion*. It had twenty-five hundred employees and during good years its profits exceeded $1 billion. In 1999, it was one of the largest corporate money managers in the world.

Now for the *but*.

But Barclays Global Investors did not employ Cesar. Cesar was the managing director of Barclay Global Invest*ments*, a division of the Barclay Consulting Group. The Barclay that spelled its name without an *s* employed a staff of one, Cesar, and maintained a checking

Half a mile (and $1.4 trillion) separated Barclay from Barclays.

account with Bank of America that had an average cash balance in the high three figures. And whereas Bar*clays* leased three hundred thousand square feet of prime real estate in San Francisco's financial district, Bar*clay*, mindful of overhead, made do with a sixty-dollar-a-month "business address service" located a few blocks west of its more profitable eponym. Not to put too fine a point on it, Barclay had as much to do with Barclays as it did with Charles Barkley, basketball's legendary round mound of rebound.

LOMPOC AND AIGLON:
A COMPARATIVE ANALYSIS

Even after prosecutors won their case, Cesar insisted he was innocent. "I would never intentionally harm anyone nor would I seek personal gain," he told the sentencing judge. The Honorable Shira A. Scheindlin wasn't convinced. Rejecting his plea for reduced jail time, she sentenced Cesar to thirty-seven months, followed by five years of "supervised release." For good measure, she saddled Cesar with a restitution penalty of $1,222,494—nearly half the advance fees the government lawyers proved at trial had been misappropriated from some of the American victims of the fraud. (Worldwide loss figures will never be known, but the milk crates suggest the Trust pocketed some $4 million in performance guaranties.)

Still, things could have gone a whole lot worse for Cesar. He landed in a cushy prison camp attached to the US Penitentiary in Lompoc, California. Setting aside the well-publicized criticism of one famous former resident, convicted insider trader Ivan Boesky, who once groused that overcrowding at Lompoc forced him to play doubles on the prison's sole tennis court, most detainees praise the minimum-security outpost. One Lompoc inmate posted this helpful review on thepamperedprisoner.com:

It's a camp, so pretty much anything you imagine as a prison, throw it out. This place is literally green grass, eucalyptus trees, and a split-rail fence surrounding it. We had sport fields, weight piles, we watched movies on the weekends, we had TV rooms; it's a summer camp. It's the federal version of community service. You work during the day, you have jobs, stay busy, then work's over, do what you want. You have over 340 guys watched by one or two unarmed guards. The whole thing operates on the honor system.

While I'd have preferred that Cesar serve time in a more austere, Shawshanky setting, I found myself marveling—more than marveling, deriving a deep sense of pleasure—in the situational irony of my former roommate's cosseted incarceration. Lompoc provides its residents with mountain vistas, well-tended fields, split-rail fences, window boxes, and cow pastures (the prison maintains an award-winning dairy farm). In short, Cesar had gone from an alpine boarding school regulated like a prison camp to a prison camp run like an alpine boarding school.

True, the prison camp doesn't allow residents to ski and hike, but its first-rate baseball diamond and bocce courts offset those prohibitions, as do its professional gym equipment and exercise bikes. (At Aiglon, cinder blocks served as leg weights.) Oh, and there's one more amenity that the school and our federal prisons have in common—foosball.

When I uncovered this parallel perk, an image popped into my head of Cesar crouching down low behind the defensemen of a prison foosball table, firing off bank shots and grimacing like a griffin while hustling cigarettes from tax cheats and embezzlers. The recurring visual eventually triggered a crazy idea: Why not fly out to California and challenge my nemesis to the mother of all grudge matches?

I downloaded the Lompoc Visiting Regulations. Guests, I learned, are authorized to enter the facility with up to twenty dollars in quarters—more than enough to fund a foosball face-off with the Shiller from Manila. (Any spare change, I decided, would be used to buy vanilla lattes from the prison's celebrated vending machines.)

I was under no illusions about winning. If I couldn't outmaneuver Cesar on the Belvedere table, I sure as hell couldn't take him in Lompoc, where I think it's safe to assume he had tons of time to train.

As it turned out, my prep work was moot. While plotting out the showdown, I discovered that the Bureau of Prisons only furnishes foosball tables in Texas and Colorado. More consequentially, a one-word update, pulled from the BOP website, derailed any and all scenarios of jailhouse retribution.

PIZZA AND SPEARS

"RELEASED."

According to a federal "inmate locator" launched in the midst of my search, Cesar had rejoined the civilian population on May 6, 2005. And while his liberty was conditional—a probation officer would be monitoring him for another five years—the reaction of my family was not.

"Whoa. Game changer," Max said when I told him Cesar was out on parole. "Let's prank him. We can call up and order a dozen pizzas sent to his house."

Françoise vetoed the idea. "*Hors de question!* He's a convicted felon. Who knows what else is on his wrapping sheet."

"It's called a *rap* sheet, Mom. And he wouldn't know the pizzas came from us. My computer has a speech synthesizer that can change Dad's voice into a girl or a robot."

I let Max down gently. "Sorry, kiddo. Payback by pizza is not an option."

"Do you know how the Warlpiri at Yuendumu would deal with someone like Cesar?" Françoise said. "They'd spear him."

"Cool," said Max. "You have that spear-thrower thing on your desk. I'll go get it."

"*Non!*" Françoise said forbiddingly. "No pizza. No spearing."

In the weeks and months following the news of Cesar's liberation, I stockpiled dozens of revenge scenarios, not all of which required props. Max's headmaster, a movie buff professionally mandated to defang bullies, suggested a streamlined response requiring neither pie-shaped carbohydrates nor Aboriginal weaponry.

"Have you considered taking your cue from the guy in *Diner*?" he said.

"I'm listening."

"Whenever the guy in *Diner* spots someone who picked on him at school, he walks over and—*bam!*—coldcocks him. The guy then ticks the bully's name off a mental checklist and goes about his business."

I needed no help when it came to revenge fantasies. I had generated plenty all on my own. The most elaborate involved luring Cesar into a karaoke bar to reenact the flogging scene from *Jesus Christ Superstar*. Except in my adaptation of the musical, Cesar would play the title role and I'd be the one holding the whip.

Karaoke comeuppance, like spearing, prison-camp foosball, and payback by pizza, provided diversion from the substance of my inquiry, but I never for a moment considered taking direct action against the ex-convict I had once roomed with in Switzerland.

Françoise's Aboriginal spear thrower.

TRUE LIES

What prevented me from satisfying the retaliatory impulses that had been roiling inside me since 1971? In a word? Risk. What did I know about taking on a felon? Hell, what did I know about Cesar? Françoise was absolutely right. I had, at best, an incomplete knowledge of my former roommate's wrapping sheet. Maybe the wire fraud conviction was part of a much lengthier, much nastier criminal history. I wasn't so reckless as to undertake real-world, lie-for-a-lie, screw-unto-others schemes of Hammurabian justice. Armchair investigation was a lot less dicey. In fact, surrounded by the criminal dossiers, rather than the criminals, made me feel in control. I knew it was just a matter of time before Cesar's story and my story would converge in the pages of a book chronicling the rise and fall of a childhood tyrant.

"It will make an *amazing* novel," Françoise said.

"I guess."

"You don't sound convinced."

"Well, it *is* a great story," I said. "A twelve-year-old bully grows up to become a con man. Hooks up with a guy claiming to be the seventy-fourth grand master of the Knights of Malta and a 'baron' who wears spats. Helps the bogus royals and their administrator operate a scam out of the biggest law firm in the world. Dupes all sorts of business types to travel the world. But here's the thing. Would you believe *any* of that if it happened in a novel?"

"What are you saying?"

"It has to be nonfiction."

"But you'll change some of the facts, no? To keep the real Cesar out of our lives?"

"How? How can I change the details of an unbelievable fraud without making it sound unbelievable?"

"*Pardon?*"

"What I mean is, I can't write a *based*-on-a-true-story story because the 'true' story is built on lies. The House of Badische was a house of cards. Start monkeying around with any of the 'facts,' the whole thing falls apart. It's a bad idea to make stuff up about guys who make stuff up."

"At least change Cesar's name," Françoise urged.

"To what? Julius? Nero? What good would that do given that the scam is on the web? The trial is a matter of public record. To mask his identity, I'd have to change his name, the name of the bank, the names of the prince, colonel, baron, and duke. Once I do that, the believability of the whole story is shot."

"So what are you planning?"

"I'm not sure. For the moment I just want to keep digging. I still don't have a sense of Cesar. Even the basics are in dispute. Goodman thinks he's American. Laurence told me she thought he might be Asian or Spanish. Glass remembers him being Mediterranean. His lawyer states he's a naturalized US citizen, but the files include an INS report that contradicts that claim. The Bureau of Prisons identifies Cesar as white. He says he's Hispanic."

"None of that changes the fact that he's a criminal. He just spent three years in prison. Now that he's out, he'll be looking for new victims. I don't want you to be one of them."

"It's a bit late for that," I joke.

Françoise fails to see the humor. "Just promise me you won't contact him."

"I'm not an idiot."

"*Promise* me," she repeats. "No contact."

"I promise."

DATA MINING

Following the discovery of Cesar's release, I became more vigilant about monitoring his movements. It came as a shock to discover that after leaving Lompoc he revived Barclay, the one-man financial group that put him behind bars in the first place. He might have been even more cavalier than that. An Internet archive indicates that his website, barclaycg.org, was updated five times *during* its founder's incarceration. In the fall of 2005, Cesar deleted his name from the site's home page and moved the world headquarters of the firm to a studio apartment near the University of San Francisco. Otherwise, it was business as usual. Barclay continued to offer "results-oriented project specific Business Financing, Offshore Company & Trust Formations" to individuals needing loans of $10 million to $100 million. Given his prepenitentiary bankruptcy filing, the $1.2 million restitution order hanging over his head, and the wages paid to federal inmates (which top out around a dollar an hour), it seemed reasonable to assume Cesar was up to his old tricks. And, as I learned from my digital surveillance, some new ones, as well.

Around the same time he updated the Barclay website, Cesar created a subsidiary entity called NextLevel, through which he offered a broad range of corporate services steeped in the language of self-improvement and personal empowerment. The spirit of the offshoot was captured in an inspirational aphorism:

WHAT LIES BEHIND US
AND WHAT LIES BEFORE US
ARE SMALL MATTERS COMPARED TO
WHAT LIES WITHIN US

Cesar credited the motto to Ralph Waldo Emerson, but I did a little checking—okay, maybe more than a little—and determined that the

actual author was a disgraced
early-twentieth-century securities trader named Henry
Stanley Haskins.* The professional dishonor Cesar
shared with Haskins wasn't
the only irony to be gleaned
from the NextLevel website.

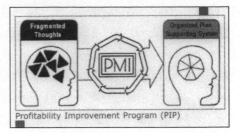

A detail from Cesar's "'Out of Your Mind' Thinking" program.

The "unique internal map of
reality" Cesar offered his clients through something he called "'Out of
Your Mind' Thinking" also resonated with unintended meaning.

Soon after launching NextLevel, Cesar further reshaped his
online persona by starting a film production company under an alias
that made use of his mother's maiden name. Cesar Augustus Viana
became Cesar A. Teague. Although I can't be sure, I suspect his ex-
periment in pseudonymity can be traced, in part, to the polynomial
habits of the Badische boys. Prince Robert juggled no fewer than
twelve aliases during his long career as a con man,† the baron at least
ten, and the colonel, though less than half the age of his royal confederates, regularly alternated among four names during the Badische loan program. (Government briefs identified him as "BRIAN

---

*Cesar is not alone in misattributing the saying to Emerson. Three successful self-
help gurus he admires (Dr. Phil, Stephen R. Covey, and Tony Robbins), a T-shirt
manufacturer, and a company that prints pithy wisdom on laminated refrigerator
magnets have all made the same mistake. Nor is Ralph Waldo Emerson the only
nineteenth-century trinomial Harvard man to receive undeserving credit. Oliver
Wendell Holmes and Henry David Thoreau are also wrongly cited as the authors of
the Haskins motto, which was first published, anonymously, in a 1940 book titled
Meditations in Wall Street.

†Besides brandishing a number of princely titles (e.g., Prince von Badische, Prince
of Montezuma, Prince Khimchiachvili, Prince of Thrace) Robert also identified
himself as the Duke of Mogolov, the Marquis de Hermosilla, the Count of Cabo St.
Eugenio, the Archbishop Metropolitan of the Holy Church of Saint John of Jerusalem, and, most frequently, the Seventy-Fourth Grand Master of the Knights of Malta
(Ecumenical).

D. SHERRY, also known as Colonel Sherry, also known as Prince Brian, also known as Brian Sherry-Berwick.")

Cesar's new surname caused me all sorts of problems. It was hard enough to track one ex-roommate. Suddenly, I had to keep tabs on two. Then, a month later, a third alias surfaced. Max alleviated some of the headache by programming an army of search engine bots to send me alerts about Cesar and his avatars.

A Stalker with Privileges

For almost a year, I obeyed Françoise's restraining order. Given Cesar's criminal record, avoidance seemed the only sensible course of action. Then, in early June 2006, one of Max's web crawlers notified me of a tantalizing opportunity seemingly free of risk.

Cesar, in the role of indie film producer, announced he was organizing a fund-raiser open to the public. The implications hit me instantly. Here was a chance to observe without making direct contact, thus satisfying curiosity *and* spousal injunction. What harm could come from an evening of anonymous reconnaissance?

Predictably, Max and Françoise held opposing views on the merits of surveillance. "You're going, right, Dad?"

Françoise shot me a look.

"I'm not really so sure I should," I told Max. "It could be a little chancy."

"But you wouldn't have to talk to the guy."

"That's true," I said. "I don't even have to sign up to attend. Cesar wouldn't know if I attended."

Françoise sighed. She knew where this was going. "What if he recognizes you?"

"It's been more than thirty years since we last set eyes on each other."

"He might not have pictures of himself on the web, but you do," Françoise noted.

"Dad can go incognito!" Max proposed excitedly. "He can grow a beard."

I rubbed my jaw. "Not a bad idea. I could start tonight."

Françoise's resolve began to falter. "You wouldn't make contact?"

"I wouldn't make contact."

"And you won't mention your name?"

"Of course not. I'll steal a page from Cesar's playbook and adopt an alias."

Françoise rolled her eyes. "And you'll take someone along with you?"

"You really think that's necessary?" That question prompted another disapproving look. "Okay, okay, I'll bring backup."

I had three weeks to prep for what Max began calling "the recon mission." I decided to use the time to find out what I could about Cesar's capacity for violence. That meant another frustrating round of calls to law enforcement officers.

All writers are stalkers. But as any freelancer will tell you, writers on assignment are stalkers with privileges. I pitched "The Search for Cesar" to a magazine editor who had published my stuff twenty years before. We'd lost touch in the early 1990s, after I started writing fiction full-time. While we were catching up over lunch, I learned that the editor was the mother of a nine-year-old girl who had just finished reading my first children's book, *Leon and the Spitting Image*. The girl liked *Leon* enough to ask her mother for an autograph from the author. The request ended well for both interested parties. The nine-year-old got a signed book, and its author got a magazine contract. Soon after that, public officials who had previously played hard to get began taking my calls.

THE KENTUCKIAN

During his eight years as an assistant US attorney for the Southern District of New York, Timothy J. Coleman prosecuted all manner of crime: racketeering, embezzlement, identity theft, narcotics trafficking. His specialty was corporate fraud. Coleman played a major role in locking up the Enron executives at the center of an accounting scandal that wiped out some $78 billion in shareholder equity. Yet Enron isn't the case Coleman remembers most giddily when asked to reflect on his career as a federal prosecutor. That honor is reserved for a minor swindle he litigated around the same time.

"Badische was in some ways my greatest case," Coleman tells me over drinks at a midtown bar. "Never did I have so much fun."

The six-foot-five-inch Kentuckian, now in private practice, figured out fifteen minutes into his first interview with the complainant, a television executive named Barbara Laurence, that something was amiss. The paperwork she presented—web pages from outfits calling themselves Barclay Consulting Group and the Badische Trust Consortium, a turgid loan agreement signed in green ink, and wire transfers for so-called performance guaranties—all suggested Laurence had fallen victim to a live-action variant of an Internet fraud commonly associated with Nigerian email hucksters.

At first blush, Coleman wasn't drawn to the case. It raised no interesting legal issues, and the sums involved were "peanuts." The cost of the investigation and prosecution would greatly exceed the sum Laurence had lost. Coleman could have followed the example set by the Manhattan DA and taken a pass. He didn't, in part, because he was impressed by the monumental chutzpah of the swindlers.

"I have to admit a measure of admiration for the audacity and manner in which the Badische boys inveigled their victims," Coleman tells me. "They managed to send their marks to remote locations all over the world. That takes a certain genius and a whole lot of window dressing. When the Trust needed an accountant, it didn't scrounge up someone's brother-in-law to play the part. It brought in a partner from PricewaterhouseCoopers." And if a multibillion-dollar deed from an imaginary African kingdom required unimpeachable validation, Badische made sure an executive from Merrill Lynch served as a witness at the signing. When lawyers were required, they called on Clifford Chance.

"And the names! Prince Robert. The King of Mombessa. Duke d'Antin. Seriously?"

Those were hardly the kind of people the future lawyer encountered growing up in Falmouth, Kentucky (pop. 2,040), a riverfront town where the kings sold burgers, the colonels hawked chicken, and all the dukes came from Hazzard.

"It was *Dirty Rotten Scoundrels* meets *Clue*," Coleman marvels between sips of a perfect Manhattan.

"Except Badische wasn't fun and games for Barbara Laurence," I point out.

"No, that's true," Coleman allows. "But that aspect of the fraud intrigued me, as well." The humiliating apology letters the victims were forced to write and revise (and revise again) suggested to the prosecutor that Badische and Barclay had a taste for degradation, as well as an uncanny ability to "calculate risk and capitalize on weakness."

I ask Coleman if he considers the Badische boys dangerous. His reply comes in two parts. Yes, if by "dangerous" I mean capable of separating a mark from his money. No, if by "dangerous" I mean violent. When I press him further, he hedges the second half of his appraisal by pointing out that he dealt with Cesar and the bankers while in the employ of the Department of Justice. "That afforded me a level of protection unavailable to civilians like yourself."

"I see."

"I had little direct contact with Cesar," he adds. "If you want to learn more about him, you should be talking to Dennis Quilty."

"Dennis Quilty?"

"The investigator on the case. He was the one who pushed me to prosecute. He was the one who did all the initial legwork."

The name takes me by surprise. None of the press reports cite Quilty, and I can't recall coming across references to him in the trial transcript. Coleman enlightens me. "Case agents tend to keep a low profile—Quilty more than most. He's no longer with the US Attorney's Office, but while he was there, Dennis was one of the best. He was finishing up an incredible career when he brought in the Badische case. He really wanted us to prosecute the Trust, and I saw no reason to turn him down. Badische," Coleman jokes, "was my retirement gift to Dennis."

Back home I plow through my files, searching for the investigator's name. It appears on fewer than a half dozen discovery documents, mostly at the bottom of federal subpoenas. The trial transcript indicates that Quilty never took the stand. He only gets mentioned in the court record when witnesses are asked who contacted them from the US Attorney's Office.

Two days after interviewing Coleman, I give Dennis Quilty a call. "Detective Quilty?"

"It's *Investigator* Quilty," he snaps. "Or was. I'm retired."

I reach the former case agent as he's speeding along I-95, somewhere north of Palm Beach. He informs me that he's late for a golf tournament and that there's no way he's going to speak to me about Cesar or Badische or anything else.

"Let me tell you something, Allen, my first boss told me a long time ago. A good fraud investigator never talks to the press and never testifies at trial. His job is to hunt for diamonds, then hand those diamonds over to the prosecutor. It's the prosecutor's job to polish them up and sell them to the jury and the public."

Quilty isn't rude, but he isn't exactly welcoming, either. Our conversation lasts about a minute.

A week later, just days before my recon mission begins, I find a more accommodating source in the Department of Justice, a high-level staffer willing to pass along criminal records on two Badische executives who never took the stand. Neither dossier references Cesar directly, but the milk crate materials suggest that he worked closely with one of the two men and sought legal counsel from the other. Since dealing with Cesar raises the very real possibility of dealing with his associates, it makes sense to read the files closely.

The Duke of Deception

The less sinister of the DOJ jackets documents the professional activities of Duke Eric Alba-Teran d'Antin, the goitrous name-dropping Badische executive with a weakness for silk ascots. From the start, I'd had my doubts about the guy. D'Antin never struck me as "credible"—the term Cesar used to describe the duke when pleading for leniency at sentencing. It seemed impossible that a senior officer of the bogus Trust could be wed to a genuine archduchess.

But much to my chagrin, I had discovered, a few months before, that d'Antin was indeed married to Michaela Maria Madeleine Kiliana von Habsburg-Lothringen, princess imperial and archduchess of Austria. The legitimacy of his matrimonial claims had compelled me to reserve judgment—until, that is, I obtained a detailed account of his criminal record.

In 1993, five years before he joined the Trust, Eric d'Antin fell under the scrutiny of US law enforcement officers by agreeing to launder the illicit proceeds of a South American drug cartel. According to his case file, this is what happened: A middleman named Thomas McMahon presented the duke with "a soft-sided suitcase containing $200,000 in United States currency in ten and twenty dollar denominations." The duke carried the suitcase into a Manhattan bank, exited minus the money, and informed his go-between that the funds were

Duke Eric d'Antin was up to his ascot in fraud long before he joined the Trust.

on their way to a numbered account in South America. Had d'Antin stuck to the terms of the agreement—he was supposed to wire the $200,000 (minus an 8 percent commission) to its final recipient via a bank in Germany—federal charges against him would have been restricted to "the laundering of monetary instruments." However, the duke chose a bolder course of action, opting to award himself a 100 percent commission on the funds placed in his care.

It's hard to know which is dumber: trying to rip off a bagman for a South American drug cartel, or trying to rip off a federal investigator *posing* as a bagman for a South American drug cartel. D'Antin discovered the consequences of the latter folly when McMahon, revealing himself to be an undercover agent working for the US Customs Service, placed the duke under arrest and, because of the failed switcheroo, broadened the charges to include the embezzlement of government funds.

Because d'Antin's Habsburg in-laws owned estates all over Europe, he was deemed a flight risk and ordered to surrender his passport.

He complied, then promptly obtained new travel documents under an untitled variant of his highborn name. Bogus passport in hand, d'Antin flew to Europe, where he ostensibly stashed his loot, and returned to stand trial in Brooklyn. The jury found him guilty. The stolen funds were never recovered.

That was hardly the duke's first brush with the law. A decade earlier, Florida prosecutors charged d'Antin with racketeering, alleging that he had woven together an elaborate daisy chain of offshore shell corporations and trusts designed to "skim on taxes." A decade before the Florida indictment, a British court convicted d'Antin on "forgery, obtaining property with forged instruments and conspiracy." Scrolling back still further, to 1971, the Italian carabinieri arrested d'Antin for "the fraudulent sale of a corporation and an industrial process for 120 million lire." That was three years after Swiss authorities detained him for bilking a German businessman out of 150,000 deutsche marks.

The archduchess of Austria appears to have tolerated her consort's European indiscretions, but her sense of noblesse oblige did not, it seems, extend to American soil. The couple divorced in 1994, soon after d'Antin's conviction in US federal court. Despite the split, the duke continued to exploit the royal name of his ex, claiming chairmanship of an unfunded charity called the Habsburg Foundation. He did so until his death, ten years later, at the age of eighty-four.

Had the marriage endured, the duke's body might have been parceled out, as Habsburg tradition dictates, among various Viennese mausoleums—his heart going to one crypt, his viscera to others. Divorce precluded that privilege. Instead, Eric d'Antin was cremated at a franchise funeral home a mile from Newark Airport, his ashes double-boxed without ritual in black plastic and recycled cardboard.

The DOJ dossier does not provide details regarding his memorial service, but d'Antin's date of death suggests that Cesar wasn't on hand. Prior commitments in Lompoc, California, would have prevented him from paying his last respects.

THE PREDICATE FELON

The d'Antin case file described the career of an incorrigible rogue, but none of its particulars suggested a taste for violence. The second DOJ file, chronicling the activities of a behind-the-scenes insurance executive and "legal adviser" to the Trust named Richard Mamarella, offered no such comfort. On the contrary, it served as a wake-up call to the dangers I was courting by traveling to San Francisco.

Richard Mamarella joined the House of Badische in 1998, after a chance encounter with Prince Robert at Cooper's, a New York cigar bar located on West Fifty-Eighth Street. At first glance, Mamarella was inclined to dismiss the prince as "an eccentric old man with a propensity to have one too many." Another Cooper's regular, the mayor of New York, allegedly set him straight. According to Mamarella, Rudolph Giuliani considered Robert von Badische "one of New York City's only royalty."

Prince Robert wasn't nearly so standoffish. In fact, he did everything in his power to ingratiate himself to Mamarella, whose business acumen had earned not one but two front-page profiles in the *Wall Street Journal*.

By all outward appearances, the two cigar aficionados had little in common. The prince boasted that his Transylvanian ancestry dated back twenty generations to Vlad the Impaler, the inspiration for Bram Stoker's *Dracula*. Mamarella, by contrast, was the son of a beat cop from the Bronx.

When the two met, Richard Mamarella was working for a "litigation service" in Weehawken, New Jersey, and billing clients $200 an hour—less than half what David Glass and his Park Avenue colleagues charged on the tonier side of the Hudson. Employing Mamarella promised to save Badische a bundle in legal fees, money the prince and his associates much preferred to spend on hotel suites and vintage champagne.

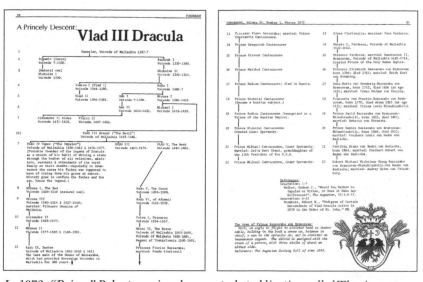

In 1972, "Prince" Robert convinced a quarterly publication called The Augustan *to publish a genealogy that traced his lineage back to Vlad the Impaler, but in all probability, Dracula's self-proclaimed heir was born Isaac Wolf, in the Jewish ghetto of Oradea, a small Romanian city.*

While the loan program was up and running, Mamarella supplied the Trust all manner of assistance. He developed anti-money-laundering policies, conducted background checks on prospective borrowers, and revised loan contracts, letters, and legal memorandums. After his colleagues started receiving federal subpoenas, Mamarella switched gears and began tutoring the bankers and their shills on how to avoid prosecution.

None of this seemed particularly noteworthy. What *did* catch me off guard was the mountain of evidence confirming that Richard Mamarella was not a lawyer employed by criminals, but rather a criminal employed by lawyers.

Some twenty years before joining Badische, Mamarella was charged with conspiring to defraud Lloyd's of London, the insurance syndicate, by diverting client premiums to personal bank accounts in Curaçao. That swindle, detailed in a seventy-eight-count federal indictment, attracted the attention of a US attorney named Rudolph Giuliani. Giuliani subsequently established that Mamarella operated a side business peddling fire insurance to arsonists. When coverage on a property he insured was discovered to have lapsed only after the building was torched, Mamarella remedied the oversight by renewing and backdating the arsonist's $300,000 fire policy. Presented with irrefutable proof of his role in a blaze that injured seventeen firefighters and left dozens of residents homeless, Mamarella cut a deal, testifying against his codefendants in exchange for five years' probation on three counts of perjury.

Soon after that conviction, Mamarella relocated his insurance business to a small town in southern New Jersey where, using as collateral a list of fictitious policies and a pad of blank promissory notes, he and some associates bilked the First Fidelity Bank of New Jersey out of $22 million. It was, at that time, the biggest bank swindle in the history of a state famed for the ambition of its embezzlers. Caught, prosecuted, and found guilty of bank fraud and extortion, Mamarella cut another deal. This one required him to provide a full account of his criminal history.

Mamarella first made a name for himself in direct sales. While still a teenager, he ran a successful business hawking "boxes of TVs" out of the back of a truck. When John Valentine Goepfert, a legendary insurance swindler, learned that the boxes of TVs contained bricks and telephone directories in lieu of the advertised consumer electronics, he saw potential in the enterprising young salesman and took him under his wing.

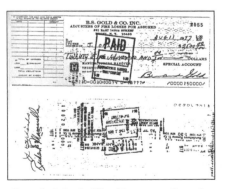

Canceled checks like this one confirmed that Richard Mamarella backdated fire insurance for arsonists.

Mamarella proved a quick study. It wasn't long before he caught the eye of Joseph Paterno, a lieutenant in the Gambino

crime syndicate. Questioned under oath about the whereabouts
of First Fidelity's $22 million,
Mamarella said he'd spent it all.
Pressed for specifics, he said, "I ate
out a lot." Although he refused to
connect his insurance scam to the
Mob, Mamarella did acknowledge
operating a highly successful loan-
sharking operation whose client
list included Antonio Turano, a
Sicilian-born footwear executive
turned narcotics trafficker with
proven ties to the Mafia.

*Richard Mamarella. The Bronx-born
Weehawken wiseguy provided behind-
the-scenes legal advice to the Trust.*

The Mamarella-Turano relationship offered troubling insights
into the business practices of the
Trust's legal adviser. After Turano was caught concealing fifteen ki-
lograms of heroin in a shipment of shoes from Thailand, Mamarella
decided to safeguard $300,000 he had lent the importer by taking out a
short-term life insurance policy in his name.

The timing couldn't have been better. While Turano was out on
bail, his bullet-riddled, plastic-wrapped corpse was fished out of a
marsh in Queens, New York. The money Mamarella collected on
the policy more than covered the outstanding principal and interest
Turano was unable to repay.

Mamarella's approach to debt collection wasn't usually that pre-
meditated. More typically, when clients failed to meet their obligations in a timely manner, he would flash a "piece" (his term) or hastily
arrange a refinancing conference with "T-Ray," a broad-shouldered
associate regularly mistaken for Chicago Bears defensive tackle William "The Refrigerator" Perry.

Not that Mamarella needed backup. As he noted under oath, he was perfectly at ease assaulting one tardy borrower with a chair ("I should have hit him harder") and disfiguring another with his ring-studded fists. The Weehawken wiseguy displayed a similar hands-on approach to conflict resolution in his personal life. According to a *Wall Street Journal* article included in the DOJ case file, "Richard Mamarella is the kind of person who, when he lends you money, is likely to arrange a life-insurance policy to repay it—just in case you don't. His own lawyer calls him a 'tough fellow.' His second wife, who left him after he broke her arm, might agree."

As I'm flying out to San Francisco, I inventory the illegalities tied to Cesar and his colleagues. The catalog has grown substantially. It now includes: money laundering, embezzlement, racketeering, arson, forgery, all manner of fraud (wire fraud, insurance fraud, mail fraud), extortion, perjury, check kiting, probation violation, grand larceny, assault and battery, and domestic abuse. All of which makes me wonder: What the hell am I getting myself into? I could have ended the search in the law-firm conference room. That would have been the sensible thing to do. Why am I *still* pursuing Cesar? Is it to uncover his story? To avoid my own? The bottom line is this: I'm not sure *what* I'm after. Nor can I explain what compels me to travel cross-country to spy on the actions of a convicted felon I have promised my wife I will not confront. All I know is it sounds nuts when I hear myself telling the yoga instructor sitting in the seat next to me the reason I'm on a plane bound for San Francisco.

PART VII

SCOUNDREL TIME

Time spent on reconnaissance is never wasted.
John le Carré, *A Perfect Spy*

Whatsoever things are true
Whatsoever things are honest
Whatsoever things are just
Whatsoever things are pure
Whatsoever things are lovely
Whatsoever things are of good report
Think on these things.
Group Captain Watts,
former headmaster of Aiglon,
invoking Philippians 4:8

"A Good Suspect"

The day before the film fund-raiser, I meet up with a spry sixty-seven-year-old Japanese American named Yosh Morimoto in the lobby of my Bay Area hotel. Morimoto was never called to testify during the Badische trial, but his name and San Jose address appeared on a restitution order listing some of Cesar's clients.

It's been more than five years since Morimoto got taken. Whatever shame or rage he might have felt at the time has been replaced by quiet reflection.

"My mother and father had a rough life," he tells me over a pot of tea. "Real rough."

Before the Morimotos were interned in a relocation camp under the shameful provisions of Executive Order 9066, they owned a pear orchard outside Sacramento. "We managed to hold on to it, but just barely," Morimoto says wistfully. The land was eventually sold to developers. Morimoto invested in real estate. His business prospered.

He remembers learning about the Badische Trust Consortium early in 1998, while trying to fund a $200 million nonprofit hospital-hotel complex in the Central American nation of Belize. Like most of the proposals Cesar presented to the Badische board, the Belize project had failed to attract legitimate investors. After dozens of rejections, Morimoto responded to an online funding offer posted by the Barclay Consulting Group. The managing director of BCG invited him to the firm's worldwide headquarters in the heart of San Francisco's financial district.

"Cesar was the screening person for Badische," Morimoto tells me. "You had to meet him first. He'd only introduce you to Colonel Sherry

Yosh Morimoto.

and the others if he thought you were a good suspect."

Morimoto passed muster.

"The next thing I knew, we were flying to New York to make a funding presentation." The visit floored him. "I never saw anything like it," Morimoto recalls, shaking his head. "Cesar introduced me to about a dozen elderly guys in the boardroom of this really fancy law firm. All of them were really, really well dressed. And all of them were really, really smooth. Most had European accents. One guy even had one of those fancy eyeglass things you hold up like this." Morimoto forms a circle with thumb and forefinger and brings it to his eye. "It made me wonder. What am *I* doing here? Why would these guys want to work with a guy like *me*?"

Cesar and Colonel Sherry assured him that he was *exactly* the kind of person the Trust targeted.

When Morimoto asked how his loan would be bankrolled, the colonel showed him a flowchart that traced the movement of funds from the anonymous investors in Europe and Africa, to the offshore trusts established by Barclay, to the project he wished to finance.

Morimoto couldn't make heads or tails out of all the boxes and arrows, but the bottom line was this: thanks to Cesar, the Trust appeared willing to loan him $30 million.

The New York meetings concluded with a dinner at Benihana, the Japanese restaurant chain noted for the showmanship of its knife-wielding chefs. Toward the end of the meal, Morimoto was again dazzled when Prince Robert introduced him to Rocky Aoki, the chain's flamboyant founder and (though less widely known) "Ambassador to the Empire of Japan" for the Knights of Malta (Ecumenical), a diplomatic honor the prince bestowed in his capacity as founder and self-appointed grand master of the for-profit chivalric order.

"With *those* kind of contacts, I figured these guys *had* to be the real thing."

Morimoto's confidence took a hit when he learned that his loan would require three offshore trusts costing "nine thousand

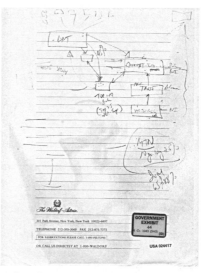

A flowchart Colonel Sherry dashed off to clarify the Trust's funding sources.

dollars a pop." Like other Barclay clients, he tried to avoid the supersized fees by using his own lawyer. The colonel nixed that idea. "He said it would complicate matters. He said the Trust had its procedures, used for generations, and that Cesar, their intermediary, was well acquainted with them."

In the weeks that followed, Morimoto gave Barclay $27,000 to form the obligatory shell corporations and another $210,000 in advance fees that the Trust called "performance guaranties." In return, Morimoto received an "irrevocable funding commitment" and a secret transaction code that was supposed to release the $30 million required to break ground in Belize.

"The only other thing I needed was the bank letter," Morimoto tells me. "But the guys rejected every bank I wanted to use. I went to the Bahamas, Germany, Switzerland, the Canary Islands. Then to Guangzhou in China, back to Switzerland, and to New York a bunch of times. What could I do? Once you get into it, you've got to make a decision. Either you bail or keep getting sucked in. And I kept getting sucked in and sucked in. I couldn't believe I got involved in such crap.

I was totally embarrassed. I didn't know what to do. I didn't know where to turn."

Morimoto kept missing deadlines, and with each holdup he was compelled to dig deeper into his pocket. "Every delay cost five or ten grand." By the time he received his "failure to perform" notice, Morimoto had blown through $500,000. Roughly half went to Badische and Barclay. The rest was spent on travel and legal costs.

"Man oh man, did they do a number on me," he says, again shaking his head.

"What was it like working with Cesar?" I ask.

"He didn't leave much of an impression. He was very noncommittal after he got his money."

"Do you remember his nationality?"

"I think he might have been Filipino, but I'm not really sure."

"Did you consider him dangerous?"

Morimoto ponders the question for a moment. "Like I said, he didn't leave much of an impression."

MY BODYGUARD

Before leaving Providence, I promised Françoise I'd bring backup to the fund-raiser. That pledge turned out to be difficult to satisfy. Unlike Richard Mamarella, I lacked ready access to professional muscle, and I couldn't see hiring someone to watch me watch my former roommate. In the end, I asked my cousin Ruth MacKay, a lifelong Bay Area local, to join me. She said sure.

Ruth rings my hotel room from the front desk two hours before the event. "Your bodyguard is here."

Measuring five foot two in sensible shoes, Ruth will never be mistaken for, say, T-Ray, Richard Mamarella's fridge-size sidekick. But with two decades of newspaper experience in and around San

Francisco, Ruth is more of an asset than any muscle-bound rent-a-cop.*

"What are your thoughts about getting a drink?" I ask when we meet in the lobby.

"I'm part Scot," she says. "Take a guess."

At the hotel bar, I provide a two-whiskey synopsis of the search.

"Sounds like you have a pretty good grasp on the contours of the con, but what do you have on Cesar?"

"Three years of his subpoenaed bank and credit card records. I know where he buys his clothes and where he gets them cleaned. I know what brand of bottled water he drinks and where he purchases his booze—a liquor store called Jugs. I can tell you where he pumps iron, where he pumps gas, where he does his banking, where he pays for massages, and where he eats. The convicted shill for the International House of Badische is a regular at the International House of Pancakes."

"That's all great," says Ruth. "But do you know what makes him tick?"

"Not really," I admit. "That's one of the reasons I flew out here. The files are full of contradictions."

"Such as?"

"I don't know if he's rich or poor. He filed for bankruptcy three weeks before he started serving time but he owns a late-model BMW that retails for $63,000."

"And you know that how?"

"A web bot. He's trying to sell the Beemer on Craigslist."

"Is it possible you're digging too deeply?" Ruth asks.

"More than possible. It's a total certainty. I can't help it. I've always been held hostage by my interests. The problem is the more

---

*By way of example: When I asked Ruth about Barclay's relocated headquarters, she shot back an email noting it was "a studio apartment in a two-unit wood-frame house built in 1940 and held in trust that a source in Tax Assessor's office suggested had 'an extremely low' valuation of $275,885."

I find out, the less I know. I'm hoping that *seeing* Cesar will clear up some of the confusion."

"Tell me about tonight."

"Cesar's raising money for an indie flick about a photographer who goes missing in Chile during the Pinochet regime."

"Is the event legit?"

"No idea." I pull out the downloaded Evite and quote from the pitch. " 'Join us on a journey back to childhood,' " I intone, "a story 'about real memories repressed for twenty years. . . . A pursuit of truth to bring peace to a tortured soul.' "

"Sounds like the film's about you, Allen."

"I'm not sure about the repressed memories part, but I suspect my tortured soul won't find peace until I learn more about Cesar. I don't even know his nationality."

"I thought he's Filipino."

"That's what he told us at school, and that's what he's told some clients. But his lawyer claims he's American."

"He could be both," Ruth notes.

"Of course. Except the files indicate the INS couldn't verify his citizenship status while the investigation was under way. And just to complicate things further, he petitioned the Bureau of Prisons to have his ethnicity changed from white to Hispanic."

"Any photos?"

I show Ruth the Belvedere house portrait from 1972.

"Anything more recent?"

"Nope. Last time I checked, his online bios all had 'Image Not Available' and 'No photo' graphics. The website for the film company includes head shots for every staffer *except* Cesar. He's represented by a JPEG of a movie clapper."

"How about yearbook pictures?"

"I contacted two universities he attended. Struck out at both."

Ruth sips her Scotch and ruminates. "So we're unsure of his

Four head shots that accompanied Cesar's early postpenitentiary web bios.

nationality or his ethnicity. We don't know whether he's rich or poor, and we have no clue what he looks like."

"Yup. Oh, and there's one more unknown. He might be dangerous."

Ruth puts down her drink. "Dangerous?"

"He's connected to some pretty nasty characters."

" 'Connected' as in *The Godfather* connected?"

"It's possible. The record indicates he received legal advice from a Gambino associate."

"Anything else I need to know?"

"Just that I won't be using my real name tonight. Refer to me as Isaac Raven."

"Isaac Raven?"

"It's something I cooked up with Max and a drinking buddy. *Isaac Raven* is Cesar's first and last name, but with the letters rearranged."

"Why not scramble your own name?"

"We tried. I couldn't see going undercover as Ezra I. Lunkwell. On the other hand, Cesar's name is an anagrammatical gold mine."*

"Fitting for a guy who's constantly reinventing himself," Ruth observes.

"Plus Isaac Raven sounds dark and brooding."

Ruth gives a nod. "And it goes well with that ridiculous beard."

---

*Rejected pseudonyms included an Armenian alias (A. Carvasian), an adjectival alias (A. Vain Cesar), a topical alias (Avian Scare), a tough-guy alias (Vic A. Arenas), and a porn-star alias (Asia Craven).

"I'm shaving it off after the party. Françoise's orders."

"That's a relief," Ruth says. And raising her tumbler, she makes a toast. "To Isaac Raven."

THE SHILL

Our nerves calmed by the genial influences of expense-account whiskey, Ruth and I catch a cab to Cesar's fund-raiser, which is taking place at a Mission District college that grants advanced degrees in political activism and women's spirituality. We arrive at the venue just as a band of South American musicians is unloading a panel truck.

"Oh Christ," says Ruth. "Tambourines."

I ask the percussionist if Cesar has arrived. He shakes his head and points to the event's cohost, a Latina filmmaker in her early forties.

"Welcome," she says. "What are your names, please?"

Ruth says, "Ruth."

The cohost turns to me. "And you are . . . ?"

"I am . . ."

"Yes?"

"I am . . ."

I know what I'm *supposed* to say. I'm supposed to say, "Hi, I'm Isaac Raven." But I can't. I can't make myself lie, at least not explicitly. Eventually I mumble, "Al."

"Sorry?"

"Al," I repeat.

"*Hola*, Al," the cohost says. "You and Ruth should get yourselves drinks."

Once we're safely beyond the checkpoint, my cousin gives me a poke. "So what happened, *Isaac*?"

"Guess I'm not cut out for fraud."

"That's pretty obvious. But you do know what I have to say now, don't you?"

"What?"

" 'Quoth the Raven, "Nevermore." ' "

The setting for the fund-raiser, a gallery space scarred by years of vegetarian potlucks, craft fairs, and cooperative art shows, is worlds away from the five-star suites into which Cesar once lured clients. There are no international financiers in matching silk ties raising flutes of vintage champagne. Mostly it's hipsters in bandannas holding red plastic cups of Two-Buck Chuck.

Ruth and I grab a couple of drinks at the cash bar, then separate. I strike up a conversation with a self-described radical vegan ecofeminist who teaches yoga and, in his spare time, promotes nonviolence toward animals ("both human and nonhuman"). I ask if he knows Cesar. He does not. My next two informants aren't much help either. They make vague references to the host's "real estate deals" and "a life-coaching thing." Eventually I approach a frail woman seated behind a card table.

"I'm the mother of the producer," she informs me proudly.

It takes a moment to figure out the implications of the claim. "Cesar's your son?" I blurt out.

"How do you know my Cesar?"

"From . . ."—I'm about to say "Aiglon" but stop before I blow my cover—"from the Evite," I improvise. Totally unprepared, and more than a little ambivalent about interviewing an elderly woman under false pretenses regarding the behavior of her felonious son, I bumble my way through the impromptu exchange that reveals, among other things, that Cesar calls his mother every day, that he takes her for long walks and occasional vacations (to Mexico, most recently), that he drives her to the supermarket, to the cemetery "to visit relatives," to the dentist, and to her doctors. When I ask the kindly woman about her son's nationality, I'm told that he is "half Venezuelan, half Asian, half Latino, and half Filipino American," which, in a way, makes sense since nothing about Cesar adds up.

I ask about his childhood, hoping to provoke some comments about Aiglon. But my unsuspecting source scrolls back further than I'd like

and tells me in consider-
able detail how she gave
birth to her only son in
the Manila beauty school
owned by her family.

"What was Manila
like?"

"*Isaac Raven*" (*left*) *and me, four hours after*
"Easier," she says with a   *my* "*recon mission,*" *no longer incognito.*
sigh. "We had servants. A
chauffeur. A laundry woman. But that life vanished after Cesar's father
died and we moved to the United States."

My discomfort level spikes abruptly—so abruptly, in fact, that I
end the interview. (Only much later do I begin to work out why. I
think it's because I'm unwilling to let Cesar's narrative of youthful
trauma bully its way into on my own chronicle of childhood despair.)

As we part company, I pick up a list of auction items and a business
card that Hispanicizes the fund-raiser's alias. Tonight he is Cesar Au-
gus*to* Teague.

List in hand, I survey the artwork hanging on the walls. A doormat-
size "meditation rug" donated by Cesar has attracted a silent bid of
$250 from "BCG." I recognize the acronym and handwriting in-
stantly. I've seen both on dozens of Barclay Consulting Group discovery documents. I find Ruth and tell her about the connection. "You're
not going to believe this. Cesar is bidding up his own stuff."

"Why should that surprise you?" she says matter-of-factly. "Isn't
that what shills are supposed to do?"

THE SIGHTING

All at once, my stomach tightens and I unleash a string of expletives.

Ruth gives me a nudge. "Settle down, Isaac."

My brain tries to tell my mouth to heed her advice, but my mouth refuses to obey. "It's him! Oh my God! Fuck, Ruth. Shit. It's . . . it's . . . it's *him*!"

The uncontrolled babbling lasts nearly a minute. The only other time I can recall losing it like that was during the memorial service for a close friend struck down by brain cancer. It's not grief, however, that's causing me to spout gibberish. Something else makes me run off at the mouth, though what exactly I can't say.

Cesar is no longer kitted out in the "armor" Barbara Laurence described. No Armani suit. No designer eyeglasses. The "double breasted or three-piece suit of high quality design" and "classy writing instrument such as Mont Blanc"—items one and ten of the Badische dress code—have been replaced by a black paisley short-sleeve shirt and a Bic holstered in a pair of pleated Dockers. And like many indie film producers, Cesar is sporting a goatee.

"How'd you pick him out?" Ruth asks after I have calmed down enough to respond to questions.

"I'm not sure. All I can tell you is that I knew before I knew."

The rattle of a tambourine quiets the audience. The filmmaker gives a brief speech about "bearing witness to the victims of violence" and "the long-term impact of short-term persecution."

Ruth jabs me again. "See. It *is* your story."

The lights dim, and a twelve-minute short is screened. It's somber and a bit too experimental for my tastes but better than I anticipated. After the lights come back on, to scattered applause, the band starts to play.

For an hour or so, I watch Cesar work the room. His manner is understated. He avoids direct eye contact as he talks to his guests. He keeps to the edges of the gallery. It's as if the hall were one giant foosball table and he's looking for an opening, for a chance to score. His demeanor strikes me both as bashful and hypervigilant. Since I can't hear what he's saying, it's impossible to tell if that's a reflection of shyness or pathology. (I favor the latter explanation.)

And what about *my* pathology? Part of me wants to run for the hills. Part of me wants to march across the room and punch Cesar in the nose. The latter impulse is not an option. Not yet anyway. Before I make a move—*if* I make a move—I will need to establish where Cesar falls on the continuum of criminality. Is he a hapless schnook? A violent sociopath? Was the work he did for Badische a onetime misstep or the tip of the iceberg? I still have no clue.

The temperature in the gallery turns equatorial once the dancing gets going. My beard, damp with sweat, begins itching unbearably.

"Hey, Ruth, I think it's time to leave."

My cousin needs no convincing. Out on the street, I'm surprised to spot Cesar taking a break from his own fund-raiser. He's standing by himself, no more than ten feet away—the distance that once separated our bunks.

"Ruth, how about a picture?"

"No thanks."

"Stay right there. Don't move."

Ruth registers the firmness in my voice and obeys.

"Smile."

Ruth smiles.

I aim my phone and snap a photo. Half of my cousin's overexposed face falls outside the picture, but it doesn't matter. She's not the one I have in my sights.

Cesar Augusto, the indie film producer. My bodyguard (and cousin) Ruth appears in the foreground.

The Silent Service

Is Cesar a career criminal? Back in Providence, I redouble my efforts to answer that question. Dennis Quilty, the retired investigator, continues to play hard to get, but I have better luck with one of his former colleagues, a US Postal Inspection Service case agent named Thomas Feeney. Enticed by the promise of a fine steak dinner, the former postal inspector agrees to meet me at a New York chop house a week after I return from the recon mission.

As soon as we're seated, Agent Feeney pulls out a fat brown envelope.

"Special delivery?" I joke.

"My Badische case file," he responds sternly. But his manner softens as soon as he begins leafing through documents in the envelope. At a certain point he even allows himself a smile.

"Something funny?"

"What *wasn't* funny about Badische?" he says. "Personally, my favorite character was the Baron Moncrieffe, Crown Prince of Serbia, born George Englert Jr., to a hotel night manager from Toledo, Ohio. What a voice that guy had. Part Ronald Reagan, part Jackie O. Hadn't done a legitimate job since the Eisenhower administration."

"He worked?"

Feeney consults his files. "He was as a window dresser at Garfinckel's department store in Passaic during the nineteen fifties."

"An actual window dresser? A prosecutor I interviewed used that exact phrase—window dressing—to describe the Trust's attention to detail."

Feeney nods. "All the crazy costumes the guys wore, the fake passports, the bogus deeds."

"How did you end up getting assigned to the case?"

"Quilty reached out for help executing subpoenas and filing forms.

Ex–Postal Inspector Thomas Feeney.

He could have used the FBI, but he preferred working with us. The guys in the windbreakers tend to be ball hogs. Quilty had no patience for their showboating. He worked for convictions, not press conferences and photo ops. Postal inspectors tend to be the same. There's a reason we're called the Silent Service."

Well, not *that* silent, thank goodness. By the end of the meal, Feeney has provided a guided tour of his case file. Here are a few highlights from my notes:

- *Subpoenas served (PS Forms MC 2001–0415, 416, and 599), May 17, 2001. Feeney executes writs to produce documents. Retrieves evidence from PO boxes and residences of Moncrieffe and Sherry.*
- *Case registered (PS Form 623), June 8, 2001. Badische investigation officially "on the books" of US Postal Inspection Service.*
- *Performance Guaranty monies received (bank check), July 11, 2001. Feeney takes custody of funds frozen in Badische client accounts managed by Gurland. ("It was strange walking around with a check for $1,222,526.39.")*
- *Warrants issued, November 7, 2001. One day after prosecutors indict Cesar et al., Feeney enters arrest data into NCIC database.*
- *Extradition request submitted, November 21, 2001. Sherry believed to be out of the country so Feeney files a "red notice" with the DC office of Interpol, confirming US Government will "pay the freight" associated with extradition.*

- *Suspect arrested, November 28, 2001. Sherry's name "pops up" at JFK during a screening of passengers coming off a BA flight from Hong Kong. Feeney goes to the airport, takes Sherry into custody, and delivers him to the main branch of the NYC post office, on Thirty-Fourth Street.*
- *Suspects arraigned (mug shot profiles), November 30, 2001. Moncrieffe, Cesar, and another Badische liaison turn themselves in to authorities. (Prince Robert formally declared a fugitive.)*
- *Luggage searched (PS Form 8164), December 11, 2001. Two weeks after Sherry's arraignment, Feeney receives a warrant to inspect impounded luggage. Discovers "fancy cravats" along with "2 DVDs which purportedly contain recordings of the films 'Young Guns' and 'Star Wars Episode 1: The Phantom Menace,'" and "3 DVDs which purportedly contain the computer games 'M Gear,' 'Diablo,' and 'Tomb Raider Chronicles.'"*
- *DVDs analyzed (PS Form 720), December 17, 2001. Encryption specialists assess if computer discs "contain what the discs purport to contain." They do. "Basically the forensics guys got to watch movies and play Diablo."*

After we go through his files, I ask Feeney if he has copies of the Badische mug shot profiles. "I'm eager to get my hands on Cesar's arrest record."

"I get that impression. But I can't help you out. I'm sorry."

I must do a pretty poor job hiding my frustration because, toward the end the meal, Feeney offers to make a few calls.

Mug Shot!

It turns out the postman *does* ring twice. Feeney gets back in touch a few days later with contact information for his former boss, a senior postal inspector named John G. Feiter ("Yeah, it's pronounced *Fighter*").

Feiter, a trim gray-haired fraud specialist, is feeling nostalgic when I meet him and a colleague at the Church Street offices of the US Postal Inspection Service. "Ah, Feeney," he says with a sigh. "He was Spock to my Captain Kirk."

"And what a vocabulary the guy had!" marvels Thomas Boyle, Feiter's new lieutenant. "Who the hell says 'sub rosa' or 'venerable'?"

I show the two postal inspectors three pictures charting Cesar's trajectory from twelve-year-old boarding school roommate (Belvedere house photo) to fictional bully (illustration of the Tank) to Bay Area film producer (snapshot of goateed fund-raiser holding bottle of beer).

"You're telling us all three of these guys are your old roomie?"

"My old roomie and your con man."

Feiter takes his time reviewing the images. "That's one helluva story," he says at last. "Sounds like you have this thing nailed."

"Not really. I need to know if he's dangerous."

"Have you reached out to Quilty? Quilty was the point person on the investigation. He'd know a lot more than we do."

"Quilty's not all that interested in talking. But Feeney told me Cesar was booked by Postal. If I could look at his arrest record, I might get a better sense of what I'm up against."

Feiter turns to his colleague. "Tom, what's in the case file?"

Boyle flips through a folder. "Most of this is administrative crap. Fingerprint cards that should have been forwarded. Hmm. I forgot about that. Looks like your guy got booked by DHQ."

"DHQ? Is that short for Dennis Quilty?"

"No," Feiter says. "Division Headquarters—the main post office up on Thirty-Fourth Street."

"That's where Colonel Sherry was booked, too," I note.

"All of 'em were," Boyle says.

"They had to be," Feiter adds. "Because of the jet fuel."

"Jet fuel?"

Feiter jabs his thumb over his shoulder. "Didn't you notice the giant hole across the street?"

"Giant hole?"

"Turn right when you leave the building. We're sitting a hundred feet from Ground Zero. When the planes hit, one of the engines broke off and landed a few floors above your head."

"Holy shit."

"We were shut down for two and a half years," says Boyle.

"I was here four days a week in my zoot suit," Feiter recalls. "Every sheet of paper had to be irradiated, cleaned, tested, and certified safe. We had PO trucks filled with case files going out to a facility in Rockaway Township ten times a day."

Not for the first time since beginning the search, I feel like a total idiot. How could something like 9/11 have escaped my attention? I check my notes. "The indictments came down about a month after the attacks."

"Sounds about right," Feiter says.

"Didn't that slow things down?"

Boyle reviews the file. "Doesn't look like it." He removes a sheet of paper and hands it to his boss. Feiter gives it the once-over before sliding it across the table.

A document I've been trying to get my hands on for the better part of two years lands in my lap. The phrase "MUGSHOT PROFILE" appears at the top. "CONFIDENTIAL FOR LAW ENFORCEMENT USE ONLY" appears at the bottom. The right side of the form is reserved for the arrest photo. The left side registers Cesar's personal data. One detail catches my attention.

"Find something interesting?" Feiter asks.

"Just an odd coincidence. It says Cesar is '5'10", 190 lbs.' That makes us exactly the same height and weight. By the way, it says he has no aliases. That info's outdated."

"Mug shot profiles are never all that accurate," Feiter notes.

"What does S/M/T stand for?"

"Scars, marks, and tats," says Boyle.

"The profile indicates he doesn't have any. And no prior arrests."

"Don't take what that piece of paper says as gospel," Feiter cautions. "Remember. It was a crazy time. A lot was going on after 9/11. Quilty would know more."

I slide the arrest sheet across the table, and Feiter slides it right back.

"Keep it," he says.

"Are you sure?"

"Sure I'm sure. Add it to the collection. I had to deal with my own version of Cesar when I was a kid. I know how memories like that stay with you."

PART VIII

"PAPER IN HIS BLOOD"

I am the Law, and the Law is not mocked!
Inspector Javert, *Les Misérables*

In order that Evil shall triumph, it is sufficient that
Good Men do nothing.
John Corlette,
founder of Aiglon College,
citing Edmund Burke

The Mongoose

Of the half dozen federal agents who worked on the Badische case, only Dennis Quilty stuck it out from beginning to end. He was there from the time Barbara Laurence lugged her paperwork into the US Attorney's Office until Cesar was packed off to FCI Lompoc. He was the only federal investigator who spoke to Cesar before he lawyered up.

If anyone could tell me whether or not my former roommate was dangerous, it would be Dennis Quilty. Yet on more than one occasion the retired investigator refused my interview requests. "Never talked to the press while I was on the job. See no reason to start now."

During one of my failed entreaties—this was in February 2007— Quilty mentioned that his grandkids were visiting him in Florida. With nothing to lose, I asked if I could send down a copy of my children's book *Leon and the Spitting Image*. Reluctantly, he said okay. "The book might interest you, too," I added. "The bully in the story became the con man you sent to jail."

Leon did the trick. Two weeks later, Quilty agreed to meet. Once again, my make-believe bully enabled me to inch a little bit closer to the flesh and blood boy who inspired him.

I expected big things from my trip to Florida. I was not disappointed. I was, however, surprised.

Dennis M. Quilty is a tall, slender New Yorker with close-cropped hair and the taut body of an avid golfer who forgoes caddy and cart. After thirty-four years of government work, he relinquished his service pistol and reached for a set of clubs. When not in use, those clubs occupy the corner of a tidy Mediterranean-style condo that abuts the second hole of a PGA course north of West Palm Beach.

"Mind if I drive?" Quilty says soon after the start of the hard-won interview.

"No problem," I tell him, sensing it wouldn't much matter if I did.

"The Quiltys tend to be civil servants," he begins. "My grandfather was a cop. My father was a heating inspector. I had one uncle who was a New York City detective, one who was a US customs inspector, and my cousin Michael was a New York City fire lieutenant who perished in the World Trade Center attack."

As a fraud specialist—first for the IRS, then with the Labor Department, and finally for the US Attorney's Office—Dennis Quilty spent the whole of his professional life hunting down racketeers, check kiters, counterfeiters, tax cheats, snake-oil salesmen, grifters, insider traders, and embezzlers. He shut down Ponzi, pyramid, and romance schemes, faux charities, and debt-elimination scams. Shortly before turning fifty-seven, the mandatory retirement age for all federal agents, Quilty identified, with mild disappointment, one subspecies of swindler absent from his trophy case of "dons and cons."

He had never bagged a bogus royal.

"I came close a couple of times," he says. But his investigations into the scams of aristocratic hustlers never met the burden of proof needed to sanction prosecution. That was before Barbara Laurence walked into his office at 1 St. Andrews Plaza.

"I was the first to interview Laurence," Quilty recalls. "Prosecutors don't have time to listen to unsubstantiated sob stories. Part of an investigator's job is to separate the crackpots from the credible witnesses. Laurence wasn't a crackpot. A loose canon maybe, but not a crackpot."

The evidence Laurence presented was robust. Still, the sums at stake—substantially less than a million dollars—made it tough to justify the cost of an investigation. That didn't faze Quilty. He was convinced that the "Marx Brothers manipulations" of the self-styled aristocrats and their California-based shill would attract the interest of a prosecutor. After all, how many white-collar crimes are adorned with monocles, Maltese crosses, and matching silk ties?

"The trick was to know *who* to get involved, and to get him involved early," Quilty tells me. Of the 170 lawyers working in his office, he zeroed in on Tim Coleman. Over the years, Quilty had helped Coleman investigate some half dozen cases. Each one ended in conviction. He knew that the slow-talking, fast-thinking assistant US attorney had a soft spot for upper-crust lowlifes. "Come on. Monocles? How could Coleman resist?"

"Clearly he couldn't."

"Yeah. Plus, when it comes to casework, I can be pretty determined. I sometimes liken the personality of the case agent to a mongoose."

I press Quilty to expand the analogy.

"The mongoose is renowned for attacking even the largest and most poisonous snakes. Say a cobra sneaks into the house; the mongoose will attack until either it or the snake is dead. I always considered the fraud investigator a mongoose that hunts snakes." Quilty's biological comparison only goes so far. He emends a little later. "The mongoose always knows when a snake slithers into view. The fraud investigator doesn't. Part of my job was to distinguish the con men from their marks. Sometimes that can be tricky. Fraudsters often claim they're the victims. (Hey, they're con men, that's what they do.) Victims often insist they *haven't* been duped. (Who wants to acknowledge getting swindled?) On top of which, sometimes genuine victims can themselves be convicted hucksters.

Dennis Quilty at the start of his career with the US Attorney's Office . . .

. . . and at the end, working the Badische case—his "retirement gift."

"It took me a while to figure out who was crooked and who was duped. The bankers, I knew from day one, were all going down. But then you had all the peripheral players. The members of the finance committee. The partner from PricewaterhouseCoopers. The Clifford Chance attorney. There was even an ambassador from South Africa who got taken in. How did all these guys end up getting hoodwinked by an elderly man wearing a monocle, claiming to be related to Vlad the Impaler?"

"Do you have an answer to that question?"

Quilty thinks long and hard before responding.

"Greed," he says at last.

I ask Quilty how he started the investigation.

"Same as always. First thing I do is subpoena the bank records. The money trail always leads you to the crooks."

The federal summonses Quilty served all began with a good-natured salutation ("Greetings") before walloping recipients into submission with a chilling, if florid, imperative: "We COMMAND YOU that all business and excuses being laid aside, you appear and attend before the GRAND INQUEST of the body of the people of the United States. . . ."

Television cop shows often suggest that grand jury subpoenas are tough to come by. Quilty corrects that impression. "I prepared my 'invites' on the computer, hit PRINT, walked 'em down the hall, and got 'em signed. Simple as that. My subpoenas flowed like water."

The documents that flowed back quickly confirmed that most of the executives drawn into the scheme—the Merrill Lynch financial consultant and the senior partner from PricewaterhouseCoopers, to name but two—were uncompensated, unknowing extras and nothing more. The innocence of the less marginal players—in particular the men on the Badische finance committee—was tougher to establish.

The subpoenaed records, bolstered by depositions, established that most committee members received "consulting fees" ranging from $5,000 to $30,000. Some of the men—Duke d'Antin, for instance—were demonstrably corrupt. Others, like the South African ambassador who credulously drafted the financial tally David Glass used to generate an "attestation" suggesting that Badische managed $90.3 billion in assets, had spotless reputations. The league of extraordinary (and extraordinarily naive) gentlemen also included the Honorable Shaun Plunket, a distant cousin to the queen of England and a godson of King George VI; Count Julien von Heisermann, the grand chancellor of the Knights of Malta (Ecumenical) and a patron of the "Millionaires of the World" Trust, an investment scheme censured by the New Zealand Securities Commission; and "Major" Mark Druck, a novelist tasked with burnishing executive bios on the Badische website, an assignment that appears to have relied heavily on his talents as a writer of historical fiction. Collectively, the finance committee challenged two platitudes commonly invoked when the

The Badische finance committee included a felonious duke, a retired ambassador, a godson of King George VI, and a writer of historical fiction.

topic of fraud is discussed: it proved that you *can* cheat an honest man and that you *can* bullshit a bullshitter.

Quilty eventually determined that even the most venal members of the finance committee failed to recognize the dizzying magnitude of the Badische charade. All got a pass.

TWO RICHARDS

Quilty had no problems letting the finance committee off the hook. The Badische lawyers presented a tougher challenge. Of the dozen or so legal experts entangled in the fraud, only four were materially relevant to the criminal investigation: Richard Mamarella, the Weehawken wiseguy; Richard Zeif, the Trust's in-house attorney; Clifford Chance lawyer David Glass; and Robert Gurland, the plummy-voiced London counsel.

The more pliable of the two Richards—Richard Mamarella—received a call from Quilty early on in the investigation. The Mobbed-up "litigation expert" with a history of turning state's evidence had no hesitation turning on his "royal" clients. He furnished Quilty with printed activity reports, invoices, and a five-page single-spaced timeline documenting every meeting, meal, letter, phone call, legal review, and consultation he undertook on behalf of the Badische Trust Consortium.

Mamarella's evidence not only corroborated the Laurence testimony, it also supplied names of additional casualties. "That was crucial," Quilty tells me. "The more victims I could find and interview, the greater the likelihood of taking the case to trial." It also helped clarify why the Trust demanded that its lawyers generate complex anti-money-laundering protocols. By tethering mandatory *transparency* to a loan contract demanding *confidentiality*, the bankers created conflicting obligations impossible for the would-be borrower to satisfy. (Logicians call this kind of incompatibility "pairwise mutually exclusive.") Irreconcilable rules *guaranteed* contractual failure.

That, in turn, allowed Badische to retain the advance fees placed in the care of its lawyers.

In view of the assistance he provided to Quilty and the paltry compensation he received from the Trust ($10,000), Richard Mamarella avoided prosecution. But because he was a predicate felon convicted of, among other things, perjury, he was of little use on the witness stand.

Richard Zeif was another matter. Discovery materials and depositions confirmed that the Trust's in-house attorney had had a recurring role in the costume dramas staged by the fraudulent bankers. Wearing a jacket bearing a UN logo and representing himself as a global peacekeeper, Zeif boasted that he had the diplomatic clout needed for Badische to hold contract negotiations in the Delegates Dining Room of the United Nations, a restaurant ostensibly exempt from American banking law.

"That turned out to be nothing but smoke," Quilty tells me.

Zeif corrected the misimpressions of the Trust's victims when he took the stand at trial. He acknowledged that he never worked for the United Nations (although he did rent an office with a UN Plaza address). That the meetings he booked in the Delegates Dining Room required no clout of any kind. (The restaurant is open to the public and is governed by the same laws as the McDonald's two blocks north.) As for the distinctive jacket he wore during loan meetings? That granted him as much entrée to the United Nations as my son's Red Sox cap permits to the Fenway Park bull pen.

Zeif testified that he began working for Badische a year before the loan program started turning a profit. That he had reviewed the $50 billion special deed of trust from the Kingdom of Mombessa, and that he had discussed its particulars with both of its principal signatories, Prince Robert and King Henri-François Mazzamba. Given his familiarity with the specifics of the scheme, it's hard to imagine Richard Zeif was entirely irreproachable. But by agreeing to forfeit some $100,000 in purloined performance guaranties (parked in a London bank account managed by Robert Gurland),

and by further agreeing to testify at trial, Richard Zeif avoided the fate of his clients.

"What Quilty Wants, Quilty Gets"

The Richards—Mamarella and Zeif—were relatively cooperative compared to the other two lawyers Quilty was determined to interview. David Glass and Robert Gurland both tried to rebuff the investigator by wrapping themselves in the mantle of attorney-client privilege. Both learned very quickly the futility of that gambit.

"I went after Glass before I took on Gurland," Quilty remembers. "He was in New York. That made him easier to pursue."

Easier but not easy. The moment the senior partners at Clifford Chance found themselves dragged into a federal fraud investigation, they reviewed their malpractice insurance and compelled David Glass to surrender all of his Trust-related materials to the firm's compliance team. A quick survey of those files revealed that Glass hadn't been the one to add the Badische Trust Consortium to the Clifford Chance client roster; two senior partners had served as liaisons before he took over. It had been their job, not his, to vet the bona fides of the Trust. Nor was Glass alone in providing counsel. At least six Clifford Chance attorneys had attached their names to documents prepared for Badische. The firm had no choice but to circle the wagons and hire outside counsel.

"When lawyers lawyer up, they *really* lawyer up," Quilty says with a chuckle. He describes one pretrial conference with particular relish. "There were two federal prosecutors, Tim Coleman and Jay Musoff, the assistant US attorney who took over from Coleman just before the case went to trial. There was Glass and *his* lawyer. There were the Clifford Chance lawyers that Glass worked with. And there were the lawyers *representing* the Clifford Chance lawyers. It was a bunch of lawyers and me."

Pressed for an exact head count, Quilty drily notes, "Let's just say there were a lot of billable hours in the room."

Soon after the investigator introduced himself, a member of the Clifford Chance defense team made a passing reference to Clare Quilty, the cryptic pedophile who appears in the more baleful passages of *Lolita*. "I always display my most stern and disapproving face when that book gets brought up," Quilty tells me. "If anything, I'm more like Inspector Javert, the cop in *Los Mizzer-whaddever-it-is*. The one who says, 'You know what is going to happen, don't you? I will take you in the end!'"

After the literary small talk had run its course, the defense lawyers invoked two superficially compelling arguments to keep mum: attorney-client privilege and the confidentiality protections that shield attorney "work product" from discovery.

That didn't go over well with the prosecutors, Quilty recalls. "Coleman told the guys straight out that the crime-fraud exception nullified all privilege.* The defense countered with all sorts of legal nuance. About what was 'privileged,' what was 'confidential,' and what was 'private information.' I don't know how many hours we wasted on that bullshit."

When he'd had enough, Quilty made an argument of his own. "'Fellas,' I told them. 'It's simple. What Quilty wants, Quilty gets. I have three years left until I retire. I'll work on this case night and day if that's what it takes.'" The investigator's good-natured swagger was bolstered by the two prosecutors, who made clear that the government would file a motion against Clifford Chance if it refused to cooperate.

In the end, the law firm relinquished thousands of pages of redacted work product and David Glass agreed to serve as a "witness

---

*The crime-fraud exception, as characterized by the Supreme Court in *Clark v. United States*, states: "A client who consults an attorney for advice that will serve him in the commission of a fraud will have no help from the law. He must let the truth be told."

of fact." In return, the government furnished a so-called proffer agreement guaranteeing that anything Glass revealed in his depositions *could not* and *would not* be used against him or his firm at trial. In the jargon of the profession, Glass was made "Queen for the Day," a fitting metaphor given the aristocratic masquerade in which he and his colleagues had unwittingly participated for the better part of two years.

Three of the four lawyers Quilty contacted responded expeditiously to his inquiries. There was only one holdout: Robert Gurland.

"Gurland was key to building the case. Fraud investigation is all about deposits and withdrawals. Who gives the money and who gets it. I had proof that Gurland handled a lot of the stolen funds. He maintained an account in London on behalf of Badische. The problem was I couldn't subpoena UK bank records."

The matter of his foreign residency presented additional obstacles. "Going after someone, especially a lawyer residing outside the country, can add six months or a year to an investigation," Quilty explains. "Extradition was not a realistic option. It costs a fortune, and you never know how it'll play out. I had to figure out another way to make Gurland compliant."

Quilty found the leverage he needed in the London counsel's background. Despite the bespoke suits and posh accent, Robert Gurland was not to the manor born. True, he had attended the very finest of public schools. But the schools in question weren't Eton or Harrow, Rugby or St. Paul's.

"The guy went to P.S. 86 in the Bronx."

The lawyer many Badische victims presumed to be an English barrister was neither English nor a barrister. He was a tax specialist with a law degree from NYU who had lived in England for thirty years.

"I knew some of the stolen performance guaranties were still under Gurland's control. I told him, through his lawyer, that those monies were the fruits of fraud and that if he failed to relinquish them, he could be charged with a felony. An outstanding arrest warrant might make it tough to visit his family in New York."

Gurland, like Glass, tried to invoke attorney-client privilege. But that argument, to use a British loan phrase favored by the Bronx-born expat, "fell on stony ground." (Translation: Fuggedaboutit.) Quilty clarified the difference between legal representation and *il*legal *mis*-representation; the crime-fraud exception trumped all privilege that might otherwise protect the lawyer-client relationship.

After six months of transatlantic negotiation, Robert Gurland signed a nonprosecution agreement with the US Attorney's Office that immunized him from all potential criminal charges stemming from his representation of the Badische Trust Consortium. In return, he promised to furnish prosecutors with redacted copies of his client files, hand over all monies in the Trust-related accounts he controlled, and testify at trial.

The Gurland materials revealed that the Trust's American loan agreements constituted only a fraction of their bogus deals. Wire transfers from all over the world flowed in and out of the Badische bank accounts he controlled like planes at Heathrow.

And where did the money eventually land? A substantial chunk covered overhead. "Imaginary banks usually cost a lot less to operate than real ones," Quilty jokes. "But Badische had higher expenses than your standard advance-fee scam. It used lawyers instead of PO boxes, and lawyers tend to cost money."

Forgoing his usual hourly fee of £200, Gurland worked for Badische on commission, taking 10 percent off the top on all performance guaranties that he handled. He later testified that the arrangement netted him some $250,000, suggesting that he managed $2.5 million in stolen funds tied to bogus loan contracts with face values totaling $2.5 billion. His records also revealed that the bulk of the stolen funds ended up in bank accounts in Switzerland, Liechtenstein, and Austria.

Quilty contacted finance officials in Zurich, Vaduz, and Vienna. Only the Viennese proved cooperative.

Following a yearlong waltz between the US State Department and Austrian bureaucrats, Quilty obtained an inch-thick dossier from the Vienna-based Creditanstalt bank. It confirmed that $2.3 million in performance guaranties had moved through a personal account controlled by Brian David Sherry. Only a few hundred dollars remained by the time Quilty received copies of the account history, but the paper trail was invaluable nonetheless. "The Austrian records helped us substantiate the existence of a conspiracy. It showed how money moved back and forth between Barclay and Badische."

"I can't believe how much energy it took to pull the case together."

"Fraud investigation is all about stamina," Quilty says. "To do the job right you have to review and re-review evidence. Patterns only emerge after you've gone over everything two, three, four times."

"I'm familiar with that sensation. But what you call stamina others might call obsession."

"Doesn't matter what you call it. It comes down to the same thing. The fraud investigator has to have paper in his blood."

CONSPIRACY

I found nearly everything Quilty said fascinating. But it was also distracting. I hadn't flown down to Florida to amplify my understanding of fraud. I was there to learn about Cesar.

"I had doubts about him from the outset," Quilty eventually tells me. "The name of his firm raised an immediate red flag. *Barclay Consulting Group?* It sounded about as authentic as the Rolexx watches—make sure you spell that with two or three *x*'s—you see guys selling on the street."

Cesar's bank records justified his skepticism. They confirmed the obvious; Cesar had no connection to Barclays of London. When he began working with the Trust, he was receiving regular biweekly paychecks from a manufacturer of laminated jewelry display cases based in Hayward, California. As for the $9,000 he charged clients for each of the offshore companies he registered, his credit card statements revealed that a Bedford, Texas, outfit took care of the paperwork for a flat fee of $595.

"Cesar told his clients he had an arm's-length relationship with Badische. That was bullshit. We proved that he received money from the baron. That he sent money to Sherry's mother. That he took out an AmEx card in the colonel's name. That he paid their bills and that they paid his.

"And there was the matter of the retainer check Sherry wrote to Rogers & Wells."

"You lost me."

"It had *Cesar's* home address in the corner. That made it kind of tough for Cesar to claim ignorance of the fraud."

"Did you establish the nature of his relationship to Sherry?"

"No, but it didn't much matter. We had what we needed to prove conspiracy."

Perhaps the most intriguing evidentiary link between Badische and Barclay surfaced during a forensic analysis of two versions of a single photograph. The altered picture, which appeared on the Badische website, showed the president of Malta receiving Colonel Sherry at the palace in Valletta. However, the original photo depicted Prince Robert, *not* the colonel, shaking the president's hand. More relevant to the charge of conspiracy was the presence of the Zelig-like figure standing at attention in the top-left corner. It was Cesar. Date-stamped 2-1-90, the photo confirmed that a relationship among the con men existed years

Evidence of conspiracy: The Badische administrator charged expenses on a Barclay AmEx card paid by Cesar.

Despite the ostensible arm's-length relationship between Badische and Barclay, Sherry's bank checks displayed Cesar's residential address.

before either Barclay or the Badische Trust Consortium existed. (The Trust, the older of the two enterprises, was only incorporated in 1997.)

Once Quilty had assembled the evidence proving fraud and conspiracy, he did one more thing. He shared that evidence with the suspects.

"I always give the defense everything—*everything*. Why? To prove the hopelessness of their situation. If they want to fight, I tell 'em, 'Go right ahead. The government pays Quilty every two weeks whether we go to trial or settle.' I tell 'em, 'Fellas, the choice is all yours.'"

"And Cesar chose to go to trial?"

"At first it seemed he might be willing to cut a deal. We talked for a while. I said to him, 'Did any of your clients ever get financing?' He said, 'No.' I said, 'Didn't you suspect something was fishy when no deals ever took place?' He said he hadn't thought to ask. I told him, 'Why don't you come in and talk?' He was about to. Then his lawyer got involved. She said her client would cooperate if the US Attorney's Office reduced the charges to a misdemeanor."

"What did you say to that?"

"I said, 'Quilty don't work for no stinkin' misdemeanors.' The proposal was ludicrous. I only consider a case a 'win' if the criminal spends more time in jail than I spend putting him there. I had two years into the case. I told the lawyer Cesar had to cop to a felony, which the government proposed offsetting with a 5K1 letter."

Named for a section of the US Sentencing Guidelines, a "5K1" is a lot less generous than the nonpros Gurland negotiated or the proffer deal signed by Glass. It promises nothing more than a *recommendation* for sentence reduction if the defendant pleads guilty and provides the "substantial assistance" to the prosecution.

The Badische website included a photo (left) showing Colonel Sherry being received at the Valetta Palace by Vincent Tabone, the president of Malta. The undoctored original includes Cesar in the background.

"A 5K1 can shave a few months or years off a sentence, but it also brands you a snitch."

Cesar found himself confronted by a variant of the classic prisoner's dilemma. Option A: Plead guilty, betray your accomplices, and receive a reduced punishment. Or option B: Keep your mouth shut and hope the jury finds you innocent.

"A lot of times it comes down to every man for himself," Quilty notes. "But these guys never ratted each other out. That's unusual."

"Could Cesar have been paid off?"

"Can't say. What I can tell you is most of the stolen money was never recovered."

"So it is possible the bankers bought Cesar's silence?"

"Possible? Sure. But I don't believe money was the reason Cesar clammed up. The impression I got was he refused to cooperate because a 5K1 compels the admission of *all* prior crimes. Not just the one being prosecuted."

"Meaning?"

"Meaning Cesar had stuff in his past."

Finally! The conversation zeroes in on the question I'm most keen to have answered. "Stuff? What kind of stuff? Violent stuff?"

"All I can tell you is that Cesar was involved in other things, criminal things, that prevented him from cooperating. When he realized he had to come clean on his *entire* criminal history, that's when he shut down."

For two or three minutes, I press Quilty, but my efforts get me nowhere, so I approach the subject from a different angle.

"Do you think Cesar has cleaned up his act?"

Quilty shrugs. "All I can tell you is that I put him out of commission for the time he was in jail. After that, guys like Cesar are usually back to their old game, or a new version of it. Fraud is an addiction and addictions are very hard to break. Fraud is what con men know. It's what they're best at. It's what they love."

"CRIMINAL THINGS"

A few days after I return from Florida, I receive an email from a Department of Justice staffer I had cold-called months before. To my surprise, he agrees to sit down with me at the headquarters of the US Attorney's Office. Although I can't be sure, I suspect some sort of back-channel intervention by one of my informants—Quilty? Feeney? Feiter? I have no clue—has prompted the outreach. Once more, I travel to New York.

Security is tight at the Southern District Headquarters of the US Attorney's Office. To enter the building it's necessary to relinquish one's driver's license and cell phone, and submit to metal detectors and inspection by a guard with a wand. Once that's done, the visitor is issued an ID sticker and directed to a waiting area.

Ten minutes after completing those preliminaries, I am escorted into an elevator filled with guys carrying sidearms. From there I'm led in silence to an overheated windowless interrogation room. Eventually, the staffer who contacted me enters the room. We speak for about an hour. What he tells me is only mildly illuminating since I already know way, *way* too much about all things Badische. I explain what I'm after: evidence of Cesar's criminal activities prior to his federal conviction on multiple counts of wire fraud and conspiracy. The staffer sidesteps the subject entirely.

"Right," he says at the end of our interview. "I pulled some files from Varick Street. These here are the public records." He sets two boxes down on a grimy Formica table. "Government exhibits entered into evidence at trial are public. As such, I'm authorized to provide these materials to you," he adds redundantly.

"Great."

"And *those* boxes over there"—the staffer cocks his head toward some cartons stacked near the door—"*those* materials were *not* introduced at trial. I am *not* authorized to release them. Do you understand?"

I give a nod, though I'm not really sure I do understand.

The staffer looks at his watch. "Right. It's eleven a.m. now. I'll be back to get you at three."

"Great," I repeat, this time more tentatively.

Then, just like that, I am left alone.

The staffer has made it clear that he has *not* authorized me to inspect the boxes near the door, so I stick to the public records on the table. Leafing through the sanctioned materials reminds me of my manic law-firm excavations during the blizzard. Five years have passed since I first figured out that my former roommate is a convicted con man. Yet here I am, *still* immersed in paper, *still* trying to get a bead on Cesar's criminal life.

The government files are scrupulously arranged. Each piece of evidence, organized by witness, is cross-referenced to a master list of the government exhibits. The material doesn't help me much, but it is exciting to hold the physical evidence introduced at trial. Using a point-and-shoot camera overlooked during the security screening, I snap some pictures:

GX 316. Wire transfer confirmation ($27,000) from Barbara Laurence to Barclay Consulting Group. [Click!]

GX 270. Contact report from Merrill Lynch on meeting with representatives of the Badische Trust Consortium. [Click!]

GX 110. Handwritten $90.3 billion tally ("Assets to Finance Deals") drafted on Clifford Chance legal stationery. [Click!]

GX 361. Creditanstalt flowchart documenting funds transferred from a Vienna account in the name of Brian Sherry to the Barclay Consulting Group. [Click!]

GX 415. Photograph showing the president of Malta greeting Prince Robert (with Cesar in the background). [Click!]

GX 967. Title and dealer invoice for spindrift-white Jaguar purchased by Brian Sherry at Manhattan Jaguar. [Click!]

Taking unauthorized pictures in a building occupied by gun-toting law enforcement officers makes me feel like a spy. More precisely, a cowardly spy. No spook worth his cyanide pill would steer clear of the restricted materials near the door.

I finish with the public records by noon. The off-limits stuff beckons. I peer around the room. There don't appear to be any security cameras, though who knows what's mounted inside the AC vents. My curiosity ratchets up, and so does my anxiety. What if someone were to catch me with my hand in the cookie jar?

For an hour at least, fear trumps temptation. Then the second-guessing begins. Why did the staffer leave me alone with material he *didn't* want me to look at? Wasn't I expected to be—what's the word I'm looking for—*nosy?*

The impulse to peek continues to grow. Actually, the staffer never said I wasn't allowed to snoop. He only said that he didn't have the authority to allow me to snoop. There's a difference. Did he make the statement to establish plausible deniability? I'm pretty sure he did. Still, I'm unwilling to face the consequences of being wrong.

Around one o'clock, my indecisiveness becomes unbearable. I slip out of the interrogation room, head down to the lobby, retrieve my cell phone and ID, leave the building, and call the magazine editor

who commissioned the search for Cesar. I update her about my predicament and ask for legal guidance. She calls back a few minutes
later. "Go for it," she tells me. "Our lawyer says it's fine."

The moment I receive her go-ahead, I feel like a complete doofus.
Suddenly it's so obvious. *Of course* I'm supposed to poke through the
files.

I race back into the building, subject myself to another round of
security checks, and reach the interrogation room with barely an
hour in which to review the unauthorized papers. At first I try exam-
ining the material in small batches. (Less to hide if someone enters
the room.) But that proves impractical when I come upon a carton
crammed with the contents of Sherry's carry-on bag.

I dump the stuff on the table and snap a bunch of pictures. The box
includes three international cell phones, one portable printer, hundreds of business cards, and a marked-up copy of the *International
Herald Tribune*. Some of the paper's classifieds, taken out by "individuals seeking funds," are circled in ballpoint, with the words *sent
letter* and *contacted* scribbled next to the names of potential marks.

The impounded bag also includes a copy of a $246 welfare check
from the public assistance division of New York's Department of
Social Services. The business cards in the box make me wonder
which name he used when depositing his welfare checks. Colonel
Brian Sherry of the Badische Trust Consortium? Sir Brian Sherry of
the House of Badische? Major Sir Sherry, Ambassador Plenipotentiary of the Knights of Malta? Colonel Brian Sherry-Berwick, Managing Trustee for Badische Anlage Treuhand? Brian D. Sherry, Doctor
of Business Administration, Finance, and Management? Dr. Brian
Sherry, Director of Highfit Holdings, Hong Kong? Or perhaps—this
was my favorite card of the bunch—Brian Shaer, Director of B.S. Financial Services?

I repack the carry-on items and move on.

The next box contains Cesar's Presentencing Report, or PSR.
Prepared by the US Probation Office in April 2003, the thirteen-page

document includes a personal history; a financial accounting ("Assets: $16,500. Liabilities: $84,800. Net worth: -$68,300"); and a brief psychological overview, which reveals another unsettling parallel between my nemesis and me ("Defendant suffers from General Anxiety Disorder, DSM IV, 300.02"). It also provides his employment record, a drug history ("The defendant admitted that he first used cocaine at 22 and last used it in June 2002. The defendant admitted that he used marihuana at age 18 and last used marihuana in September 2002"), and a list of prior crimes.

It's in this last section that I finally hit pay dirt. Quilty's vague reference to "criminal things" is clarified with telegraphic efficiency: "Date of arrest 8/16/90 'Possession of 30 grams of cocaine.' Oslo Police Dept., 2 Years custody."

Later, when I tell Max about the cocaine smuggling, he expresses dismay (and a knowledge of drug laws that he assures me is gleaned from *The Wire*): "Two years for thirty grams? Cesar caught a break. He'd be serving a dime if he'd been busted in Baltimore."

Sherry's confiscated carry-on, the Trust's mobile office, included business cards with a half dozen aliases and a marked-up Herald Tribune.

PART IX

ON YOUR MARK

Revealing too much information weakens your positional power.

Cesar Teague,
"Negotiate Your Way to More Sales"

One has to mature gradually towards one's enemy as towards one's best friend.

Hans Keilson,
The Death of the Adversary

The drug conviction came as a relief. It was a victimless crime, which suggested that whatever danger Cesar might pose was unlikely to involve overt acts of violence. I had known for some time that if I had any hope of getting a better sense of the guy, we would have to meet. That meant convincing Françoise (and myself) that the benefits of a reunion—if one could be arranged—outweighed the potential risks.

I waited a few weeks before making the pitch. I told Françoise pretty much what I'd told myself. *Yes*, Cesar was a felon twice over—convicted on multiple counts of fraud in US federal court and for bringing illicit drugs into Norway. And *yes*, he had ties to a thug who had been employed by the Mob. But since he himself had no known record of violence, I'd concluded that a properly planned and cautiously executed tête-à-tête posed only limited danger.

Françoise disagreed. Vehemently. She pointed out that Cesar could retaliate *non*violently. "That's how con men work."

"I'm pretty sure I can handle whatever he throws my way," I claimed.

"*J'espère*," she said. *I hope so.*

So what next? Even under the best of circumstances, there was no reason to think Cesar would be willing to talk. We weren't exactly long-lost friends, and his recent prosecution only increased the likelihood that he'd tell me to fuck off.

Compounding those concerns was the practical impediment of not knowing *which* Cesar to contact. If I got in touch with Cesar *Viana*, as he was called before he was released from Lompoc, he'd probably assume I knew about Badische. Web searches for that name now pulled up dozens of links to press accounts of his conviction. But if I reached out to Cesar under one of his postpenitentiary aliases, that would preclude bringing up Aiglon and thus nullify the whole point of the meeting.

I was similarly indecisive about *how* to make contact. Should my opening salvo be framed as a request or an offer? What, if anything, would make Cesar *want* to talk to me about our shared experiences and his subsequent life? Should I introduce the possibility of financial gain?

It was impossible to ignore the irony of the situation. The questions I was asking myself are the very questions a swindler poses before closing in on his mark. Why should that have surprised me? Spending a few years thinking about hustlers is bound to throw your moral compass out of whack. Lie down with dogs, get up with fleas.

I wasted a few months evaluating various ornate come-ons before realizing that any attempt to con a con man would end disastrously. Best to leave such contrivances to filmmakers and professional cheats. If I did get the chance to confront Cesar, I would do so without artifice: as a writer and a former roommate working through memories of childhood trauma.

While I was dithering, Cesar kept himself busy. After Lompoc, he became, in quick succession: a producer of feature films, a "Lifestyle Entrepreneur" promoting seven-figure income opportunities in four-minute YouTube clips, the international marketing manager for an IT company based in Bangalore, a health adviser, a scriptwriter, an essayist on matters of business negotiation, a motivational speaker, a home business coach, and the regional distributor for a line of aloe vera products manufactured by an Arizona billionaire named Rex. His ceaseless self-transformation reminded me of a clever board book Max had as a kid; it lets the reader flip tabs to replace a Stetson with a tiara on the head of a cowboy and put a pair of leather chaps on a queen.

"Find Someone in Your Network"

In April 2010, I find the opening I'm looking for. Around the time Cesar is wrapping up his five years of court-mandated probation, he joins a social networking site called Plaxo under an alias. That, in itself, isn't useful. What *is* useful is that he includes Aiglon College among his educational affiliations. Why the revived association? I can't know for sure, but I have a theory: he's trolling for new clients.

Whatever the motive, the commingling of Cesar's past and present identities gives me an unthreatening answer to a question he's sure to ask when I attempt to make contact: How did you find me?

I sign up for Plaxo and include Aiglon in my educational profile. But before I have a chance to plot my next move, something unnerving happens. Cesar deletes his boarding school affiliation while keeping the rest of his profile page intact. From one moment to the next, my unthreatening access point slams shut. Has Cesar removed his name from the alumni group because my name now appears on it? Is it possible he knows I'm pursuing him? After all, I've spoken to dozens of people connected to his case. One of them might have squealed.

I fret over the digital disconnection until Max points out that it doesn't matter. I can still get in touch. "You could have downloaded his info and waited to get back in touch. You don't have to know he changed his profile."

Bolstered by my son's logic, I fire off an innocuous email:

> *Dear Cesar,*
>
> *Are you the same Cesar who went to Aiglon College with me in 1971? . . . If you are send signs of life. Tell*

me what you're up to. (I write children's books and
make science kits for kids.)

All the best,

Allen (from Belvedere)

Because of the time difference between Providence and San Francisco, I dispatch my seemingly innocent query in the afternoon. I want Cesar to be awake when it lands in his in-box. I'm hoping for a quick reply. Crazy, I know, given how much time has elapsed since last we spoke.

Well, I don't get a quick reply. In fact, I get no reply at all.

Is he blowing me off? The prospect of never talking to him unsettles me. Man things have changed. For the longest time, I was afraid of confronting Cesar. Now I'm afraid of *not* confronting him.

A few months after the failed Plaxo overture, Cesar opens a Facebook account. (Actually, he opens two—one under his original name and another under an alias.) He apparently likes jazz, hiking, martial arts, and self-help best sellers containing numbers in their titles: *The Tenth Insight*, *The 7 Habits of Highly Effective People*, *365 Days of Richer Living*. More significantly, he again joins the alumni group of our alma mater.

Renewed opportunity buoys my mood. I'm determined not to blow it. Instead of emailing Cesar directly, I decide to let Facebook make the introductions by friending a few dozen Aiglon graduates—some of whom I don't even know—and waiting for the social network's algorithm to play matchmaker. Sure enough, after two weeks of promiscuous outreach, I receive an auto-generated message encouraging me to friend Cesar. I wait a day before clicking the button that executes the request.

Four hours later, Cesar clicks the thumbs-up icon. His acceptance comes as a huge relief and dispels my earlier worry that he knows what I'm up to. (The Plaxo query, I suspect, landed in a junk folder.)

The timing couldn't be better. My publisher is flying me to San Francisco in a couple of weeks to promote a science kit I developed with Max. That presents me with the perfect backstory, as well as a convenient reason to propose a face-to-face reunion. I send my new Facebook friend another bland email:

> *Dear Cesar,*
>
> *Wow, it's been nearly forty years since we last saw each other. You've gotten thinner and I've gotten, well, let's just say I've gotten LESS thinner. I see you're in SF. I'll be there next week for Maker Faire (in San Mateo). It'd be a blast to catch up.*
>
> *Cheers, Allen (from Belvedere)*

Two days go by with no reply, so I resend the message, tacking on a question in the hopes of teasing out a response: "P.S. Where was that Facebook picture of you taken? I'm guessing that's the Golden Gate Bridge in the background."

The postscript query does the trick. Six hours later, I receive this response:

> *Hi Allen,*
>
> *Cool and I'm in town next week. . . . We can meet for lunch or happy hour!*
>
> *The photo was taken up on the other side of the Cliff House.*
>
> *Thanks and call me Monday afternoon when you're in town and let's chat then!*

REUNION

I arrive in San Francisco on a Tuesday and arrange to have lunch with
Cesar that Thursday. On Wednesday, I scope out the setting of our
rendezvous, a Thai joint in the Panhandle called Phuket. The food
is pretty good and the two uniformed cops eating curry a few tables
away from me give the place a reassuring vibe. The night before our
meeting, I sleep horribly. By six a.m. Thursday I'm standing over an
open travel bag, worrying about what to wear. (Once more, shades of
senior prom.) Tie and jacket might play to Cesar's formal side. After
all, the Badische dress code endorsed "French-cuff shirt, with tasteful
cuff links" and "Conservative silk necktie with clip or tack." But that
was before Cesar changed his name, grew a goatee, and embarked on
a career in film. I decide to wear what makes me comfortable. And
since I'm the type who protects dress shoes with plastic bags, I opt for
jeans, sneakers, and a no-iron button-down.

I reach Phuket way too early and end up biding my time in a hardware
store until an alert goes off on my phone. As I'm entering the restaurant,
I find myself wondering if the cops from the previous day will be back.
It couldn't hurt to have backup. Then another thought hits: What if the
cops *are* inside and one of them says something to me? Given Cesar's
recent legal difficulties, even a casual nod of acknowledgment from a law
enforcement officer could sabotage the reunion before it begins.

My fears turn out to be unfounded. The patrolmen aren't on hand.
In fact, their table is now occupied by a convicted felon—*my* convicted felon. Hunched over a menu, Cesar doesn't see me come in. I
give him the once-over before approaching. The goatee is gone, but
he's wearing the same black paisley shirt he had on four years earlier,
while he was raising funds for a film. (According to the web, he's still
looking for financing.)

He soon spots me and waves. When I reach his table, Cesar smiles,
extends a hand, and says, "We've got to stop meeting this way."

Robert von Badische, Seventy-fourth Grand Master of the Knights of Malta, and his wife, Princess Audrey, posed for Mathias Braschler in 1999, while the loan program bearing his name was in full swing. When I showed my son this photo, he called attention to the prince's provocative hand gesture.

Before serving as the figurehead for the Badische Trust Consortium, Prince Robert conducted dozens of bogus knighting ceremonies at various churches around Manhattan. The more ambitious events included engraved announcements, a boys choir, and (as seen above right) a white-gloved, sword-wielding honor guard.

The theatricality of the investiture ceremonies relied on the talents of the Baron Moncrieffe (seen above). Moncrieffe claimed to be a Serbian aristocrat, but a birth certificate unearthed by criminal investigator Dennis M. Quilty revealed that the onetime department-store window dresser was born in Toledo, Ohio, and that his name was George Ritchie Englert Jr.

The roster of celebrities duped by the prince and the baron included (clockwise, from top left) Pope Paul VI, the Queen Mother, "Sir" Anthony Quinn, and "Sir" Sammy Davis Jr.

Before his fraud conviction in 2002, Brian Sherry identified himself as Colonel Sherry, Major Sherry, Sir Brian Sherry, Prince Brian, Graf von Sherry, and Colonel Sherry-Berwick. After completing his prison sentence, he shed the regalia and royal titles, founded a synagogue, and started calling himself "Reb Benzi."

As the check to the left shows, welfare payments supported the administrator of the multibillion-dollar loan program.

Like his colleagues, Sherry came from nonaristocratic stock, as the document to the right confirms. My wife, noting that the future felon was ushered into the world by a man named Port and a woman named Sherry, said, "I guess Johnnie Walker and Dom Pérignon were out of town."

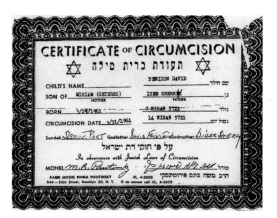

Fraud is in the details. To give their scheme the air of legitimacy, the swindlers named their nonexistent Trust after a defunct financial institution. The real Badische Bank failed in 1935.

The Kingdom of Mombessa, the principal source of the Trust's fictive assets, had no such backstory. As this fax from King Henri-François Mazzamba suggests, logos and letterhead had to be designed and tweaked before the $50 billion deed could be printed, signed, and witnessed.

Mombessa may not exist, but its capital does. That said, the only image I could find of the "City of Mondimbi" appears on a postage stamp issued by the Belgian Congo in the early 1930s.

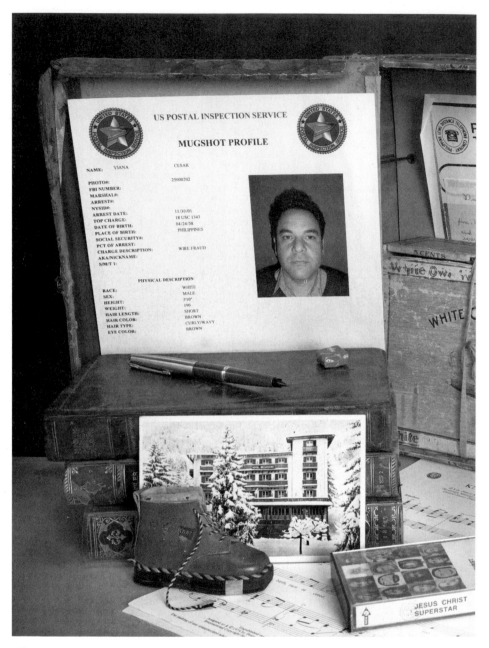

The "Cesareum." My file box of search ephemera includes a mug shot of my roommate; a postcard of our dormitory; a 1971 cassette recording of Jesus Christ Superstar; *a ski boot match safe; the sheet music for an anthem composed for Prince Robert's sham order of knights; a Parker 45 fountain pen; a Sugus candy; . . .*

. . . a cigar box containing forty-year-old trinkets; a foosball man; the patch from my Aiglon blazer; my rank badge; the notebook my father filled as a ten-year-old (in 1920); letters I wrote while a boarder; a page from a Manila phone book; Sir Brian Sherry's gold-embossed visiting card; and a replica of Augustus of Prima Porta, a gift from my son, Max.

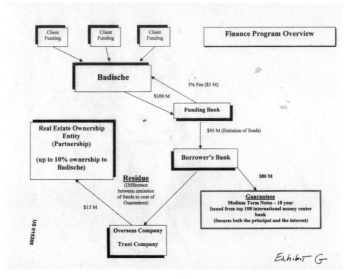

This is probably the clearest graphic expression of the loan program Cesar pitched to his clients. None of the projects he represented received funding.

Self-styled knight of Malta, Robert von Badische (age unknown) in 1998.

Self-styled knight of Malta, Maximilian Kurzweil (age four) in 1998.

House Photo

"Long time no see," I respond. "You're looking good."

That's a lie, the first of many we will exchange. Cesar is not looking good. He's looking hungover. And the fact that he's wearing a shirt that's at least four years old suggests his current professional activities aren't nearly so lucrative as the ones that landed him in Lompoc.

"What've you been up to, Allen?"

"I'm a writer. Novels, mostly. Children's books. A little journalism. Oh, and I just released a science kit I developed with my son." I hope I'm sounding calm. It's hard to know. If the Badische fraud has taught me anything, it's that deception makes me awkward and self-conscious. I provide a brief rundown of my promotional schedule, grateful for the cover story. "Anyhoo. What about you?"

"I do a couple things," Cesar says. "Mostly in sales and marketing." He pulls two business cards from his wallet and places them on the table.

I reach for the closer of the two. "'Founder, NextLevel Consulting'?"

"I manage a team of experts who offer a broad range of strategic services to small- to medium-size businesses."

"Impressive. What kind of services?"

"Whatever's needed. We target firms generating revenues of fifty million and up. Companies that have an interest in expanding to, let's say, Europe or Australia."

I'm tempted to say he's being modest since his consulting website lists Xerox, McDonald's, Cisco, Apple, British Telecom, Hewlett-Packard, Disney, Sony, and DreamWorks among its clients. Instead, I pick up the second card, which indicates that Cesar moonlights as the regional sales manager for something called Forever Living Products. "Pretty ambitious name."

"We're the world's largest grower, distributor, and producer of aloe vera. Allen, are you familiar with the health benefits of aloe vera?"

"It's for sunburns, right?"

"Not only. It can be taken internally, as well."

While I'm learning way, *way* too much about the nutraceutical benefits of a proprietary aloe vera hybrid grown, harvested, and bottled in the Dominican Republic, a waitress comes by to take our orders. I go with a Pan-Asian chicken special. Cesar opts for a spicy seafood dish. It seems he still has a thing for hot sauce.

I use the interruption to end the medicine show and explain, in general and unmenacing terms, why I've asked him to lunch. "I'm planning to write about my experiences at Aiglon. . . . Trying to resurrect everything I can about our time there."

"I recall a lot," Cesar says amiably. "But just in bits and pieces. There are some things that people have told me about that I really don't remember. You might need to prod me a bit."

"That's not a problem," I assure him. "I'm more than happy to prod."

I pull out the Belvedere house photo and place it between us. Cesar scans the image while sucking on a shrimp. After resting the peel next to his plate and wiping his fingers daintily on a napkin, he begins stabbing faces.

"That's me. That's the kid who built a little gas airplane that made a friggin' racket. That's the kid who got care packages of fluff and peanut butter. That's what's-his-name, the Pakistani with the stutter. Remember what we used to call him?"

I shake my head.

Cesar twists his wrist as if turning the ignition key of a car that refuses to start. "*T-t-t-t-t-ta-yub!*" he sputters as he cranks. "*T-t-t-t-ta-yub! . . . T-t-t-t-t-ta-yub!*" The gesture brings to mind the two-fingered rebuke he deployed whenever he called me Nosey.

Cesar's memories of Aiglon turn out to be both extremely exacting and highly selective. He recalls his laundry-tag ID number ("I was 323"); the mimeographed list of Briticisms that JC compelled speakers of American English to learn ("Who the hell says 'fortnight'?"); his favorite pocketknife, a wood-handled Opinel ("with a little metal ring that turned to lock the blade").

"Remember the boy with the toaster?" I say.

"Sure I do."

Together we reconstruct a memory of breakfast in Belvedere. Each morning, one of our older housemates—we can't come up with his name—would enter the dining hall carrying a two-slice toaster under his arm. As soon as he sat down, the fellow would start making toast, and he'd keep making it throughout the meal, distributing toast to every boy at the table without regard to age, rank, or personal affection.

"I always buttered my toast on both sides," Cesar says.

"I usually slathered mine with blackstrap molasses, butter, and cocoa powder."

There is one huge discrepancy in our composite memory of the toaster boy. I remember him with great fondness. Not only did he transform an inedible bread product into a delicacy worthy of a French bakery, he subverted, ever so slightly, a culture of hierarchy and privilege. Cesar, by contrast, recalls the frustration of never receiving a second slice.

"Speaking of bread," I say awkwardly, "remember the pellets you guys forced me to eat? It was—"

Before I have a chance to mention the chili sauce, Cesar cuts me off. "I don't. But remember Bean Day? How JC was always trying to raise money for famine victims?"

"Oh, right." I vaguely recall the founder's well-intentioned initiative—a day during which the whole school ate nothing but beans—and its inevitable consequences: a dorm-wide fart-a-thon of epic proportions. "Maybe that's why we were forced to keep our windows open at night," I joke.

While Cesar is chuckling, I tap the face of my best friend.

"Anderson," he says. "I always thought he was a little slow."

I bristle. "That's not how I remember him."

Breakfast in Belvedere, circa 1971. Cesar is seated at left.

Cesar recalibrates. "I'm not saying mentally. But the way he *acted?* He was like . . ." Cesar throws himself into an impersonation of Woody that includes denigrating guttural sounds impossible to represent in print.

"You may not know what happened to him," I say. "When I went back to the school in 1991, I learned that Woody fell down the—"

Cesar again cuts me off. "I know *all* about it. I was right next to him when it happened."

"Next to him?"

"Well, nearby."

"Was he really dead by the time he hit the ground? That's what Mrs. Senn told me."

"Yeah. Instantly. Like that." Cesar snaps his fingers. "He landed on his head." Then, as he reaches for a mussel, Cesar adds, "I had to help scrape up his brains."

"*What?* Are you kidding?"

Cesar sucks the meat from the shell. "Nope. I got stuck having to scoop his brains into a bag."

Shocked by the self-directed nature of the revelation and the unself-conscious slurping that accompanies it, I watch Cesar add the shell to the shrimp peels beside his plate.

He misreads my stare. "Want to try one?" he asks, picking up a mussel.

"Uh, no thanks," I manage as I try to shake the chilling image of Cesar bent over my buddy Woody's lifeless body at the base of the Belvedere stairwell.

ATTACK OR RETREAT?

The rest of the meal, while not nearly so macabre, is no less eye-opening. At one point, I pull out a school directory from 1972. Cesar scans the list and quickly pounces on the name of a girl I never knew. "We used to tease her all the time," he says with a hearty chuckle.

"We used to punch her because she was really, *really* fat. I mean, I was chubby, but she was *huge*!" The remark, in itself, is unsettling. What disturbs me more is the curiously good-natured comment that follows: "She was great and really very nice."

As we swap stories, I'm struck by how many of our shared memories provoke profoundly different feelings. Take showering. I recall hating every aspect of the daily hose-downs, both the cold ones that followed PT and the warm ones that preceded dinner. But for Cesar, the shower room is a locus of pride. "Remember how I was the chief shower checker?" he boasts. "I took the job seriously. I got prizes."

"And I got verrucas."

"Verrucas?"

"Ingrown warts. Matron tried removing them with a scalpel. And when that didn't work, she coated them with pepper paste."

"I liked Matron," Cesar says of the nurse with the daguerreotype looks. "She was very . . . matronly."

"How did you end up at Aiglon?" I ask midway through the meal.

"Some guy with a name like George Winterthorpe III told my mom about it."

"Was it easy leaving Manila?"

"God, no. I was sheltered. When I first got to Switzerland, I was a fish out of water. I believe my mom thought Aiglon was going to be a wonderful experience. She got super feedback from all these people who had been there before. Well, guess what, Allen. It *wasn't* wonderful. It was like the military. Like a concentration camp. I actually had to go to therapy because I felt like my mom abandoned me. I turned around and just like that"—Cesar again snaps his fingers—"she was gone. The whole Aiglon thing was really tough. 'Do this! Do that! Make your bed! Tip your chair? Fifty centimes!'"

Much of Cesar's misery appears to be rooted in the daunting physical demands placed on students. Overweight while at Aiglon, he loathed the weekend hikes that I loved. "I got snow blindness one time," he complains. "And remember how you had to report on what you saw? And don't get me started on the sleeping bags. Man, they stank!" (Regarding this last grievance, he raises a valid point. The school-issued bags were notoriously malodorous and crusty for reasons better left unexplored.)

Cesar recalls enjoying only one hike, a short ex that required him to lead a small group of boys up and down three mountains. On the first day of the expedition, he set himself up at a base camp and mustered the troops.

"I told them, 'We're gonna have to work this smart,'" he remembers.

That meant abandoning the itinerary sanctioned by the expeditions master, disregarding a sacrosanct safety policy spelled out in the *Rules*—"Never get separated"—and persuading his charges to undertake solo climbs of the peaks that the team was supposed to tackle in unison. When his charges returned to the base camp, Cesar cobbled their separate field notes into a report chronicling an expedition ostensibly undertaken as a group. The work-around shaved a full day off the ex, which the boys spent in a village bar. "We had some wine, laughed our heads off, and played foosball. It was a lesson in leadership," Cesar adds with no apparent irony.

Sometimes the two of us recall despising the same things but for different reasons. When I ask Cesar if he remembers the pine tree that provoked my nightmares, he says, "Sure. Crows used to nest there and *caaaaaw* in the morning. I hated how they'd wake us up."

"I don't remember the crows. What I remember is worrying I'd be tossed into the tree if a fire broke out." I stop short of pointing fingers, worried doing so might end the interview prematurely.

Cesar has no such qualms. His catalog of boarding school assailants is a lot lengthier than mine. There's the classmate who swiped the pocket money from his bedside cash box. The "klepto" from Finland who stole his knives. The two upper-schoolers who *tried* to beat him up. ("They couldn't," he notes proudly. "I studied judo.") The boys who whacked his legs with nettles during a game of capture the flag ("Man, that stung like hell"). The duty prefect who forced him to strip and submit to an ice-cold "punishment shower" until his "skin turned red," all because of some unspecified late-night mischief.

And that's only the students who made his life hell. The roster of abusive adults is just as long. An assistant master gave Cesar laps for cursing—"even though I'd just gotten stung by hornets!" Our history teacher hit him over the head during class. (Here our recollections again diverge, if only on a minor matter. Cesar is certain the teacher in question meted out justice with a wooden ruler. I'm equally sure he made use of a hardcover textbook, which, by year's end, was as flexible as a paperback.) Even Lady Forbes, my seemingly irreproachable elocution tutor, earns a reprimand: "She ate french fries with her fingers!"

Of all the tormentors Cesar endured during his three years at Aiglon, he reserves his greatest ire for our housemaster, the volatile Irishman who tore into me when my grades were in the gutter. "That guy was *always* on the warpath," he says.

"I remember him the same way."

"Once I skipped a punishment run because I had to buy stuff for a long expedition. The prick came to my room and said, 'What are you doing here?' 'Well, I had to go shopping,' I said. And he said, 'No, you're supposed to be on your punishment run. You were about to make silver [rank]. You just blew it.'

"Another time, I told him I had fifty francs stolen, and he said, 'Where'd you get all that money? You're not supposed to have that much.' It's like *I* became the person that was guilty!"

"Technically you were guilty. The *Rules* prohibited us from having more than five francs at any time."

"I guess that was a problem," Cesar admits.

Asked about his absolute worst memory of Aiglon, he says, "Probably the time I was quarantined with German measles. No one visited. I was all alone. I spent my birthday in the freakin' hospital."*

"Is *that* the reason you disappeared? I've always wondered about that. One moment I'm rooming with you and Paul, and the next thing I know you're both gone. Are the two of you still in touch?"

"Nope," Cesar says. "I don't even know if he's still alive."

"Oh, he's alive," I say. "Google his name. Last time I checked, half the photos online had him at New York and Palm Beach charity events. The other half were from mugshots.com."

"I had no idea," Cesar says. He shows no interest in learning the specifics of his childhood henchman's grown-up slipups—two arrests

---

* There's some ambiguity regarding the disease that led to Cesar's extended isolation. At different times during our talks he mentions German measles, a mild virus that clears up quickly, and measles, which can be much trickier to treat. A letter submitted by a relative prior to sentencing compounds the confusion by citing smallpox as the cause for his hospitalization.

and some bench warrants involving a stolen vehicle. From the way Cesar nervously redirects his gaze to the photo, I get the impression that the mention of mug shots hits too close to home.

"Paul's not in the picture," I say. "It must have been taken after he left and before you got sick." I take a deep breath. "Remember how Paul swiped my father's watch?"

Cesar doesn't respond, at least not directly. "I remember him being pretty harmless."

"Paul? Harmless? That's not my memory. I lived in fear of the guy." *And what you made him do.* "Remember how he helped tie me to the bed to reenact *Jesus Christ Superstar?*"

"I think everybody picked on somebody," Cesar says flatly.

I mention getting whipped to the sound track of "The Thirty-Nine Lashes."

Cesar doesn't respond.

Not for the first or last time, I'm faced with a choice: attack or retreat. And not for the first or last time, I choose the coward's course of action, diverting the discussion into a thicket of meaningless detail. "The music was played on Timothy Kann's tape recorder," I say. "A portable Philips about yay big." I spread my hands a foot apart.

Cesar doesn't recall the whipping, the interlude, or the tape recorder. He doesn't even recall Timothy Kann.

The last lapse is especially curious. How can someone who knows his boarding school laundry-tag number forget the name of a roommate? I give him a

Cesar's sidekick in 2004. His profile, as an adult, is exactly as I remember it at school.

few prompts. "New York kid. Father worked for Bache and Co. Liked Broadway musicals. Neat freak. Had a fancy electric toothbrush."

"Like I said," Cesar says, "there's a lot I don't remember. I got an email from a Turkish kid in Belvedere. I have no recollection of him either." (I never knew the Turkish kid. He arrived at the school a few months after I left. But his views of Cesar surfaced on a Facebook alumni page: "Don't you remember me?" he asked my former roommate in the public forum. "You composed a jingle about how I picked my dick every day?" I contacted the alum and we exchanged five or six emails that corroborated many of my memories. "Yes, Cesar was a problem to all those not as big as he was," he wrote. "But he made sure to stay away from me after seeing me take down another bully within hours of my arrival at school. Since first grade I've never taken crap from anybody.")

I ask Cesar to name the boys he roomed with during his time at Aiglon. He mentions six or seven.

"You missed one," I say.

"Who?"

"Um. I roomed with you, too."

"Really?" Cesar gives me a doubtful look.

"There were five of us living together."

He still appears skeptical.

"In a room at the top of Belvedere."

"That's right," he says at last. "And people would pick on you, right?"

People? I let it go. No, that's not right. I'm not letting anything go. I'm keeping everything bottled up—to prolong the conversation and to keep myself in check.

"Are you in this?" Cesar asks, tapping the house photo.

At first, I think he's joking. He has correctly identified nearly every boy in the picture. His failing to find me is like Professor Moriarty failing to recognize Holmes. But when he repeats the question,

I know he's serious. I point to the sad-looking, mop-topped, cross-legged eleven-year-old at the base of the pyramid.

"That's you?" Cesar says, shaking his head.

"That's me."

"Man, you were little."

"I was," I say with a sigh. "I was the littlest kid in the school."

A FEW MORE MEETINGS

Is it really possible that a boy I will never forget has all but forgotten me? I believe it is. I'm pretty sure Cesar isn't lying. Not about the photo, anyway. After all, if he were up to his old tricks, he'd pick me out of the lineup, recall the happy times we shared, then attempt to rope me into one of his schemes. He doesn't do any of that.

I feel foolish for so grossly exaggerating his capacity for evil. Cesar is not the All-Knowing Menace I anticipated. Truth be told, if anyone deserves that title, I do. Far from resisting my questions, he welcomes them, even going so far as to suggest that we meet again before I fly home.

At our next get-together, I continue to lob softballs. My approach resembles the Gradual-Length Method developed by Monsieur Stump, our ski instructor at Aiglon. Monsieur Stump always started beginners on short skis that were easy to maneuver. Only as our confidence grew would he introduce longer skis. He recognized the value of incremental challenge. By the same logic, I guide Cesar over unthreatening terrain. No talk of felony or flogging. No further mention of stolen watches.

At a certain point, Cesar tells me he's writing a screenplay.

"What's it about?" I ask.

"It's about these two people, and they're both living a lie."

"Both living a lie?"

Cesar nods. "He's a construction worker posing as a wealthy banker. She's a shampoo assistant in a beauty salon posing as a famous movie actress. When they meet each other, they're pretending to be people they're not. They get to know each other really well and fall for each other. But what will they do when they find out who each one really is?"

That's an excellent question, one I'm starting to ask myself. "How did you come up with the idea?"

"It's basically about the relationship between me and my wife—just exaggerated to the max. There's a certain formula that seems to work in Hollywood. I'm trying to stick to part of that formula, but I'm also trying to break away from it. Add some cachet. Towards the end, I want to have a little twist or something."

"Everyone loves a little twist at the end," I say. "What are you calling it?"

"*Parallel Lives.*"

"That's a good title. I read an essay collection called *Parallel Lives* a while back."

"No, not *lives*," Cesar corrects. "*Lies*. Parallel *lies*."

"Wow. That's even better."

"Thanks."

"*Parallel Lies*," I repeat. "That's *really* good. Just be careful someone doesn't swipe it."

During our second exchange, Cesar brings up his expertise in something called NLP. "It stands for neurolinguistic programming. It's a very interesting way to break out of certain patterns or blockages. Athletes use it. NLP allows you to reframe your thoughts—to have total control. Basically, it teaches you that all behavior is positively intended."

"Really?"

"Really. People always intend to do things for positive reasons. Even Hitler. Hitler's intentions were positive. They just didn't match his outcomes."

"You're saying *Hitler* was a do-gooder?"

"In his own mind, yes." Sensing my skepticism, Cesar hedges. "Probably not a good example. NLP is pretty complicated."

And also controversial. Wikipedia cross-references it to crop circles, crystal healing, dowsing, and urine therapy. Less neutral sources invoke brainwashing.

NLP, I soon discover, is just one of the many self-improvement tools Cesar uses to tap his "core reality" on behalf of the executives he tells me that he coaches. "I use a little bit of this and a little bit of that."

"What specifically?"

Cesar mentions qigong breathing, tai chi, brain wave therapy, biofeedback, and Buddhist meditation, relational public speaking ("to get grounded, to get connected"), EST, an EST offshoot called Landmark ("Human behavior is governed by a need to look good"), and a program known as Family Constellations, which teaches its practitioners that "there is no 'right' and 'wrong' when it comes to past transgressions"—a lesson that seems tailor-made for a felon who believes he's been unfairly prosecuted.

Cesar attributes his personal growth and professional success to many masters, but he privileges the insights of Tony Robbins, the square-jawed "leadership psychologist," above all others. ("Forget your past," Robbins advocates. "Don't think about who you have been. Who are you *now*?") Cesar tells me he has attended numerous Robbins events and owns a complete set of the speaker's motivational tapes. He has even uploaded, onto his consulting website, a photograph of his personal (Robbins-inspired) "vision board"—an aspirational collage composed of, among other things, a beachfront Mediterranean-style home, an Aston Martin convertible, and a snapshot of Cesar posing in front of Machu Picchu. "I look at the board every day and tell myself, 'That's where I want to go. That's where I will be. That's where I already am.'"

"Already? How has the vision board already helped you?"

"Okay, here's an example," Cesar says. "About ten days ago, I cut Tony Robbins's head off."

"Excuse me?"

"I cut off Tony Robbins's head," he repeats. "I found this picture in a magazine of Tony giving a presentation at Carnegie Hall. There must have been five thousand people in the audience." I'm pretty sure he means Radio City Music Hall. "So I cut his face out and taped my head on top of Tony's body. Okay, now here's the freaky part." I'm thinking we're well past the freaky part. "I cut off his head ten days ago, right? And so what happens yesterday? I'm unexpectedly asked up onstage at a conference to help *run* a leadership class."

Cesar acknowledges that the turnout at his event was smaller than at Tony's. (Twelve entrepreneurs attending a free seminar on "The Best Kept Secrets of Modern Day Heroes and Leaders" in the break-out room of an airport hotel.) But that does nothing to diminish his zeal. "Visualization is a *very* powerful tool," he declares. "Don't question how the subconscious brings about your goals. It doesn't matter how. Besides, it's beyond our conscious comprehension."

"Killing Me Softly with His Song" wafts over the café's sound system while he's telling me all this. The bluesy lament does a fine job capturing my reaction to his life lessons, but doesn't help me to visualize how I'm going to get him to open up about Badische.

My first ploy is to introduce the topic of aristocrats, hoping that might prompt Cesar to mention his own royal connections. I scroll through my phone and pull up three pictures of Aiglon alums bearing noble pedigrees: Prince Leka of Albania, Princess Marsi Paribatra of Siam, and His Highness Muhammad Jahangir Khanji, the Nawab of Junagadh. When that fails to provoke the intended reaction, I reminisce about a Belvedere housemate who comes from a long line of Florentine nobles. But all that gets me is a long tirade about the Italian aristocrat's unwillingness "to explore various international IPAs" (income-producing activities) Cesar is trying to put together.

Once I've used up my royal bait, I chum the waters with a tale of wrongful imprisonment. "Do you know about the current headmaster?" I ask.

Aiglon's aristocratic alums have included Prince Leka of Albania, Princess Marsi Paribatra of Siam, and His Highness Muhammad Jahangir Khanji, the Nawab of Junagadh.

"What about him?"

"In 2000—this is while the guy was headmaster the first time—he was jailed."

"Why?"

"His wife falsely accused him of molesting one of their sons. It took him two years, *two whole years*, to get the charges dropped. Can you imagine what that must have been like? But the most incredible thing is that the school rehired him despite the scandal. Talk about redemption! Extraordinary how he bounced back, don't you think?"

Again, Cesar refuses to be drawn in.

"Have you ever revisited the school?" I ask.

"Never."

"What about Switzerland?"

"Never."

"No?"

"No," he repeats. Then he corrects himself. "Wait. Sorry, I've been to Zurich. I went there for meetings."

At last, a nibble. "Oh?"

"I was doing partner financing back in '99 and 2000."

I nod, trying to appear interested, but not too interested.

"A couple times a year, I'd go to New York and Switzerland to meet with this lending group headed up by a prince."

"A prince? That sounds fancy." I resist the impulse to say more. Cesar eventually begins to open up.

"What happened was the group would lend money to people. But in order to borrow, you had to put up a bank guaranty. And there ended up being a lawsuit because they were signing contracts to lend money, but they didn't have money in their account to lend it. They were going to syndicate the funds from various sources. Anyway, it became a big stink, which they're saying was a fraud, which I don't believe. It wasn't a fraud, but they're saying it was a fraud, and I didn't make any money on it."

It would be so easy to dispute Cesar's rambling defense by pulling up the mug shots stored on my phone. But that would be cheap and foolhardy. I need to reel him in slowly.

Our second conversation ends soon after he brings up the fraud. I fly back to Providence knowing I'll have to put some time between us before we talk about it again.

THE TASTING

A year later, I return to San Francisco and arrange another meeting with Cesar. This time I really go to town, booking dinner for two at an upscale Moroccan restaurant famous for its eight-course tasting menu. I figure a meal like that will provide ample time to probe the criminal activities Cesar mentioned in passing at the end of our previous exchange.

The first thing I find myself thinking when Cesar arrives at the restaurant is that his black paisley button-down must be in the wash. Tonight he is wearing a polo shirt with an embroidered eagle, the logo of the aloe vera company that employs him. Unlike the avian emblems associated with Aiglon and Badische, this raptor is posed in a stance of midpredation, its talons clutching at a single word stitched in gold: "Forever."

After we order drinks, I try to soften Cesar up. "I read your web essay 'The Art of Persuasion.' Amazing piece of writing." I quote a line from memory: " 'Information is power, so gather it well and manage it very carefully.' That's excellent advice. It's advice I plan to follow."

Cesar acknowledges the compliment with a smile.

"Oh, and dinner's on me," I tell him. "I'm on assignment."

"What assignment?"

"Don't you remember? I'm writing an article, maybe a book. About Aiglon. About the boys of Belvedere and the men they became."

"Oh, right," Cesar says. "Brilliant."

I pull out pen and paper as the waiter arrives with our drinks. "Do you gentlemen wish a few minutes of face time before we begin building your meal?"

"That's not necessary," I tell the waiter.

"Very good. Then let's get started. Tonight, our chef begins his tasting with a soup course. In addition to the lentil, we have available but not printed"—the waiter interrupts himself to lean forward and reveal with the conspiratorial delight of a black-marketeer—"the cauliflower soup, which we serve tableside, poured over a garnish of two raw almonds, a few dehydrated capers, a little bit of raisin puree, and a crispy fried individual floret of organic broccolini. . . ."

After he completes his oration and we make our selections (anchovies, lamb shank, tuna and squab, etc., etc.), Cesar launches into an account of his recent trip to Spain.

"Barcelona was incredible," he says. "I wouldn't mind living there."

"What would you do?"

"Same as what I'm doing now." He pinches the eagle on his shirt. "It'll be my five-year Forever Living anniversary in November. I get a gold ring with an onyx and a little diamond in the middle, and that's pretty cool."

"So you'd live in Barcelona and work in the Bay Area? That's a helluva commute."

Cesar, the night he talked about his screenplay, Parallel Lies.

"I could get away with it. I'd come back one week a month."

"One week in four? Really?"

"I don't think I could do two weeks a month," Cesar says, misinterpreting the reason for my skepticism. "But a week I could manage." He explains how: a German film producer who's helping him finance a feature-length psychological thriller ("No, not *Parallel Lies*, another project") told him that if you fly between Barcelona and San Francisco via Zurich in "business class three times, you get the fourth flight free."

It's at this point that I write the letters *DQ* on my notepad, a coded reminder to myself that Cesar displays about as much common sense as that other Iberian fantasist, Don Quixote.

"But commuting would only be temporary," he assures me. "Forever Living has an office in Madrid."

"How's your Spanish?"

"Not fluent," he says. This comes as a surprise, given that his father was Venezuelan. Still, it might help explain why he failed to convince the US Bureau of Prisons to change his ethnicity from white to Hispanic.

"And if the Forever Living gig doesn't pan out?"

"I found a financial services job in Barcelona. I've sent them two emails."

"That's right. You've done financial stuff before," I say leadingly.

Cesar nods. "I started my career at Merrill Lynch in '82. Got my license in securities. Then I became a broker at Charles Schwab. Then I traded currencies. I was the manager for a foreign exchange outfit in the early nineties—before there was any Internet, before the euro. We used Knight Ridder equipment. Viewtron screens. Teletrac terminals." (More specifically, Cesar worked for Infoex International, a short-lived day-trading operation that the Commodity Futures Trading Commission charged with "fraud" and "material misrepresentation.") "I was basically overseeing executives. I wish I could do that again. After all, sales management is sales management."

"Isn't selling aloe vera different from trading currency?"

"*Totally* different," Cesar says, seemingly unaware that he's contradicting what he just told me. "But what I *really* want to do is more international sales and marketing."

"Which is what you were doing with that prince you told me about, right?"

Cesar shifts in his seat.

I prime the pump a little more. "That whole business sounded very, very . . . *dramatic*. What happened, exactly?"

"You want to know what happened?"

"I do."

And so, ever obliging, Cesar opens up about his ties to the Badische Trust Consortium.

PART X

PARALLEL LIES

Truly I was born to be an example of misfortune, and a target and mark at which arrows of adversity are aimed and directed.

Miguel de Cervantes, *Don Quixote*

Most of the world today is governed by Caesars. Men are more and more treated as things. Torture is ubiquitous. And, as Sartre wrote in his preface to Henri Alleg's chilling book about Algeria, "Anybody, at any time, may equally find himself victim or executioner." Suetonius, in holding up a mirror to those Caesars of diverting legend, reflects not only them but ourselves: half-tamed creatures, whose great moral task is to hold in balance the angel and the monster within—for we are both, and to ignore that duality is to invite disaster.

Gore Vidal, "The Twelve Caesars"

"We used to stay at—where was it in Zurich?—at the . . ." Cesar struggles for a name I have no trouble remembering. "The Dolder Grand," he says at last. "A six-star hotel on top of a hill."

It's a five-star hotel, actually, but I resist the impulse to correct him.

"That's where we'd have meetings and see clients. The group I worked with was called Badische Anlage Treuhand."

I fake a confused look.

"*Treuhand* means *trust* in German," Cesar explains. "Prince Robert von Badische was the chairman of the Trust."

I start writing. *B-A-D-D*—

"No," Cesar corrects. "It's spelled B-A-D-I-S-C-H-E."

"Got it. Thanks. And how did you meet this Prince Robert fellow?"

"Through the administrator of the Trust. We used to do import-export involving urea fertilizers and debt-for-equity swaps on behalf of the Venezuelan Development Corporation in the Lincoln Building. I introduced the administrator to his current wife. He loves Latinas."

"What kind of company was Badische?"

"A hundred-and-fifty-year-old investment house based in Baden, Germany."

Hardly. It was a Delaware corporation, established in 1997, operating out of a rent-stabilized one-bedroom on Central Park South.

"What was it like, working for a prince?"

"It was an incredible experience," Cesar says. "Incredible. I served as Prince Robert's aide-de-camp on a diplomatic mission to Malta. He even knighted me."*

"In Malta?"

"No. The ceremony took place in New York, at a restaurant on Fifty-Fourth or Fifty-Fifth Street, upstairs in the Knights of Malta room."

I realize at this point that I'm starting to sound like an interrogator, yet I don't sense Cesar minds. "What did you do for the investment house?"

"I helped clients prepare business plans and loan documents."

"What kind of clients?"

"High-powered types. There was a German guy who wanted to turn used plastics into new desks." (If memory serves, he lost about $750K.) "Another guy, from Japan, had this epoxy invention that got hard underwater. I had one client who wanted to start a tire-recycling facility." (He was referring, I knew, to Masimba Musoni, a Zimbabwean engineer compelled to submit a loan request for $100 million even though he needed only $1 million. With Cesar's help, Musoni lost his shirt and, soon after, left the United States.)

"How did you vet potential borrowers?"

"There was a whole qualification process," Cesar says. "These were big, *big* projects, generally requiring loans in the tens of millions of dollars. Project proposals are like a dime a dozen—you can find 'em anytime, anywhere. So one of the things I did for Badische was screen, say, four hundred submissions to find maybe four or five people that were really prepared. That had their act together. That they could put their own money in."

I suspect the last criterion was the only one that mattered.

---

*"Sir" Cesar was in good company. Robert also dubbed (and duped) Oscar-winner Ernest Borgnine, action stars Steven Seagal and Chuck Norris, and the Russian poet Joseph Brodsky.

"Typically, we'd meet at the top of the MetLife Building, in the boardroom of Clifford Chance, the largest law firm in the world."

"And if the prince deemed your client acceptable?"

When that happened, Cesar explains, he would shepherd the prospective borrower to "Zurich or France, usually Zurich," to hammer out funding details and sign contracts.

Again I press for specifics.

"The transactions involved bank guaranties."

"What are bank guaranties?"

"So say you're a client. Badische lends you money—more than needed to fund your project. The balance is used to purchase bank notes that mature at a certain rate of interest that end up covering the principal amount you needed."

"Sorry. I'm not following you."

"It's complicated. My understanding of the way it works is that the larger sum is held by the bank that funds the transaction. So they end up earning the interest on the money and end up covering the principal released to you to begin with."

I'm still confused, but I see no reason to ask for further clarification since I know the whole point of the loan program was to confuse would-be borrowers into parting with their money. I find it interesting that Cesar describes the scheme in the present tense, as if it's an ongoing and viable loan program. "How many deals did you complete?" I ask.

"None."

"None? What happened?"

Cesar lets out a sigh. "My clients kept promising me, 'I have a bank. I have a bank. I have a bank.' See, it's the responsibility of the borrower to have a project *and* a bank—and it has to be a 'top-twenty-five-class bank.' Not some small branch. The bank, to be acceptable, has to be willing to back things up with a bank guaranty to support this money. Anyway, a lot of banks, I guess, told my clients they could do it—or the clients *thought* they could do it—and they couldn't."

"I imagine that frustrated them."

Cesar brushes aside my concern. "Look. They signed contracts with their attorneys present. Their attorneys double-checked it all out. There was a schedule, a very strict schedule, that everybody had to follow. Everybody was clear on that. Painfully clear. Badische said, 'Don't even *think* about signing unless you're sure you can perform, because after you sign, you have three weeks to present us with a letter from your bank stating you can take possession of the funds.' You figure the client can do it, right?"

I shrug noncommittally.

"Well, for one reason or another, the client comes back with 'The bank changed their mind.' Or 'They don't really want to do it.' Or the client never really had a banking relationship in the first place."

"So what happened?"

"The shit hit the fan is what happened."

Annus Horribilis

"Y2K was one of those years where one thing happens, then another thing happens, and then another," Cesar says grimly.

"I had one of those once a long time ago." On my notepad I scribble, *Y2K = C's annus horribilis.*

"I ended up getting into trouble with the law because of a woman from New York who lost money to Badische."

Enter Barbara Laurence. "How much money did this woman from New York lose?"

"A half million dollars. It was a performance guaranty, which she would have gotten back if she and Prince Robert had closed their transaction."

"But that didn't happen?"

"No."

"What did?"

"She complained to the US attorney. Next thing I know, I get a phone call. 'Hi, this is Detective So-and-So from the US Attorney's Office. Blah, blah, blah, blah, blah. I'm calling about this and that.'"

"'This and that'?"

"He said that Prince Robert was not really a prince."

"Was he?"

"I believe he was. The guy was a gentleman and *very* straightforward. I saw the people he hung out with. I mean, you can tell if someone is a prince, right? The way they act?"

Apparently not. Robert was a serial con man who regularly got dragged into court. "I don't know. Lots of people pretend to be something they're not. You do have to be cautious. We live in a world of con artists and frauds. Consider Madoff."

Cesar scoffs. "You can't compare what Madoff did to my situation. Madoff was a one-man show. Badische was an international bank. Did we sign deals in the back of a dark alley? No way. We were meeting in the boardroom of Clifford Chance, the largest law firm in the world! How could Badische *not* be on the up-and-up? Besides, like I was saying, these guys wouldn't sign a deal unless you brought along your attorney or your adviser. They insisted on it. Would an illegitimate organization do all that?"

"It seems the prosecutors thought so."

"Yeah," Cesar allows.

"Did you talk to the feds?"

"I had an appointment to meet with their detective, but I was advised by three different lawyers not to go. They said, 'Nothing good comes from talking with US attorneys. For *them* it's good—but not for you.' Everyone told me, including my sister, 'If you testify, you'll get fried, you'll absolutely get fried. Whatever you say, they'll end up using against you.' Basically, the prosecutors wanted to meet with me to build their case."

"So what did you do?"

"I canceled. I guess they didn't like that."

"I imagine not."

"Their attitude was 'If you're not with us, you're against us.' And so that was that. The beginning of my end, so to speak. They wound up throwing me together with the other defendants." Cesar lets out another sigh. "They needed to," he adds.

"Needed to?"

"In order to prove conspiracy there have to be five defendants," Cesar claims.

"Really? The prosecutor couldn't charge, say, four people? Or three?"

"No, there have to be five."

"I never knew that," I tell him, keeping my doubts to myself. "Who were the other four defendants?"

"Prince Robert. That's one. The baron, that's two. The administrator who coordinated everything. Three. There was another broker who turned out to be the half brother of the administrator. That's four. And me. That makes five."

"What were you charged with?"

"Up-front fraud scheme . . . something fraud . . . something with *up-front* in it . . ."

The charges were "conspiracy to commit wire fraud" and "wire fraud"—violations of Title 18, Sections 371 and 1342, respectively, of the United States Code.

"Collecting fees up front is illegal," Cesar says. "If you apply for a loan and they charge you an up-front fee, apparently, that's against the law. I had no idea. Also, the money has to be in the account when you sign the deal."

"*Did* Badische have the money they were proposing to lend your clients?"

"Badische never had the money in their account when they signed the contracts. But the contract didn't say anything about the money being in the account. They were using *syndicated* funds."

"Meaning?"

"In other words, Badische didn't have the money lying around waiting for someone to sign a deal. *That's* why there was a schedule. Three weeks for clients to provide the bank letter. A month for Badische to then pull funds from different accounts to meet the loan obligation."

Cesar still hasn't answered the $90.3 billion question. I rephrase it. "Did Badische have *access* to the funds they were promising your clients?"

"The prosecutor claimed they had no money, period. That Badische was a fraud."

"And was it?"

"At first I was kinda wondering that myself. I asked myself, 'Is this thing for real? Are these guys for real?' But, Allen, when a Badische executive walks you into the headquarters of Credit Suisse in Zurich to meet one of their senior VPs, and that senior VP says, 'Yes, this transaction is possible. Our bank will accept your client,' well, it seemed legit to me. I still, to this day, believe it was good and real. But according to the prosecutors, I knowingly brought clients to Badische"—he pauses to bracket the phrase that follows in air quotes—"'like lambs to be slaughtered.' But that's *not* what happened. I brokered deals because I felt good about the bankers. What I found interesting is there was a whole finance committee, and none of those guys had fingers pointed at *them*. Somehow the fingers were all pointed at myself!" Cesar slumps in his chair.

"Did the members of the finance committee cooperate with the prosecution?"

"As far as I know, they didn't."

The trial transcript tells a different story. No fewer than five of them testified at trial. So did the senior partner from PricewaterhouseCoopers roped into client meetings, the Merrill Lynch analyst convinced to endorse the special deed of trust from the Kingdom of Mombessa, and David Glass, the Clifford Chance lawyer routinely exploited by the Trust.

"Sounds like maybe you got bad legal advice."

"My attorney started off being good," Cesar says. "Then I found out she was having an—that she had a boyfriend in Florida. That made her distracted. I'm not sure she was taking care of my situation. But man, she was pretty."

"Probably not the best measure of competence."

Cesar shrugs. "I told her I didn't want to go to trial. That I didn't *need* to go to trial. I wanted her to meet with the prosecutors and just talk to them. She told me it doesn't work that way. This is all news to me. I don't know the legal process, right? So here I am, saying, 'Wait a minute. I'm innocent. I'm trying to fight this.' My lawyer goes, 'Well, it's kinda past that point already.' And I'm like, 'No, it's *not* past that point.'"

"Was it?"

"Who knows? Anyway, it didn't matter. The US Attorney's Office used illegal tactics to scare off potential witnesses."

"How so?"

"Okay. So there was a great guy from Texas. He was actually going to testify on my behalf. He was actually going to say positive things. The US attorneys hid him in his hotel room. No one could find him. Nobody knew where he was.

"And there was another client, from Hong Kong. Her family owned a hotel in Manhattan. She was told, 'If you testify, we're not going to be renewing the license for your hotel. Oh, and by the way, we're going to do some really serious investigating into the taxes you filed on your businesses in the US.' She never showed up, either. Then I come to learn that one of the jurors bullied the others during the trial."

"*Bullied?* How exactly did he do that?"

"He said, 'Everybody, we'll do this' and 'Everybody, we'll do that.' And come Friday afternoon, he said, 'We could be stuck here all weekend, or we could just decide.'"

"So what happened?"

"You know, at any trial, there's always three parts to the story. There's the one side, there's the other side, and the truth somewhere in between."

There's another part Cesar is forgetting. "What was the verdict?"

"Bottom line? I lost. But it took the jury like three days to decide. They asked many, many questions, and 90 percent of the questions were about me."

The last observation seems to offer Cesar some comfort, if only briefly. "And to add insult to injury, I was stuck with a $44,000 bill on my AmEx card and ended up having to file for Chapter 7." This last statement is true. I called the automated California Bankruptcy Court hotline to confirm Cesar's insolvency: "No assets recorded. *Beep.* Disposition: Discharge granted. *Beep.* The case is closed. *Beep.*"

"What put you $44,000 in the hole?"

"It had to do with the meetings in Zurich. Badische said, 'We'll assemble some of the directors to come in and meet. But you have to front the costs, and we'll reimburse you later.' I said, 'I don't have a problem with that.'"

"The Badische bankers didn't pay you back?"

"It wasn't their fault," Cesar says protectively. "They *wanted* to provide reimbursement, but their attorney in London refused to let go of the money. I'm wondering if he was working for himself."

Enter Robert Gurland, the London counsel who earned $250,000 in legal fees. I throw gasoline on the fire: "Did the guy in London get arrested, too?"

"No!" Cesar exclaims. "It really was rather unfair, which of course is nothing new to me. I've got to accept that that's the way the universe works."

The more he opens up, the more it becomes clear: Cesar has been on a hamster wheel of self-pity and delusion all his life. His father neglected him. His mother abandoned him. Aiglon abused him. The Cornell University Admissions Office rejected him. A bouncer at Studio 54 barred him from entering the disco ("This was in 1978"). Prosecutors shanghaied him. An aunt refused to put up bail after he was charged with fraud. A fiancée betrayed him by calling off their wedding after his conviction. And soon, I am confident, he'll be adding another name to the list of traitors and turncoats.

SABBATICAL

"So you lost your trial?"

Cesar nods.

"Then what happened?"

"I had a sabbatical."

"A sabbatical?"

"Three years cut to seventeen months. Good behavior and all that."

"What was prison like?"

"Ever heard of Lompoc? The original Club Fed?"

"Rings a bell."

"Tennis courts, basketball, military-style dorms with bunk beds. I remember saying at the time, 'This reminds me of Aiglon.'"

"Interesting analogy."

"Only Aiglon was stricter. You got to chew gum at Lompoc."

"Was there foosball?"

Cesar laughs. "No, but we had a decent weight room."

"Was it dangerous?"

"There was no 'Don't drop the soap' stuff, if that's what you mean. But fights broke out all the time, mostly in the TV room over what to watch."

"What did you like watching?"

"Formula One racing and concert specials. Sade was a favorite of mine."

"Sade?"

The question prompts Cesar to start singing:

> *He's a smooth operator*
> *Smooth operator*
> *Smooth operator*
> *Smooth operator.*

Mother of God! Is he actually serenading me with a ballad about a con man? "What else did you do in Lompoc to keep busy?"

"Well, I never went in for the whole refilling-ink-cartridges thing. You had to be up at like seven in the morning to do that kind of work. I took a job shelving books in the prison library for five bucks a week. That gave me plenty of time to read. Tony Robbins, Deepak Chopra, Wayne Dyer. Also, I taught a class on résumé building."

Résumé building strikes me as something Cesar is more than qualified to teach. "Who were your students?"

"Tax evaders, people who did drugs, white-collar criminals. Basic folks."

"Basic folks?"

"Basic folks."

"And how did that go?"

"Not great," Cesar acknowledges. "They all kept asking me, 'Who's gonna hire a convicted felon living in a halfway house?' Anyway, I gave that up to work on a currency-trading system I developed. I'd get the *Financial Times* and the *Wall Street Journal*. Another inmate had a subscription to *Investor's Business Daily*. The opening, the high, and the close—that's all my system needs."

But day trading from prison didn't pan out, either, so Cesar reconnected with Sherry. "When I was still actually in jail, I asked for a list of client contacts from the administrator."

"Did the administrator give them to you?"

"He sent me a bunch."

"And did you end up reviving the loan operation?"

"No. I wanted to, but I never did. Probably best. The administrator's name was mud."

"Are you guys still in touch?"

"I am. His wife uses my products."

"Is he still in finance?"

"No," Cesar says. "He's doing a religious thing now."

"Sounds like you miss the Trust."

"I do. I loved it. I wish I could do it again. I mean, all I need is to find lenders willing to fund projects without charging an up-front fee. Real lenders—lenders that can really deliver." Cesar puts down his fork and leans across the table. "So if you know anybody, Allen. Or come across anybody. I'm still looking for credible backers to do projects."

"Sure thing," I manage before redirecting my attention to the squab in nettle cake and foie gras emulsion. Then, glancing upward in the awkward silence that follows, I spot it, if only for the briefest moment: the grimace—that unsettling rictus I first observed forty years before.

That's when I know things have gone too far. It's one thing to tally up our parallel lies, quite another to allow those parallel lies to converge. It comes as a huge relief when the waiter reappears tableside with the bill.

"I appreciate you inviting me out," Cesar says as we part company.

"My pleasure," I tell him, though of all the emotions that have accompanied the tasting, pleasure isn't on the list. "The whole business with Badische is an amazing story."

"And it'll make a brilliant book," Cesar says. "I guarantee you."

"I wish I had your confidence."

"NOT BY ANY STRETCH OF THE IMAGINATION"

I already had Cesar's confidence—I had wormed my way into his life—but lacked the other, more conventional, kind of confidence, the assurance of mind about the story I wished to tell. Looking through my notes on the flight home, I wasn't even sure I had the wherewithal to wrap things up. I felt caught between weariness and obsession. There were so many leads still to follow. Too many. I started crossing names off my list of potential interviews, and I kept cutting the list until only three remained: Prince Robert, the Baron Moncrieffe, and Colonel Sherry. I didn't know how to reach the first two: the prince was still a fugitive (if he hadn't passed away) and the baron had dropped out of view soon after leaving prison. But Sherry presented no such obstacles. After completing his forty-one-month sentence, he established a New York–based nonprofit with a Facebook page that included an active cell phone number.

I call Sherry and request an appointment, withholding, at least initially, the reason for the rendezvous. Like Cesar, he agrees to meet without hesitation, proposing that we join up in the visitor's center of the American Bible Society, a light-filled atrium on the Upper West Side of Manhattan.

The religious setting is only the first of many surprises. When we get together, I discover that the colonel is no longer a colonel. He has mothballed his uniforms and tailored business suits. Gone, too, are the Maltese crosses and military ribbons. He now wears a yarmulke under a golf cap and a lapel pin honoring Yad Vashem, the Jerusalem Holocaust memorial.

"Call me Reb," Sherry says at the outset of our interview. "Although I am a rabbi, I find the word self-important and pretentious." The onetime colonel, prince, major, knight, administrator, and ambassador plenipotentiary tells me that he now tends to the spiritual needs of a congregation of Messianic Jews, blending evangelical Christian theology with teachings from the Torah, an interfaith work-around that allows him to practice a form of Judaism that assigns the burdens of atonement squarely on the shoulders of Jesus Christ.

Soon after we find a spot to sit, under a plaque bearing a quotation from John 10:10—"The thief comes only to steal and kill and destroy"—I tell Sherry I have no need for his religious counsel.

"So how can I help?"

"When I was ten, I attended a boarding school in Switzerland. It was both a joyous and traumatizing experience. So much so that I decided to track down my roommates—actually one roommate in particular."

"Did you find him, this roommate of yours?"

"I did. His name is Cesar Augustus."

I wait for a reaction.

"That's his real name?" Reb asks.

"It is."

"That's interesting."

It falls to me to keep the conversation going. "For a while, my search was waylaid by false positives—by men who shared my room-mate's name. There was a flute player, a distinguished professor of electrochemistry, a set designer in Belgium. But it turns out that *my* Cesar Augustus was your"—the word *confederate* is on the tip of my tongue, but I catch myself and opt for a more dispassionate term— "colleague."

"Oh, yes?" he says after another long pause.

"Yes. And since I'm writing a book about my search for Cesar, it makes sense to talk to you."

"Your book, is it fiction?"

"No. No one would believe the details of the story, yours or Cesar's, if they appeared in a novel."

"The details you *think* you know, Allen," Sherry snaps. "What you may have read in the newspapers is *not* an interview with me. It's *not* an interview with the chairman. It's not an interview with Cesar. Not by any stretch of the imagination."

There's no reason to hold back any longer. "Are you saying Badische was legit?"

"Absolutely."

Sherry senses my disbelief.

"Look. I want to be clear, Allen. I've done some things in the past that would have gotten me stoned to death in the time of Moses. But my work on behalf of the Trust and its clients was not one of them. I did nothing wrong. Cesar did nothing wrong. Badische was *not* a fraud. The quote unquote *crime* was nothing more than a contract dispute—the result of one disgruntled client, a woman named Barbara Laurence, who defaulted on an obligation and who used the US Attorney's Office as her personal collection agency. What she did, and what the prosecutors did, was unjust. Worst-case scenario, the dispute should have been arbitrated by the International Chamber of Commerce in Paris."

"If everything was on the up-and-up, why did the government go after you?"

"The prosecutor wanted to get a big feather in his cap. He wanted to build a big résumé of convictions so that he could get a job at a big firm and get paid buckets of money. Conviction, Allen. That's all that mattered. Guilt or innocence was beside the point. *That's* why we went to prison. The prosecutors twisted what Cesar and I did to fit their charges. Wire fraud? What the *hell* are they talking about?"

"The government argued that you hoodwinked the lawyers at Clifford Chance into using their offices."

Sherry lets out a rueful laugh. "The top law firm in the world? Filled with the sharpest legal minds? Hoodwinked? How is that even possible? It was Clifford Chance who drew up the contracts. It was Clifford Chance that tallied up the total worth of the Trust based on the individual asset portfolios."

"Were those assets real?"

"Of course they were real. Not all of them were tangible, but they were real."

"Including the special deed of trust from the Kingdom of Mombessa?"

"Absolutely. A forestry company from Canada assessed the value of the kingdom at $50 billion—and that's just for the timber. Minerals and diamonds weren't even part of the calculation."

It's tempting to mention what I find "special" about the deed in question. That its asset valuation is five times the GNP of the region in which it's supposed to be located. That its capital city, Mondimbi, is a sparsely populated fishing village. That no kingdom called "Mombessa" appears on any map of Africa. Instead, I continue to present the case argued at trial. "The prosecution said there was no king."

"Not true," Sherry counters. "I met him. He has a name—Henri-François Mazzamba. He's a genuine king from the Republic of the Congo, which used to be called Zaire."

Again, that's total baloney. For starters, Sherry is mixing up the Republic of the Congo with the *Democratic* Republic of the Congo, formerly known as Zaire. And as for the so-called king? He was teaching at a grade school in Ottawa when he signed his name to the deed.

"What about the other signatory, Prince Robert? Was he the real deal?"

"As far as I know. His family at one time owned BASF. The *B* in the chemical company's name stands for Badische," he says, repeating the balderdash the Baron Moncrieffe fed David Glass. "It's true that he had fallen on hard times, and for a while he was offering knighthoods for $25,000 a piece. But how is that any different from what the Vatican does? Or the Order of the Knights of Malta overseen by the Queen of England?"

"Why didn't you tell the jury everything you're telling me?"

"I wanted to, but I couldn't. My lawyer said, 'If you testify, you'll come off like Dr. Evil.'"

"Cesar told me his lawyer said the same thing."

"Cesar was baffled that there was even a trial. He's *still* baffled."

For nearly two hours, I listen to Sherry's narrative of victimhood. How he was a casualty of incompetent clients. ("None of them could perform.") Of unscrupulous prosecutors. ("They were scum, no better than human garbage.") Of a jury misdirected by a prejudicial judge. ("Fourteen out of the fifteen witnesses were on our side. Only Barbara Laurence was against us.")

"The government spun it like it was a con job kingdom *we* created. But if anybody was a victim of a con job kingdom, it was *us*. Me. Cesar. I was—we were—convicted for crimes we did not commit. We just couldn't compete with the prosecution's craftiness."

It's tough not to marvel at how uncannily Sherry's account dovetails with Cesar's. Both blame the victims. Both show no real remorse. Both express outrage and disbelief that their seemingly minor contract dispute with Barbara Laurence had ended up in federal court. Where their views part company is in the roles they see themselves having played. Cesar portrays himself a hapless liaison with a peripheral connection to the work of the Badische Trust Consortium. Sherry, by contrast, positions himself proudly at its center.

"I was the one who put all the pieces in place," he boasts. "The one who made it all happen. In a certain sense, I *was* Badische. And I'll tell you something, Allen. If our deals had gone through, if our clients had been able to perform, I'd be the king of Wall Street right now. People would be lining up at my door with wheelbarrows full of money, asking me to help them invest. Instead, they treat me like I'm a sort of Madoff."

As he's making his case, I notice Sherry doing something very weird with his hands. He wraps his fingers around the back of his neck, places his thumbs against his Adam's apple, and squeezes.

I can't decide if the gesture is his way of unconsciously asserting that the government had him by the throat or if (again obliviously) he is attempting to stop himself from talking. I suspect it's a bit of both.

FEAR, DISGUST, PITY, REMORSE

The conversation with Sherry, like the talks I'd had with Cesar, went better than I expected. Sherry had opened up about the fraud, something I never thought possible. After the interview, I retreated to my office and began writing, finally confident that no further communication with him or Cesar would be necessary.

A year went by before I realized that was total bullshit.

Troublesome questions about my conversations with Cesar kept asserting themselves: What stopped me from bringing up what he had done to me? What stopped me from revealing what *I* was doing to him? Why did I pull my punches?

Part of my restraint, I figured out, was rooted in fear. Cesar, I eventually admitted to myself, scared me. And to be clear: it was not the felonious drug-mule-turned-con-man with the Mafia ties who terrified me. It was the childhood version of that man, the twelve-year-old, who filled me with dread.

I was, even on the far side of fifty, still the boy in the tower mimicking the habits of the chamois, bouncing from one spot to another to avoid potential peril.

But that hard-won realization only partly explained why I continually gave Cesar a pass. So much more was going on. I also avoided direct confrontation because of a growing sense of self-loathing. I hated that I had developed an aptitude for duplicity. Cesar had no idea what he was in for; a two-time loser was about to get indicted for a third time, if only in the pages of a book. Although I never thought it possible, I pitied my unsuspecting mark. Curiosity was giving way to compassion. Rancor was getting sidelined by remorse.

By failing to confront Cesar I had failed to confront myself. The story I wanted to tell had systematically undermined the story I needed to tell. Oddly enough, the predicament was captured in the lyrics of "Smooth Operator," Cesar's Lompoc prison anthem:

Face-to-face, each classic case
We shadowbox and double-cross
Yet need the chase

It was time to stop shadowboxing and double-crossing. Coming clean was the only way I would be able to end a chase that I started more than half a lifetime ago.

"DEFEND THE 10 YEAR OLD!"

On May 1, 2013, I screw up the courage to give Cesar a call. "We've got to meet, and I won't take no for an answer."

"Great," he says amicably. He doesn't ask why, and I don't tell him.

Two weeks later, I'm once more in San Francisco, sitting in a Tenderloin café, staring at a framed movie poster for *The Thief of Bagdad*. To pass the time, I read over some of the reminders that I typed into my phone during the flight from Providence: "Avoid parallel lies. No monocles, no knights. Confess the pain."

When Cesar enters the café, I do a double take. He has bulked up considerably since we last met. The goatee is gone, and so is the rest of his hair. Head shaved, dressed entirely in black, he gives off an Oddjob vibe, minus bowler and mustache.

After hearing about the "personal branding workshops" he's been running in São Paulo and Mexico City, I get down to business.

"This is very hard even to bring up," I say, my voice quavering.

Cesar leans across the table. "What's wrong?" he asks. "What's happened?"

"Actually, it's what *hasn't* happened. I know that you forgot about me after Aiglon, but I—"

"No offense, Allen. There are a lot of people I don't remember."

"—but I never forgot you. That's why I'm here."

"Really? I assumed you flew out for a book signing or something."

"Nope."

"Why not just call?"

"It wouldn't have been the same. I needed to look you in the eye to say what I have to say. It's about Aiglon."

"I get it."

"You do?"

"Absolutely. It's like with my wife. One of the reasons she healed from cancer is by coming to terms with certain family issues. Reconciling with her mother and her father face-to-face really helped her. You're doing the same thing."

"That's right," I say, surprised by his wisdom.

"You know, neurolinguistic programming can be *really* useful in dealing with this sort of thing. It's an amazing way to reframe one's perspective. I've gone back to the kid I was at Aiglon and told him—told me—that I was loved. That it was my mother's *intention* to provide the best for me. Of course, I didn't feel that way at the time, but that is what she intended. It's what I told you before. Everyone has a good reason for doing what they're doing."

"You truly believe that? You believe *everyone* is well intentioned? Prince Robert? Colonel Sherry? . . . You? . . . Me?"

Cesar nods. "Actions may not reflect that intention. But the *underlying intent* is still always good."

"I'm not convinced. You know what they say about the road to hell?"

Cesar looks at me blankly.

"That it's paved with good intentions. Look where you ended up. I mean, Lompoc isn't exactly a holding pen for saints."

It takes everything I have in me to leap the chasm of silence that opens up between us. "I have to get something off my chest, Cesar. You really did a number on me at Aiglon."

"Well, lots of kids did a number on me, too," he responds blandly.

I suppose the "too" could be taken as an acknowledgment of guilt, but I didn't fly to San Francisco to squeeze meaning out of vague implication. "You've told me a ton of stories of your mistreatment, Cesar. But I haven't done a good job telling you about mine. *That's* why I'm here. To say, 'Hey, this is what I remember. This is what you did.' That's what my book is about."

"Am I in it?"

The question throws me. "In the book? Yes, Cesar, you're in the book. In a certain sense, you *are* the book."

"Wow," he says, chuckling the same way he chuckled when recalling the nice fat girl he enjoyed punching at school. As he's chuckling and I'm remembering the nice fat girl, an alarm goes off on my phone. I glance down and see that the screen is telling me:

> **Defend the 10 year old!** now   Close   Snooze

"AND I WAS JESUS CHRIST"

The prompt isn't necessary.

"I don't think I've told you this, Cesar, but I spent my first four Christmases in Villars. My dad was alive then. After he died, I never returned—until I went to Aiglon, until I was ten years old, rooming with you at the top of Belvedere. One of the first things I recall you saying is that if a fire broke out in the dorm, you'd have to throw me out the window. After—"

Cesar cuts me off. "Remember the fire drills we had?"

"Sure. But what I'm trying to say is that the threat of—"

"It was near the showers."

"That's possible, but I—"

"That's really all I remember about that, Allen. Like I've said before, I only recall bits and pieces."

"Do you remember calling me Nosey?"

"Nosey?" Cesar chuckles.

"Nosey," I confirm.

"Why? For what reason? Is it because you *were* nosy? Because of the kind of inquisitive person you are now?"

For the first time, I hear the tiniest hint of aggression creep into Cesar's voice. I ignore it and barrel ahead. "Well, I guess I was nosy. And obviously, I still am. I'm also still Jewish, which might have had something to do with the nickname." I curve my thumb and index finger around my nose.

Cesar looks at me blankly. He appears to have no recollection of the gesture he invented to silence a pesky roommate.

"And at one point, you and Paul—I've tried to bring this up before—you guys tied me to the bedpost and pantomimed a whipping sequence from *Jesus Christ Superstar*."

Cesar titters and slaps the table with his palm.

"You can laugh, Cesar, but it was fucking traumatic for me!"

"Sorry," he says. "I *do* remember the song. It was a big deal at the time."

That's something, I suppose. Previously, he had no memory of it at all.

"But I don't remember any of the other stuff."

"You performed 'The Thirty-Nine Lashes.'"

"And you were Jesus Christ?" Cesar says, unprompted, suggesting that he might recall at least some tiny portion of the incident.

"Yeah, Cesar. And I was Jesus Christ."

I have the song cued up on my cell phone but resist the urge to play it. There's something more important I need to say before Cesar bolts. "The worst thing that happened to me at Aiglon wasn't *Jesus Christ Superstar* or the nicknames. Do you remember what I told you about my watch?"

Cesar shakes his head.

"What happened was I left the watch under my pillow and went to take a shower. When I returned, it was gone. I cherished that watch. It had been my father's. It was by far the most meaningful thing I inherited from him after he died."

"Wow, that stinks," Cesar says. "Do you know what happened to it?"

"I do. Paul tossed it out the window."

"Paul? That doesn't sound like him. My memory of Paul is of protecting him from getting bullied."

"You're joking! Paul didn't need protection. He was huge."

"Huge but weak," Cesar says.

"I don't—"

"Hold on! Something makes me think it might have been Winn who took your watch. He stole money from me. I don't know how I remember this all of a sudden, but I do."

"Winn *was* bad news. He was always calling me Kikewheel. But he had nothing to do with my watch getting stolen."

"I remember blaming Winn," Cesar insists.

"You may have blamed Winn, but Winn didn't swipe my watch. It was Paul."

"Are you sure? Did he confess?"

"He told Group Captain Watts that he launched it out the window on a dare. He left Aiglon soon afterward."

"I thought he was kicked out because he didn't have the grades. Or because he just wasn't mentally all there."

I shrug. "I don't know the specific reason for his departure."

"Was the watch found?"

"Nope."

"But what does your missing watch have to do with *me*? That's what I want to know."

"*Stolen* watch," I correct. "Paul only ever did what you told him to do. He was your henchman. You were his—"

"So you're saying *I* had something to do with it?"

I give a nod. "You made my life hell."

Cesar's jaw tenses. His brow furrows. "So, basically, I'm being blamed for your memories? That's what's happening?"

"Pretty much."

"Well, it doesn't sound like you're writing about *me*. This is really only *your* interpretation based on *your* recollection of events."

"I wouldn't disagree. But that doesn't change the fact my father's Omega was hurled out the window."

Cesar turns pensive. "Well, all I can say is I'm sorry you remember losing your watch or whatever it was that happened."

"It wasn't lost. It was stolen," I say testily.

"If you wanna blame me, that's fine," Cesar says. "I don't remember any of this. But clearly, you do."

The back-and-forth continues for a few more minutes, but try as I might, it's next to impossible to grab a bullshitter by the horns.

"Look, Allen. We see things the way we want to see them. Especially when it comes to memory. We put things together that have absolutely no relation to one another. We take one plus one and we get a hundred. I know. It's like that with me and Badische. It's easy to draw negative conclusions after the fact, but I know that what I did for my clients, I did with good intentions."

"And at Aiglon? Were your intentions 'good' there, too?"

"You shouldn't focus on Aiglon. Think about the good times *before* you went there. *That's* where you should target your energies. Let the positive memories overwhelm the negative ones. Don't harp on the bad stuff. That's what I try to do." Cesar's tone turns conciliatory. "I'm glad we've had a chance to clear the air. I'm just sorry I don't remember more."

"That's okay," I tell him. "I remember enough for the two of us."

"There. Was. No. Trust."

Our conversation doesn't end there. After working through my shortlist of juvenile complaint, I turn again to Badische. But before the gloves come off, I tell Cesar I know far more about his criminal career than I've been letting on. That I am, in fact, thoroughly versed in the details of the fraud.

My disclosure doesn't seem to rattle him. And whatever the reason—obtuseness, chutzpah, friendship, nostalgia, amnesia, confidence, naïveté, delusion—he has no qualms answering a whole new set of questions about his ties to the Trust.

I jump right in. After recapping what I know about his client Barbara Laurence, I ask if she complained to him directly before reaching out to the authorities.

"Sure. Many times."

"And what did you do?"

"What can I do?" Cesar says, again privileging the present tense to describe a decade-old crime. "I'm not in control. Barbara Laurence is the one who started the whole thing. She can't meet the conditions of the loan agreement, so she complains to the prosecutor. The next thing I know, the prosecutor goes after me."

"You're saying he made you the fall guy?"

"Exactly. They needed to fry me to prove conspiracy."

"Yeah, about that, Cesar. That's not how things work."

"Yes, it is," he insists. "When you have five defendants, the government can ignore legal procedure. Rules get thrown out the window. That's why I was indicted."

"No, it's not." I resist the urge to quote *Black's Law Dictionary*, which defines *conspiracy* as "a combination or confederacy between *two* or more persons."

"What about Quilty?"

"Quilty. Quilty. Quilty," Cesar says. "I know that name."

"Dennis Quilty. The investigator who helped put you in jail."

"Oh, yeah."

I ask Cesar if he realized Prince Robert was a career swindler.

"He wasn't a swindler when I first met him."

"Yes, Cesar, he was. Do you know about Colonia?"

"What's Colonia?"

"An imaginary micronation Robert helped establish three hundred miles from Manila."

"Sorry, Allen. I'm pretty good at geography. I've never heard of the place."*

"It was part of a passport mill he operated around the time he began claiming to be the Grand Master of the Knights of Malta."

"Wow. You know a lot."

"Guilty as charged," I say. "Oh, and while we're discussing Manila, I've been meaning to ask. What was it like living under the specter of an eighteen-year lawsuit?"

"What lawsuit?"

"The lawsuit caused by the fire."

"What fire?"

"The one that broke out next to your family's beauty school. The one that took the lives of four students."

"This is the first I've heard about a fire or a lawsuit."

I move on. "Were you aware that the Badische scam was an exact

---

*Colonia was probably Robert's biggest coup, geographically if not criminally. In 1978, under one of his many royal appellations, Robert quietly claimed possession of an uninhabited patch of the South China Sea previously abandoned by a crackpot adventurer named Tomás Cloma. The territory, a collection of guano-rich outcroppings on the western fringe of the Spratly Islands, had little commercial value until Robert, partnering with another ersatz royal doing business as the Prince de Mariveles, began selling diplomatic passports (unit price: $20,000) to individuals wishing to bypass customs inspection. Four Corsican drug runners arrested in Israel were among those who attempted to benefit from the diplomatic protection of the nonexistent nation-state.

blueprint of a fraud that Brian Sherry's father pulled off in Europe?"

"What? When?"

"In the mideighties. The earlier version was called the Nikon Trust. It used the same loan agreements as Badische and required the same performance guaranties. It even included a guy claiming to work for Barclays."

"I don't know anything about that. But I can tell you what I *do* know. I reviewed all the Trust agreements signed by my clients."

Before Robert served as the figurehead of the Badische Trust Consortium, he helped run a passport mill associated with the Kingdom of Colonia, a nonexistent micronation located three hundred miles from Manila.

I ask about Richard Mamarella.

"Who?"

"The Mob-connected fixer Prince Robert hired. The guy who broke his wife's arm, swindled a New Jersey bank out of $22 million, and underwrote a life insurance policy on a drug dealer who then got whacked."

"Mamarella wasn't part of Badische."

"Yes, he was."

"I never met him."

I ask Cesar if he feels bad about his clients' losses.

"Look. You're always going to have people who will say good things about you and people who don't have positive things to say." I'm reminded of Laurence's less than positive assessment: "A schmucky, nebbishy lying sack of shit."

I ask if he still thinks about Badische.

"Sure. All the time. Like three days ago, I'm lying on my couch, trying to rest, and my wife says she's going on a trip for business and staying in a six-hundred-dollar-a-night suite. And I start thinking, wow, six hundred bucks! That's how much my room was in Zurich when I was with the Badische thing. And then my minds starts in with, what if I had testified?"

"Why didn't you?"

"Are you kidding? I would *love* to have testified! I was *dying* to testify! But my lawyers and my family all told me not to. They said that I'm too emotional. That I'm too defensive."

I ask about his drug-smuggling troubles.

"Norway had nothing to do with Badische, but they would have used it against me."

I ask about his longtime friendship with Brian Sherry. "Do you think he was a colonel?"

"That's how he was introduced."

"Maybe. But it was total bullshit. I have a copy of his military records. Sherry was discharged from the army for 'financial hardship.' He was a private first class."

Cesar shrugs.

"Is it possible that Sherry lied to you?"

"Sure, it's possible."

I ask Cesar how his home address found its way on to the retainer check Sherry wrote to Rogers & Wells, the law firm absorbed by Clifford Chance.

"I have no idea."

"Do you know that Sherry ripped off John Kearns while his wife was dying of multiple myeloma?"

"That's insane."

"Were you at your trial?"

"Of course."

"Kearns testified about it."

"I don't remember that."

When I note that the fraud netted some $4 million, Cesar scoffs. "There was no $4 million."

"Yes, Cesar, there was. Sherry laundered *at least* that much through personal bank accounts all over the world."

"They weren't *personal* bank accounts. They were Trust accounts."

"No, Cesar. They were *personal* accounts."

"The Trust wouldn't—"

"Cesar. Listen to me. There. Was. No. Trust. The Trust was a myth."

"What about the finance committee? The Swiss bankers? The lawyers at Clifford Chance?"

"Window dressing."

Cesar releases a long sigh. "Okay. Let's say I'm full of shit. Let's say I'm totally guilty. That means Sherry's totally guilty, too. And that he's more guilty than I am."

"He *is* totally guilty. That's why he went to prison. And yeah, he is probably more guilty than you."

"All I know is I didn't get paid."

After sustaining an hour of cat-and-mouse, I look Cesar straight in the eye and ask point-blank, "Were you guilty of fraud?"

"No! I am *not* guilty of fraud."

"The jury disagreed," I counter calmly.

"Juries don't make decisions based on fact. They make decisions based on emotions. But hey, that's the way the cookie crumbles."

"There Is No Time"

A huge sense of relief washes over me after coming clean. I have shed the pretense of friendship and have challenged Cesar head-on about his criminal transactions. Of even greater consequence: I have

defended the ten-year-old, or more precisely the ten-year-old has defended himself. He has confronted his childhood menace. Mission
accomplished, I tell myself as I leave the café. Case closed. No further
action required.

Wrong. Cesar calls soon after we part company. I decide not to
answer. I assume he wants to vent. Hell, he has every reason to vent;
he was just blindsided with a one-two punch of childhood and adult
recrimination.

He leaves a voicemail on my phone. When I play it back, I discover, once again, that he confounds expectation. Here's a full tran-
scription of his message:

*Hi, Allen. Cesar. It's one fifteen, about. I'm back home. Just re-
alized that the most important thing hasn't been said. And that
is that I apologize to you for whatever pain I may have caused.
I'm sorry about that. I really didn't realize until you told me that
you've been looking for me since '91, and how important this is
for you. I fully respect that. I know how it feels because, as I told
you, I'm also still dealing with it myself—still looking for closure.*

So, I apologize to you.

*I was very nice. . . It was nice to discuss your issues and mine
as well. [Badische is] of course painful to bring up again and revisit. But thanks for doing that. We'll see, we'll see what happens.*

*And oh, by the way, Norway was totally my fault. I went to
visit my buddy Lars, and he asked me to bring him some cocaine,
which I did. Everything was fine until the evening when they arrested everybody. Of course I denied it. The police tricked [Lars]
and told him that I'd admitted it. And he thought, me being such
a nice guy, that I did. But I didn't. I brought it [the coke] for him.
(I took some for myself—but not much. I'm not a big drug user.)
But bottom line is it was my fault. I was in for fourteen months
in a country with a different language. It was interesting.*

Then I find myself some ten years later back at a trial and not expressing my side of the story and being very frustrated to this day about not [testifying]. I was advised by five different people not to take the stand. That I would be just too emotional. That the jury would convict me based on my emotions and not because of any facts. Irrespective of everything else, it just doesn't look good on paper. Half the stuff you're telling me, I'm not even aware of. Of course, all this comes out after the fact, but anyway. It's worth talking some more about, certainly for me.

I don't know if you're writing anything about it or doing anything about it—probably not—but I hope you get closure on your book. And for yourself. I think that's very important.

So I just want to call you and apologize for anything that may have happened in the past. It may seem like a long time ago, but it's still perfectly valid and very important. Because there is no Time. We created— Man created Time. There is no such thing as time.

And I'm happy to be able to assist you. Call me anytime you want to talk further. I'm honored that you came out here just to talk to me. Okay, thank you.

After listening to the voicemail, I find myself overwhelmed by a primal urge to run—an urge I satisfy by scrambling up a hill overlooking San Francisco Bay. At the summit, surrounded by a dozen frolicking dogs and their owners, I replay the message while catching my breath.

I apologize.

Cesar's simple, all-powerful avowal strikes like a thunderbolt, releasing me from a prison of vengeance that I've inhabited since the Nixon administration.

Ω

The first few times I listened to Cesar's mea culpa, I heard what I want to hear. What I *needed* to hear—the remorse of a man whose childhood degradations changed my life forever. The deeper consequences of his equivocal recording only emerged later, back in Providence.

After much deliberation, I figured out what now seems absurdly obvious. The search for Cesar had always been, at its core, a search for someone else. Observing him through a two-way mirror for as long as I had ultimately enabled me to catch reflections of myself in the glass. And who stared back? A victim. An obsessive. A boyfriend. A husband. A father. A journalist. A completionist. A stalker. A frightened five-year-old gripping the hand of a dying father.

Cesar found himself in my crosshairs because of a timepiece once owned by that dying father. Boarding-school cruelties, however baroque, cannot explain my sustained fixation. Nor can the jaw-dropping fraud that landed Cesar in prison. (The dirty-rotten-scoundreldom of the Badische Trust Consortium was never anything more than a detour, albeit one embellished by some truly amazing props.)

Part talisman, part shield, the lost Omega was also—how else to put it?—a time machine, a device that transported me back to a moment when my family was intact and I was profoundly happy.

So forgive me if I reject the notion that there's no such thing as Time. Without Time, we cannot remember. Without Time, we cannot learn. Without Time, we cannot heal.

When I told Françoise and Max that I was sending Cesar packing, they were overjoyed—for themselves and for me. He, we all agreed, had overstayed his welcome. And they marked his long-delayed eviction by giving me an extravagant gift. I am wearing it on my wrist.

Me, age three. My father took this photo of me in Villars, Switzerland, the year before he died.

ACKNOWLEDGMENTS

An alpine trek lasting some forty years—okay, half that, if one pinpoints its start to my return visit to Aiglon in 1991—is bound to generate a mountain of indebtedness. The list of thanks that follows, while lengthy, is not, I'm sure, complete. I apologize in advance for any omissions.

There has never been anything neutral about my Switzerland. Although this chronicle was born out of trauma, it has been offset by countless acts of generosity rooted in, and routed through, the village of Villars and the precincts of Aiglon College. I spent just 304 days at Aiglon—from September 1, 1971, to the following July 4—yet even now, I can recite the morning roll call of Belvedere ("Aikman, Anderson, Benjamin, Blane . . . Kiefer M., Kiefer T., Kurzweil!" . . . "HERE!"). I am grateful to most, though obviously not all, the boys whose names I carry around in my head. Memories of the school—for reasons made clear at the outset of this book—reverberate like the haunting echo of the mountain yodeler, except that the reverb seems to defy physics by growing louder and more distinct over distance and time. This is due, in no small part, to the hundreds of conversations I have had with many Aiglon alums. Special thanks, in this regard, go to Erik Friedl, Christopher Grove, Doug Hillen, Nino Zamero, Rana Sahni, Wes Green, Andreas Kehl, Harold Summers, Joe Lasheen, Sandro Corsini, Sabina Hickmet, Michael Feron, and the late John Vornle. The catalog of helpful teachers and administrators I encountered at Aiglon is just as long, and includes: Rachel Davies, Joelle du Lac, Karen Sandri, Patrick Roberts, Group Captain Watts, Tony

Hyde, Norman Perryman, Elizabeth and Theodore Senn, Phillip and Bibi Parsons.

Among the witnesses who testified at the trial of the Badische boys and their principal shill, three warrant special mention: John Kearns, Barbara Laurence, and David L. Glass. Each one helped clarify the often confusing testimony generated in *United States of America v. Brian D. Sherry et al.*, 01 CR 1043. Yosh Morimoto, another of Cesar's victimized clients, although absent from the court proceedings, also furnished important insights into the protocols of the Badische Trust Consortium.

Not all those duped by the convicted hustlers wished to be quoted by name. I have honored those requests. However, I have not, despite current editorial custom, "changed names and identifying details." No facts that appear in this book have been finessed. No identities have been modified. Nothing good comes from taking such liberties—especially when one's efforts are focused on a narrative steeped in falsehood and deception. Wherever possible I have verified memories and statements—my own, Cesar's, and those of the individuals dragged into the fraud—against the court record and other reliable sources, both public and private.

While trying to make sense of the swindle, and the federal case that brought it to light, I was helped by three former assistant US attorneys—Timothy J. Coleman, Jay K. Musoff, and Alexander H. Southwell—as well as Dennis M. Quilty, the relentless criminal investigator who pieced together the evidence the government produced at trial. Officers from the US Postal Inspection Service further helped flesh out the criminal activities of the Badische boys. In particular, I am grateful to three first-class postal inspectors: John Feiter, Thomas Boyle, and Thomas Feeney. I am also beholden to two senior partners from the firm of Debevoise & Plimpton—John H. Hall and Mark P. Goodman—and to Mark's longtime legal secretary, Diane Bletterman.

Dozens of research institutions assisted me during this investigation. Of particular note: the John Carter Brown Library (under the aegis of its former director Ted Widmer and current deputy director Margot Nishimura); the Rockefeller Library at Brown University; the New York Public Library (and, more specifically, Pamela Leo, formerly of the Center for Scholars and Writers); and the Providence Athenaeum, a once dormant member-supported library recently reawakened under the stewardship of Christina Bevilacqua and Alison Maxell.

Even though a list of photographic credits appears elsewhere, I would like to offer special thanks to: Matt Sherwin, for schlepping to a Manila slum to take pictures of Cesar's childhood mail drop; Mathias Braschler, for graciously allowing me to reproduce his timeless portrait of the Prince and Princess Khimchiachvili; Harold Summers and Patrick Roberts, for forwarding hi-res versions of images originally posted on the web; Norman Perryman and Bret Bertholf, for permitting me to reproduce their art; Erik Friedl (again), for digitizing stills from the 16mm film he shot at Aiglon College in 1972; Patrick Conner, for his beautifully composed still life of the Cesareum; US Postal Service Senior Technical Surveillance Specialist Larry Ghorsi, for unearthing an image of his colleague Thomas Feeney; Bruce Metcalf of the Augustan Society, for allowing me to reprint a genealogy establishing the ties between "Prince" Robert to Count Dracula—a genealogy that Guy Stair Sainty, with equal aplomb, has discredited; and finally Rob Walker, an illustrator and designer whose digital competencies find expression throughout this book.

· I could shorten these acknowledgments by mentioning only those family members who did *not* support the search, but I'm no fool; I know what's good for me. To all the Kurzweils who gather at my sister-in-law Nancy's Long Island Seders: *Todah rabah.* To all the Schmidts, Dussarts, and Howorths who gather at Françoise's Christmas dinners: *Merci infiniment.* Special thanks also go to: my cousin (and West Coast bodyguard) Ruth MacKay; to my mother, Edith Kurzweil, for preserving, among other things, fifteen linear feet of my father's photo albums, a ten-year cache of his private notebooks, dealer invoices for every car she has owned since 1965, and pretty much all letters and photographs she has ever received from her children (Ron, Viv, and me) and her stepchildren (Anna and Antonia, Lenny and Peter). Kurzweils and Schmidts tend to be pack rats, a weakness I have shamelessly exploited while piecing together the early sections of this chronicle.

My son might not possess the archival predisposition of his older relatives, but he, too, has helped me greatly, serving as my in-house editor on matters of popular culture that might otherwise elude a guy in his fifties.

A few dozen friends also offered editorial counsel. Thanks go out to Paul Hechinger, Dan Dubno and Lisa Bernstein, Jay Kernis, Andrew Kerr and Cyndi Doyle, the Joukowskys (every last one of them), the aptly labeled "geniuses" and "creatives" at the Providence Place Apple Store, Steve O'Shea, Rosemary Mahoney, Becky and Dan Okrent (the latter a master of pacing, punctuation, and bone-dry gin martinis), David Nishimura (who deepened indelibly my knowledge of fountain pens), Bill Powers and Martha Sherrill, Malcolm Pollack and Nina Phillips, Harvey Sachs, Jonathan Barzilay, Arthur Riss (for his steady supply of Melville quotations and anagrammatical aliases), Kirstin and Michael Allio, Al Venditto and Rachel Atlas, Heather and Ronald Florence, Linda Carter, Carrie Cook, Alec and Liz Stansell, Ashley Dubois, Dan Miller, Grace Shohet and David Brownstein, Michael Spalter, and Michael Boyer.

Students and teachers at dozens of schools offered unfiltered insights into the nature of bullying. I received especially nuanced assistance from fourth, fifth, and sixth graders at the following schools: the Ten Acre Country Day School, the John D. Runkle School, the Hunnewell School, the Dalton School, the Wheeler School, the Moses Brown School, the J. F. Deering Middle School, the Fenn School, the Field School, the Meadowbrook School, the Paideia School, the Weston Public Schools, and the Bates, Shutesbury, Wenham, Bonner,

Brooklyn, Buker, Hanaford, Gardiners Avenue, Merrill, Garvin, and James H. Eldredge elementary schools.

I've been racking up editorial debt ever since a crude iteration of this book reached the in-box of my editors at Harper, David Hirshey and Barry Harbaugh, and their indefatigable assistant, Sydney Pierce. The structural and stylistic improvements they made to the manuscript were reinforced later on by copyeditor Mary Beth Constant and by the intermittent counsel of Beth Silfin and Jonathan Burnham. In inventorying the assistance I received from Team Harper, I'd be remiss if I failed to insert a special callout to Fritz Metsch, the book's designer. For those readers who share Fritz's (and my) love of colophons, I'd also like to give a nod to William Martin (1757–1830), the type designer responsible for Bulmer, the transitional typeface in which this book is set. Bulmer, like the Harper staff, is distinguished by precision, balance, and a seraphic pizzazz that's just a little bit edgy. Two other editors beyond the publishing house helped remove countless blemishes: Susan Morrison, of *The New Yorker*, and my dear friend Karyn Marcus.

Finally, I would like thank the three most patient women associated with the search for Cesar: my assistant, Alex Dunwoodie (for all things administrative); my literary agent, Liz Darhansoff (for all things transactional); and my wife, Françoise Dussart (for all things full stop). The very first day I met Françoise near the widow's quarters at Yuendumu she rescued me from trouble. She has been rescuing me ever since. As her Warlpiri aunties would say, *Yati!*

And finally—yes, that's right, the last *finally* was premature—there's one more individual who needs to be recognized. I do so without irony.

Thank you, Cesar. You have taught me that the lies we tell others always begin with the lies we tell ourselves.

PERMISSIONS

Grateful acknowledgment is made to reproduce the following illustrations:

p. 5: Courtesy of Aiglon College, Switzerland
p. 9: Courtesy of Edith Kurzweil
p. 10: Courtesy of Edith and Len Kurzweil
p. 13: Courtesy of Edith Kurzweil
p. 15: © Patrick Roberts
p. 16: Linda Color, Geneva, Switzerland
p. 19: Courtesy of Aiglon College, Switzerland
p. 20: Courtesy of Aiglon College, Switzerland
p. 22: Courtesy of Aiglon College, Switzerland
p. 23: Courtesy of Aiglon College, Switzerland
p. 25: Courtesy of Aiglon College, Switzerland
p. 26: © Erik Friedl from the film *Aiglon College*
p. 28: Courtesy of John Vornle
p. 31: © Norman Perryman
p. 35: Courtesy of Edith Kurzweil
p. 39: Courtesy of Edith Kurzweil
p. 40: Courtesy of Edith Kurzweil
p. 42: Courtesy of François Dussart
p. 49: Linda Color, Geneva, Switzerland
p. 51: Courtesy of Aiglon College, Switzerland
p. 61: © Bret Bertholf
p. 64: United States Navy
p. 65: © Matt Sherwin
p. 75: © New York Post
p. 97: Illustration from the title page of *Forty Years a Gambl*er by George H. Devol, 1887
p. 105: Courtesy of Barbara Laurence

p. 115: Universal Studios, 1960

p. 139: Courtesy of John Kearns

p. 165: Courtesy of www.barclaycg.org

p. 172: © Dora Espinoza

p. 175: © 1968, 1972, The Augustan Society, Inc.

p. 177: Courtesy of Jacqueline Hankins

p. 182: Courtesy of Yosh Morimoto

p. 194: © Larry Ghiorsi, Senior Technical Surveillance Specialist, New York Division, U.S. Postal Inspection Service

p. 203: Courtesy of Dennis Quilty

p. 204: Courtesy of Dennis Quilty

p. 232: © Erik Friedl from the film *Aiglon College*

p. 237: Courtesy of Mugshots.com

p. 243: Keystone/Getty Images (*left*), Courtesy of the Marsi Foundation (*center*)

p. 277: © Rob Walker

p. 283: Courtesy of Edith Kurzweil

INSERT ONE

p. 1: Courtesy of Aiglon College, Switzerland

p. 2: © Laurent Brodier

p. 3: Courtesy of Edith Kurzweil

p. 4: Courtesy of Edith Kurzweil (*top*), © Ronald Schmidt (*bottom left*), © Patrick Jantet (*bottom right*)

p. 5: Courtesy of Aiglon College, Switzerland, © Erik Friedl from the film *Aiglon College* (*top right*)

p. 6: Courtesy of Aiglon College, Switzerland

p. 7: © Patrick Roberts, courtesy of Edith Kurzweil (*center*)

p. 8: Courtesy of Edith Kurzweil

INSERT TWO

p. 1: © Mathias Braschler

p. 2: New York Post (*top left and bottom left*)

p. 3: Bernard Gotfryd/Getty Images (*bottom left*)

p. 4: New York Post (*top left*)

pp. 6–7: © Patrick Conner

p. 8: Courtesy of Edith Kurzweil (*bottom right*)

ABOUT THE AUTHOR

ALLEN KURZWEIL was educated at Yale and the University of Rome. He is a novelist, journalist, teacher, and inventor. He has written for numerous publications, including the *New York Times*, the *Wall Street Journal*, and *Vanity Fair*, and has received fellowships from the Guggenheim Foundation, the Fulbright Commission, the National Endowment for the Humanities, and the Center for Scholars and Writers at the New York Public Library. He lives in Rhode Island. To learn more, visit allenkurzweil.com.